# UPLAND BRITAIN

# UPLAND BRITAIN

Roy Millward & Adrian Robinson

**DAVID & CHARLES**
Newton Abbot    London    North Pomfret (Vt)

British Library Cataloguing in Publication Data

Millward, Roy
   Upland Britain.
    1. Scotland – Description and travel – 1951–
    2. England – Description and travel – 1971–
    I. Title II. Robinson, Adrian
    914.11'09' 43         DA867

   ISBN 0–7153–7823–6

Typeset by
Northern Phototypesetting Co., Bolton
Printed in Great Britain
by Butler & Tanner, Frome, Somerset
for David & Charles (Publishers) Limited
Brunel House Newton Abbot Devon

Published in the United States of America
by David & Charles Inc
North Pomfret Vermont 05053 USA

To Professor Emrys Bowen
pioneer of research in
the historical geography of the uplands

# Contents

# Acknowledgements

We would like to acknowledge the source of the following air photographs used in the book: plates 12, 36, 37 and 48, Aerofilms; plate 9, C. H. Wood Ltd and plate 29, Peter Baker. We are also indebted to our colleagues on whose work we have drawn or whose advice we have sought. As in our previous books, we have relied on our wives for the preparation of the index and the drawing of the maps and diagrams.

*Jacket photograph* North-West Highlands of Scotland: a Lewisian Gneiss landscape near Laxford Bridge (*photo Roy Millward*)

# Introduction

Upland Britain, the parts of these islands where one can find oneself at more than 1,000ft above the sea, has often been described as the better half of Britain. Its chief and most obvious attraction is the absence of far-spreading conurbations, though in places the juxtaposition of city and upland wilderness is remarkably close. The desolate peat hags of Kinder Scout and Bleaklow in the southern Pennines, where men have died of exposure in winter blizzards, lie only a few miles from Manchester town hall and the heart of the city of Sheffield, but the remoter parts of highland Britain must rank among the loneliest places in Europe. On a clear day the prospect from one of the summits of the North-West Highlands of Scotland contains little evidence of the works of man. From Ben More Assynt, at more than 3,000ft, the eye can take in the whole of northern Scotland, a blunt peninsula filled with mountains and framed by the sea. Around one is the seemingly endless emptiness of deer forest – stony, rain-soaked and unproductive. To the west stretches the lower country of the Lewisian gneiss platform in coastal Sutherland, a landscape largely denuded of its population in the clearances of the last century. Beyond, in the distance, the Minch gleams gold and silver in the afternoon sun, and the far western horizon is closed by the dark silhouette of the Outer Hebrides.

The outstanding viewpoints of upland Britain help one to appreciate the variety of the landscapes of the westernmost parts of these islands. Ben More Assynt, at the very heart of the most extensive wilderness left to us on this crowded raft of offshore Europe, holds out enticing prospects of neighbouring mountains, each with its individual characteristics. Suilven, a huge bastion of Torridonian sandstone, compelling to the eye from any viewpoint, rises from a lonely, loch-bespattered platform of Lewisian gneiss. To the north, the grey-white slopes of Foinaven, a mountain of Cambrian quartzite that looks like a permanent cover of snow under the grey lid of northern cloud, seem to present the ultimate desolation. And the distant view from this Sutherland mountain hints at still more and different groups of mountains. To the south-west, 60 miles away, the jagged lines of the Cuillins in Skye may be discerned on good days, and across the Minch are the conical forms of the hills of Harris.

9

1   The dramatic qualities of a highland landscape in North-West Scotland as viewed across the ice-scored platform of gneiss towards the long ridge of sandstone forming Suilven

The essential individuality of our mountains is emphasized in their distant prospects. There is no better place to appreciate the personality of the northern Pennines than in the eastward view from the summit of Helvellyn in the Lake District. Across the green and ordered expanse of the Vale of Eden the long western wall of the Pennines fills the far horizon. The spaciousness of the Pennines, the long, even skylines that form an essential part of the topography almost anywhere between the Peak District and the outskirts of Carlisle, are foreign to the mountains of the Lake District, which plunge with suddenness to valley troughs shaped and deepened by glaciers of the last Ice Age. There is a dominant vertical element in the topography of the Lake District that is shared by all the heavily glaciated uplands of the most western parts of Britain.

Britain's upland scenery must also be seen in its relation to neighbouring lowlands and the all-embracing western seas. The hills that rise from the plains of the English Midlands foreshadow the landscapes of the upland west. The Wrekin, an island in the Severn plain, is a fragment, both geologically and historically, of upland Celtic Britain. Even the Cotswolds, in their highest places rising to just over 1,000ft and in almost every sense an epitome of the landscapes of lowland England, reveal a fine prospect of the western uplands from the lip of their steep escarpment above the Vale of Severn. From the heights above Broadway and Chipping Campden the shapely line of the Malvern Hills shows one of the oldest fragments of Britain's geology — rocks whose true affinities are with the remote Hebrides. And even further west lie the high hills of the Welsh Marches, the Black Mountains, of an incredible blueness on a fine summer day when seen from the pastoral summits of the Cotswolds.

It is on the western fringe of upland Britain, in the juxtaposition of sea and mountain, that the most dramatic elements of our highland scenery are encountered. Even as the crow flies, the Atlantic coast extends for almost 1,000 miles from Land's End to Cape Wrath. The absolute length of that coastline is immensely greater, with the far-reaching estuaries of Solway, Clyde and Severn and the numerous sea lochs, fjords in all but name, of Highland Scotland. The images that form in the mind as one meditates upon the extent of upland Britain inevitably involve a prospect of the western seas as well as of mountains.

In the Penwith peninsula of south-west Cornwall, where upland Britain is finally submerged in the sea surge around the granite reefs of Land's End, the blue line of the Atlantic's horizon forms a continuous, ever-present background to the prospect from those hills that are rich with the relics of prehistory. Here upland Britain ends in a shelterless façade of cliffs, storm-racked in countless winters. The apparent emptiness of the sea around Penwith, the blankness of the Atlantic's horizon to the casual visitor, disguises the importance of the seaways of the west in the evolution of highland Britain. Across the western approaches over the past five thousand years have come peoples, commodities and ideas — ideas about the organization of life, the laying out of fields, hamlets and houses, and perhaps too about man's place in the order of things. The relics of this exchange and intercourse with Europe are still written on the landscape in the great megaliths that look out to sea from Penwith's high places, in the patterns of prehistoric fields and the clustered ruins of Iron Age villages. The memory of the past remains too in the long-abandoned tin workings that were engaged in trade with the Mediterranean in the first millennium BC, and also in the heroic tales of the Dark Ages when the tragic Tristan sailed the seas between Ireland, Cornwall and Brittany.

The varying relationship between sea and land contributes largely to the great diversity of Britain's upland scenery. For the greater part of the cliff-bound coast of north Cornwall a harsh divide is drawn between the two elements. Tintagel's Celtic monastery, perched on its forbidding cliffs, would seem to be the last outpost of a lost culture. But in North Wales sea and land have combined to nurture one of the oldest and most distinctive cultures of upland Britain. Here, from the summit of Snowdon or those two princely mountains, Carnedd Dafydd and Carnedd Llewelyn, one looks westward across the heartland of Gwynedd, the strongest of the Dark Age kingdoms of Wales. The topographical foundations of Gwynedd lie in the narrow coastal plain between the mountains of Snowdonia and the sea and in the isle of

11

Anglesey – Mam Cymry, the mother of Wales – beyond the Menai Strait. The winding strait between Caernarvon and Beaumaris, composed of drowned valleys from late Ice Age times, is the very opposite of the hostile, exposed cliffed coasts found in so many parts of upland Britain. Here lush pastures, rich woodlands and private parks planted with exotic species run down to the water's edge. Mountains, the sea and a sheltered lowland have conspired in shaping an environment that favoured the development of a distinctive Celtic community, one that is still evident in the strength of Welsh as a spoken language.

The cultural distinctiveness of upland Britain rests in the pockets of lowland between the western seas and the encircling hills. The plain of Cumbria, reaching from the foothills of the northern Lake District to the salt marshes and mudflats of the Solway Firth, has long acted as a focus of settlement. Long since vanished from the living landscape but still clearly apparent on aerial photographs are the estates, the British farms, that flourished here in the Roman centuries and that were tributary to the garrisons of this imperial frontier and the town of Carlisle. Further north still, in western Scotland, the same relationship between early cores of settlement, lost kingdoms and the disposition of coastal lowland, sea and mountains may be sensed. The lower Clyde valley, a dramatic pattern of long, branching fjords set against the backcloth of the mountains that lie west of Loch Lomond, was the setting of the Dark Age state of Strathclyde, a political entity that vanished with the emergence of medieval Scotland, but whose past importance can still be felt in the primitive shape of Dumbarton Rock rising out of the dull clutter of a Victorian industrial town and its shipyards.

The Clyde estuary ushers in a fresh element in the topography of upland Britain. Fjords, the sea-drowned troughs scoured out by the Quaternary glaciers, are overshadowed by the highest mountains of Britain. The head of Loch Linnhe lies 60 miles from the open Atlantic; here the sea is within sight of the summit of Ben Nevis, our highest mountain. Every element in the landscape of Fort William is dwarfed by the mass of this mountain. Even on the many days when cloud sheets roll in unceasingly from the west, hiding all but the lowest few hundred feet of the mountain, one feels the presence of Ben Nevis in the streets of the little town at its feet. With the rare clarity of a fine day in late winter the mountain is seen to dominate every object for miles around in the countryside of Lochaber. The huge crust of snow above the northern precipice provides a fitting background to the war memorial above Spean Bridge; more magnificent still, the profile of the northern face, with deepest black of bare rock and crystal white of snow, towers over Corpach and its huge pulp mill across Loch Linnhe. In the last few years much has been done in the way of the economic development of Fort William and its neighbourhood – hydro-electric power, pulp and paper making, aluminium smelting – but all is dwarfed by the immensity of the mountains that overshadow Loch Linnhe, and by the sheer extent of the encompassing upland wilderness.

If the landscapes of upland Britain along its western margin are the product of an ever-varied relationship between sea and mountain, it is true to say that the scenery of the highest parts of the uplands, particularly in the east, is composed of only two visual elements – rolling, treeless land surfaces, seemingly infinite in their extent, and over all, stretching to the far rim of the distant horizon, the great dome of the sky. Such landscapes – empty, calm and breathing peace – are one of the most precious elements in the topographical heritage of a nation that has to earn its living in cities. Fortunately some of these tracts of upland with an elemental simplicity of scenery lie close to our greatest centres of population and industry. The gently sloping tableland that leads to the crest of the Brecon Beacons is within sight of the busy, congested valleys of the South Wales coalfield. The gritstone moors of the Dark Peak rear their heads above a ring of conurbations comprising the towns and cities of the West Riding, Manchester, Sheffield and the Potteries. There, within the rim of Kinder Scout's plateau, is only the intricate, trackless maze of wandering streams among the peat hags, the sound of the curlew and the close presence of an ever-shifting cloudscape.

Upland Britain is in most senses Atlantic Britain, and because of its great extent of latitude – more than 10° separate Land's End from the most northerly point of the Shetland Islands – this vast region of mountains, moorlands and the interpenetrating seas may be regarded as the bridge between northern and southern Europe. The North-West Highlands of Scotland are part of the world of the North Atlantic, sharing many of the topographic and cultural features of Scandinavia, the Faeroes and Iceland. The trackless shores of Loch Nevis and Loch Hourn are most easily accessible by boat, a characteristic of the communications of the Norwegian fjords. The long valleys that have provided age-old routes from east to west across the backbone of upland Scotland are matched by the seemingly endless troughs that break the monotony of the high plateaux of eastern Norway giving access to the sombre, enclosed recesses of the western fjords. And high above the eastern valleys stretch the moorlands: Ben Wyvis, whose long, level summit at more than 3,000ft above the sea dominates the view across Cromarty Firth; the Monadhliath Mountains, an empty land of rock and heather, moor and winding glen to the south of Loch Ness; and, first and foremost among the surviving fragments of wilderness in upland Britain, the Cairngorms – a mountain tract whose grandeur is surpassed only by the more extensive emptiness of the wild tundra of northern Scandinavia.

Here the traveller can enjoy a northern climate as well. On many days of the year northern Britain is enveloped in air from more northerly sources – fresh polar maritime air that has crossed the North Atlantic from Greenland, or a much more biting Arctic air that finds its source in polar regions. The high mountains lie under a thick blanket of snow for many weeks in winter. Even as late as the first weeks of April the deep corries that hang above Glen Shiel keep their accumulations of winter snow, and the famous summer snow patch in a sunless cleft of the northern face of Ben Nevis is a visible reminder of the Ice Age that was lately responsible for the shaping of so many features of our northern landscapes. The cultural links of northern Britain, as we show in the later pages of this book, are also with those even more northerly lands. Place names, legends and the stuff of early Scottish history that sounds more like mythology reveal the indelible imprint of the Viking, of close connections with Scandinavia that lasted for half a millennium.

At the southern margin of upland Britain the relationships of both land and peoples are with Brittany, Iberia and the western Mediterranean. The granite uplands of Cornwall and Devon – smooth moorland landscapes whose skylines are broken by the jagged outlines of tors – can be matched in the highlands of the interior of Brittany, likewise of granite, or in the bare hill country of northern Portugal baked by a summer sun. The climatic affinities too of Cornwall and Devon are with south-western Europe. The occasional severe winter brings paralysing blizzards to the hills of south-west Britain, but statistics show that the mild, wooded estuaries of south Cornwall can expect snowfalls as infrequent and fleeting as those on the coasts of Brittany. Not without some grounding in truth did the Great Western Railway in its heyday advertise the coastal resorts at the end of its main line as the Cornish Riviera. In the good years – and there are many – spring comes early and the heat of summer lingers on into late October. The cultural links of the south-western uplands with Iberia and Brittany are explored in later pages. The prehistoric tin trade from Mounts Bay reached out to distant markets in the colony that the Greeks had founded on the site of Marseilles. Brittany itself derives its name from the migrations of Britons from the south-west peninsula that took place in the post-Roman centuries; and the wandering saints of the early Christian period took as their territory a world that encompassed all the lands in the western approaches of the English Channel.

Despite the communications of the twentieth century – radio, television, and the outstretching tentacles of a motorway system focused on lowland Britain – the distinctive character of the lands of the former Celtic world is still apparent. Debates about devolution and campaigns for the preservation of the wilderness and the creation of national parks are only two of the many aspects of the individuality of the upland regions of Atlantic Britain – regions which have displayed a personality of their own from prehistoric times to the present day.

# 1

# Landscape of Rock and Stone

Few concepts have made such an impact on our understanding of the geography and landscape history of Britain as the suggestion of Sir Halford Mackinder that there are two contrasting halves to the country – highland and lowland. It is a theme taken up and developed by others at a later date when seeking to explain differences in the whole character and personality of the two regions in terms of contrasting rock types, destructive and formative processes and even the expression of day-to-day weather. For simplicity, Mackinder proposed that his dividing line should run diagonally across the country from the mouth of the Tees to that of the Exe, and for many subsequent generations of schoolboys the Tees–Exe line became a fundamental feature of the geography of Britain. Mackinder never thought of his line as a sharp 'frontier' but rather as a zone of transition where the lowland basins and lines of gentle hills of the south-east gradually gave way to the harsher contours of mountains and high plateaux of the north and west.

Apart from an obvious difference of altitude there were other factors which tended to reinforce the fundamental contrast between the two areas. In highland Britain there is a greater preponderance of older rock types, often tenaciously resisting erosion and standing out defiantly in bare, exposed crags as if to assert their authority. Lowland Britain, on the other hand, is moulded out of softer material – clays, sandstones and chalk which nearly everywhere lie concealed beneath a rich and verdant cover of vegetation. In their weather and climate the uplands of the north and west are subject to the maritime influence of westerly winds: the conditions they bring to the area are wet, though relatively mild for the latitude. In contrast, lowland Britain is prone to a Continental influence which shows itself in icy blasts from Siberia in a cold winter or in the weeks of settled summer weather of the occasional heatwave. The uplands have their own distinctive features of weather largely as a result of the rapid change of altitude.

Man, too, has been affected; the whole history of these islands over the past five thousand years shows a response to this major sub-division, whether in the spread of Christianity by the Celtic and Roman Churches or in the impact of the Industrial Revolution. The distinctiveness of our upland regions is perhaps most clearly expressed in the way man has wrestled with and adapted himself to the physical environment. The availability of local rock has led to a preponderance of building in stone in highland Britain, and with it a much greater chance of survival than was enjoyed by the early wooden structures of the lowlands. The types of material used also led to variations in the style of architecture adopted, adding yet another distinctive facet to the man-made landscape of our upland regions. Even today, after a hundred years of improved communications which have seen the breaking down of many economic and cultural barriers between the uplands and lowlands, highland Britain is still very much a landscape where rock and stone assert themselves either as bare, ragged skylines or more humbly in modest cottages or farmland carefully apportioned by loose stone walls.

The discovery of upland Britain by the ordinary traveller, tourist, artist and, latterly, industrialist came relatively late. The sixteenth and seventeenth centuries provide plenty of evidence of sea captains willing to sail to the distant corners of the globe but, except in the case of a select band of hardy adventurers, the more mountainous parts of Britain were shrouded in secrecy and left to those who, by accident of birth, had to wrest a living against the odds. Even the intrepid woman traveller Celia Fiennes, who in 1685 started a journey on horseback through Britain which was to last for twenty years, adopted an indifferent attitude to the more hilly parts. Her diary – really a series of jottings on any subject that took her fancy – contains little specific reference to life and landscape of the highlands; she always regretted leaving the industrial towns for what she considered untamed and uncivilized parts. As her long tour was coming to an end, the hack journalist Daniel Defoe was beginning the first of three tours which carried him the length and breadth of the kingdom. Defoe was happy enough amidst the ordered landscape of lowland England, for he could equate good farming practice with his view of beauty. Even the industrial towns of Lancashire had some merit, but as he made his way northwards to the Lake District he felt he was 'leaving the pleasantest part of Britain and entering a land of unhospitable terror, barren and bleak, no use to man or beast'. Celia Fiennes had enjoyed the waterfalls on the edge of the Lake District but was happy not to penetrate the interior, where 'the hills were farre worse for height and stony-nesse'.

Attitudes were to change considerably during the next century, when travellers in search of the picturesque suddenly found mountain scenery quite acceptable. Under the influence of the ideas of people like William Gilpin, any natural scene could qualify as picturesque provided that it was well composed and harmoniously coloured. As a result, the mountainous parts of the Lake District and North Wales became part of the itinerary for an ever-increasing number of tourists who were willing to combat the hostile elements, bad roads and primitive accommodation in pursuit of their goal. The poet Thomas Gray first came to the Lake District in 1769 and his description, written in the form of a journal to a friend, was later incorporated in Thomas West's *A Guide to the Lakes* when it reached its second edition in 1780. The account is clear and precise, though at times it lapses into bouts of exaggerated writing which might have deterred rather than encouraged any would-be-visitor. His description of Borrowdale is typical of the whole work and, though blissfully ignorant of nature's handiwork, is at pains to stress the fears that might overcome any unsuspecting traveller:

> The whole way down and the road on both sides is strewed with piles of fragments, strangely thrown across each other, and of dreadfull bulk; the place reminds me of those passes in the Alps, where the guides tell you to move with speed, and say nothing, lest the agitation of the air should loosen the snows above, and bring down a mass that would overwhelm a caravan. I took this counsel here, and hastened on in silence.

Not everyone took Gray's account seriously, and even the author of the guide dismissed it as 'the spoils of fancy he was pleased to indulge himself at'. The guide apparently was not adversely affected by the excesses of Gray's writings, and by 1812 it had gone into its tenth edition. Much of its success was due to the list of viewpoints from which the tourist could observe the mountain scenery, fully equipped with a Claude glass and sketch pad.

All the early guide books covering mountain areas suffered from a lack of basic knowledge about the fashioning of the landscape by nature as well as the time scale involved. Stones and boulders lying at the foot of cliffs had inevitably just arrived as the result of a recent earthquake. There were, too, those who believed that active volcanoes still existed in the Highlands of Scotland. Dun Caan, whose flat-topped summit dominates the island of Raasay and was specifically sought out by Dr Johnson and James Boswell during their Hebridean tour of 1773, was thought to be a volcanic cone which occasionally emitted puffs of smoke from vents (caves) on its southern flanks. It was not until the early decades of the nineteenth century that a sense of realism took over from fanciful accounts. The growth of the science of geology and the recognition that landscapes had evolved over millions of years, often by processes long since completed, represented a tremendous breakthrough. William Smith (1769-1834), a civil engineer, had begun working on the rocks of the Bath district before the eighteenth century was out and soon found that similar formations could be identified in other parts of the country by their fossil content. His first geological map, dated 1799, was of the Bath area only, but as he began to study other areas he decided to produce a map of the rock formations of the whole country. This he achieved in 1815 'after twenty-four years of intense application', as he himself put it.

Strata Smith, as he became known, was not the sole originator of this new school of geology, but his work undoubtedly influenced men like John Farey, working in the Peak District, and Jonathan Otley, busy in the Lake District unravelling the geological succession of an area increasingly under the gaze of a new breed of tourist. Even Wordsworth, in his expressive *Guide to the Lake District*, felt obliged in the editions published after 1842 to include an appendix on the rock types of the area, in this case written by no less an authority than Adam Sedgwick, the Professor of Geology at Cambridge. Jonathan Otley, a local guide, had already published in the *Lonsdale Magazine* for 1823 an essay in which he set out the main outcrops of the various rock types present and their influence over the scenery. The Borrowdale Volcanic Beds, for example, were brought to the attention of the visitor because all 'our fine towering crags belong to it and most of the cascades among the lakes fall over it'.

Elsewhere in Britain the close relationship between the type of rock and the resulting landscape was becoming more widely accepted. Not only were characteristic landforms found to occur time and time again with a particular rock type, but there was also a distinctive human response reflected in the whole appearance of the landscape. Apart from the areas which, because of their complex rock types, do not fall into a single distinctive category, there are five individual scenic types which can be distinguished in upland Britain on the basis of their underlying rock formations.

## Granite landscapes

Granite has such a reputation for toughness and solidity that it is not surprising that it plays a prominent role in the geography of our upland regions. Being formed deep down in the earth's crust, it was able to cool slowly and therefore develop a prominent crystalline structure. On Dartmoor the rock has large finger-like crystals of white felspar which give it its overall colouring. In the Shap area, on the eastern fringes of the Lake District, the felspar is pink so that the resulting stone has a warm appearance when used in cottage building. Cairngorm granite is similar in colour, though so little of the rock has been quarried in the past that its impact on the man-made landscape is much less.

Of the succession of uncovered granite domes which make up the backbone of the South-West Peninsula, Dartmoor is the best known, partly because of the 200 square miles of countryside where the rock occurs at the surface. At Yes Tor in the north the gently rounded contours of the upland plateau rise to a height of almost 2,000ft, but over much of the moor the tops are well below this level. Compared with the areas around, the granite heartland has resisted erosion so that it stands well above the marginal countryside, often ending in a well-defined edge. In many ways this granite margin is a cultural boundary as well, for within it cultivated fields gradually disappear and the number of settlements and individual farms decreases rapidly. This outfield area, beyond the present limits of enclosed farmland, has not always been neglected, for both prehistoric man and the early medieval colonists, intent on pushing the frontiers of habitation well beyond the 1,000ft contour, settled here. Plentiful supplies of moorstone scattered over the surface were readily available for building homes and field boundaries. If subsistence farming was to be

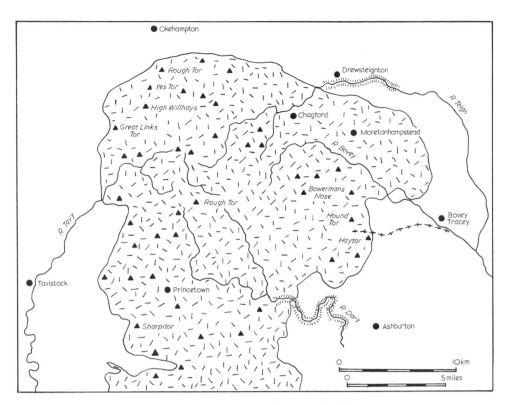

Fig 1    The Dartmoor granite outcrop with the principal tors

successful, fields had to be hewn out of the waste, and this usually involved a preliminary clearance of the scattered boulders littering the surface – boulders that were incorporated in the dwelling house, barns and other outbuildings as well as the field walls. Some of the stones were so huge that teams of horses were used to drag them from the fields. For use as cornerstones in buildings they were lifted into position by means of a chain and pulley system, again with the aid of horse power. Hansford Worth, a noted Devon geologist and antiquary, summarized the part played by granite in the life of the region in a series of papers collected together under the title of *The Moorstone Age*. Apart from the dressed stone used in churches from the fourteenth century onwards and in the great rebuilding period of manor houses and farm buildings which took place in the reign of Elizabeth I, the granite found innumerable other uses. Small everyday objects like the quern or the farmhouse cider press were also fashioned from it.

The qualities of granite as a building stone in the world outside the moor only came to be recognized at a much later period. Quarries like those of Haytor on the eastern fringes of Dartmoor or De Lank on the margins of Bodmin Moor were to send their hewn stone all over the kingdom. Their development coincided with the recognition that in granite there was a crystalline rock of an almost uniform character that rendered it impervious to water and resistant to

19

2   The tramway of granite rails which served the Haytor quarries

the smoke pollution of the industrial towns. Within a few years of this realization it was sought by engineer and architect alike. Stone from Haytor found favour for building the quays of the nearby port of Teignmouth in 1820, and it was not long before these same quays were exporting the granite blocks to London for use in the pier supports of the old London Bridge as well as in Nelson's column. The Georgian architects, laying out new precincts in the towns, used granite for both public buildings and private houses, particularly in Devon and Cornwall where transport costs did not prove an insuperable barrier. Even in this century the architect Sir Edwin Lutyens built Castle Drogo near Drewsteignton of granite – perhaps the last time the stone was used for a private house. Today the Haytor quarries lie abandoned amidst the heather and bracken of the moor which is gradually closing in on them. The old tramway, with its granite 'rails', is also largely overgrown and needs seeking out by the enthusiast with an eye for the unusual.

Granite so dominates the man-made landscape of the interior of Devon and Cornwall that we are in danger of overlooking the way in which it shaped the basic form and detailed features of the region long before prehistoric man entered the scene. Vertical joints in the granite, perhaps dating from the time of its cooling many millions of years ago, are believed to control the present rolling surface of the moor. Where the joints are closely spaced the rock has proved more susceptible to wearing down and so open basin-like valleys have formed.

In contrast, the broad-backed ridges tend to have survived where a wider joint spacing exists. This same wider joint system is believed to have influenced the development of that other granite landform, the upstanding tor, which stands as a sentinel on many an upland skyline. Even the casual observer can see how the vertical joints which divide up the tor vary in spacing from about 1ft to 20ft apart. Combined with the almost horizontal false bedding planes, they make each tor look as if it were made up of stone blocks, like a roughly constructed and half-finished building. Some of the 'building blocks' have obviously been displaced in the past and lie littered around the foot of the tor. Sometimes the tor has virtually disappeared under the debris of its own destruction. Movement of the broken-off blocks took place in the past when Dartmoor was subject to the fullest effects of soil flow (solifluction) due to Arctic-type conditions during the Ice Age. It is because of this that extensive boulder fields, made up of angular rock fragments known as clitter, make an apron around many of the tors, especially on their north-facing slopes. Vegetation has masked the clitter slopes to some extent, but one cannot fail to be unaware of the broken rock fragments underfoot as the tor is approached.

While a whole series of granite plutons were being emplaced in the south-west of England, another great mass of the same rock type was cooling slowly at depth in the Highlands of Scotland. This, too, was later to be exposed to form the present day Cairngorm and Lochnager mountains, the former representing the largest area in Britain above the 4,000ft contour; individual summits reach to over 4,200ft, the highest being Ben Macdui at 4,296ft. Everywhere the same pink boulders litter the tops. Unlike the Dartmoor granite, the rock here has not

3   Houndtor, with its weathered granite showing the false bedding planes and vertical jointing to perfection. Around are dislodged boulders forming the clitter

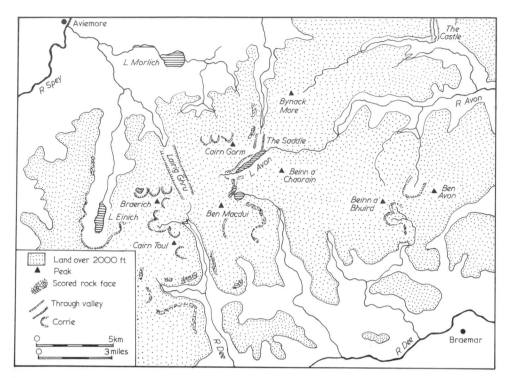

Fig 2  Landscape features of the Cairngorms

found favour either for building purposes or as a road metal, largely because the
area was so inaccessible until its development as a winter sports centre based on
nearby Aviemore. In winter there are ski runs available on the mountain slopes
of the Cairngorms and an access road up to 2,000ft now serves a number of
chair lifts to the top. There are difficulties in promoting skiing in this area, not
the least being the unreliability of a thick snow cover in milder winters. Even
after a heavy snowfall it may not cover the granite boulders which lie scattered
over the slopes, especially in exposed areas subject to wind drifting. In spite of
these inherent difficulties the region seems destined to become a major leisure
centre, not only for winter sports but for summer pursuits as well. Walking and
camping holidays are well catered for in what is one of the few remaining wild
and unspoilt parts of Britain. A walk through the great trench of the Lairig
Ghru – a result of ice erosion during the later phases of the Pleistocene
glaciation – following what was once a drover's route right through the
mountain heart to Braemar 20 miles away, is an exhilarating experience
without parallel in this country. Even on one of the hot days of the fine summer
of 1976 it was possible to walk through the Lairig Ghru from the
Rothiemurchus Forest in the north to the Dee headwaters in the south and
meet only a handful of fellow travellers. For hours the loneliness of the walk
provided a view of mountains unblemished by human form or influence. Few
climbers venture into this part of the Cairngorms, for granite weathers badly on

22

the surface and therefore gives few safe handholds. Where climbing is possible, gulleys, fissures and ladders provide the only safe and acceptable means of reaching the top.

The summit plateau of the Cairngorms above the 4,000ft contour has become very accessible since the building of the chair lifts in the 1960s. A first-time visitor will be immediately struck by the scatter of pink granite boulders which lie prostrate all over the surface. In one or two places there are wart-like protruberances of solid rock – the equivalent of the Dartmoor tors. Although not as widespread or as large, the Cairngorm tors are believed to have a similar origin dating back to the Ice Age. Glaciation must have been much more severe here than in the south-west of England, so the survival of tors on the Cairngorm summit is something of a surprise. It is possible that the tors here represent the remnants of much larger masses of partially rotted granite, perhaps formed under warmer climatic conditions than at present. When the freeze–thaw processes were operative during glacial times, the remaining solid rock was still able to withstand complete wearing down. Under the severe conditions then in operation great masses of the granite must have been prised away from the parent rock and in this way the extensive boulder fields of the summit plateau came into being. Miraculously, some of the granite outcrops managed to withstand the glacial onslaught to the extent that after it was over they were able to survive as tors.

4   Cairn Gorm summit with its surface covered by granite boulders around one of its many tors

## Volcanic landscapes

It is hard to imagine a greater contrast in the geological history of these islands than that which took place early in the Tertiary period, perhaps twenty-five million years ago. While the present lowlands of south-east England around London and Southampton were in a tranquil state, receiving deposits of sand and clay from the waters of a shallow sea, parts of north-west Britain, especially in the Inner Hebrides, were in the throes of considerable upheaval, with volcanoes pouring forth great lava flows and ejecting dense clouds of dust and ash. This intense activity was probably associated with the movement of one of the great crustal plates that form major elements in the earth's plan. A series of active volcanoes centred on islands like Mull and Skye were responsible for vast flows of mobile lava which completely blanketed the surrounding countryside. In some areas, a succession of flows built up, rather like layers of icing on a cake. Earth movements were taking place at the same time and the surface was rent apart. Sometimes hot magma (molten rock) entered superficial cracks and when it cooled it formed a distinctive dyke rock. Much of western Scotland is crossed by dyke swarms which converge on the centres of vulcanism. Many of the volcanic vents were later to cave in, and in this way great sunken cauldrons came into being, similar to features we see today in active volcanic areas.

The various lava flows, even though they took place millions of years ago, have left their mark on the character of the Inner Hebridean islands as well as on Antrim in Northern Ireland. In the northern part of the island of Skye the long peninsula known as Trotternish has more than 400 square miles of lava with individual flows up to 50ft thick. Tabular hills with terraced slopes marking the edge of individual flows dominate what would otherwise be a dull terrain. An individual flow often has a weathered upper surface and this gives a reasonable thickness of soil available for cultivation. On the south-west coast of Mull there is a curiosity preserved in the lava cliffs south of Rudha na h-Uamha, where a fossil tree 40ft high stands upright amidst the columnar basalts. The trunk of the tree is represented by a cast filled with a bleached basalt which has taken the place of the original wood burnt out as the lava flows enveloped it. Although it is difficult to reach, the unique fossil is ample reward for those prepared to scramble along a rough coastal track in the area aptly named the Wilderness.

Impressive though this feature is, the best volcanic scenery occurs in the Trotternish peninsula of Skye where over 2,000ft of lava flows are piled one on top of the other. The whole backbone of this northern peninsula is made up of lava which reaches its most impressive form in a high east-facing escarpment. The basalts here overlie Jurassic sediments, but as these have moved they have undermined the lava beds, causing them to slip forward. The result is one of the finest examples of landslip topography in upland Britain. The Old Man of Storr, a 160ft pinnacle of rock standing isolated in front of the scarp face, invites comparison with its namesake, the sea stack off the west coast of the island of

5 Past landslipping of great rock masses from the lava crags has given rise to this tormented landscape known as the Quirang

6 Bare, heavily glaciated country fashioned out of the volcanic beds of the central Lake District. The view is across the Buttermere Fells towards Scafell in the distance (*Aerofilms*)

Hoy in the Orkneys. Further north there is the feature known as the Quirang, a succession of rock slips where the lava has broken away from the towering crags of the main escarpment. Much of the slipping must have occurred during the glacial period as there is little evidence of mass movement at the present time. Today it is a scenic curiosity to whet the appetite of those prepared to venture away from the better-known part of southern Skye centred on the Cuillin Hills. In times past the rumpled ground of the Quirang served as a natural hiding place for cattle rustlers.

Vulcanism of a much earlier period of geological time has played its part in fashioning the details in the scenery of two of our finest mountain areas, the Lake District and Snowdonia. In the north-west corner of Wales with its succession of peaks topping the 3,000ft contour, the core area around Snowdon itself is made up of the products of past volcanic activity, not so much lava as the finer ashes and tuffs. Where these have been compressed the result is a tough rock which weathers slowly. Not surprisingly, therefore, the highest peaks like Snowdon, Glyder Fawr and Glyder Fach are largely fashioned out of the volcanic beds, thrown into a series of gentle folds. The folded strata are best seen in the back wall of the corrie basin of Llyn Idwal, where glacial erosion has bitten deeply into the northern face of the Glyder Range. It is difficult to pinpoint the exact centre from which this volcanic material was ejected, but one suggestion is that it lay close to Foel Gras, a mountain in the Carneddau Range away to the north-east.

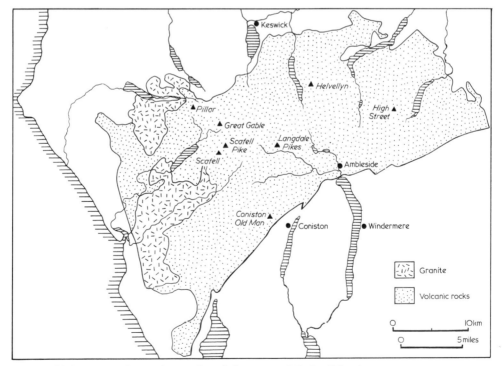

Fig 3    Volcanic and granite rocks of the central Lake District

26

7 Typical vernacular architecture of the Lake District seen in a house in Old Ambleside. Local stone has been used for both the walls and the roofing slates

The impact which the volcanic rocks have had on the scenery of an area is even more strikingly seen in the Lake District. Running across the region from south-west to north-east is a broad band of the Borrowdale Volcanic Series, a succession of ashes, lavas, tuffs and breccias. As in Snowdonia, they form an extremely tough and unyielding group of rocks, and as a result the highest mountains – Scafell, Scafell Pike, Great Gable, Coniston Old Man, Helvellyn and the Langdale Pikes – all belong to this formation. One reason for this is that some of the tuffs have been partly altered by heat and pressure to become much harder, and flinty in character. Together with the lavas, the bands of flinty tuffs are responsible for many of the bare rock crags in areas like Borrowdale and the Great Langdale valley. The impressive wall of Walla Crag, towering above Derwentwater, is composed of a succession of lava flows. The broken and much-weathered edge of Hallin Fell, a fine viewpoint noted for its prospect over Ullswater, developed as a band of hardened tuffs and has consistently resisted erosion by water and ice, both past and present.

Much of the volcanic activity which gave rise to the rocks forming the present landscape of the central Lake District took place under water so that, in addition to truly volcanic beds, the Borrowdale Series also contains beds of hardened mudstones. As a result of compression these have been altered into the famous green slates which are still quarried in a few places. Many of the beds are finely cleft and therefore of use as a source of slate for roofing and

27

cladding. Less suitable beds have been worked as a building stone, and nearly all the older cottages of the central Lake District have this green and brown rough stone in their unmortared walls. The old centre of Ambleside, lying tucked away up the hill from the bustle of the busy tourist town, has a fine group of old cottages and houses built of the local stone; most of the farm buildings of valleys like Borrowdale or Great Langdale are constructed from it, as are the galleried spinning cottages of Troutbeck or West Hartsop. Even new bungalows and houses make use of the local building material, so that the industry is still an important source of employment, both in the quarries and the dressing sheds. About 15 per cent of the quarried material is used for roofing slates, but by far the greater proportion consists of flat slabs for the building courses of cottages and houses. Having adopted local styles of architecture as well as the local material, the Lake District has not suffered to the same extent as many of our mountain areas from past excesses of unplanned building. Now with the planning controls exercised by the National Park Authority the future seems assured.

Long before man began to exploit the volcanic rocks of the Lake District as a building stone, some of the beds had been sought out and used for making stone axes. The flinty tuff bands were found, perhaps by chance, to be especially suitable for shaping, and as a result Neolithic man established his 'factory' on the slopes below the Langdale Pikes and in the area around. Past glacial activity had already loosened the rock so that early man found it relatively easy to prise it away from the outcrop and then fashion the fragment by splitting it to form a fine cutting edge. The discovery of the five-thousand-year-old industry dates from 1947 when the slopes below the Pike of Stickle were found to be littered with thousands of flint chippings, roughly shaped axeheads and many rejects. Subsequently other working areas were found around Scafell Pike and Glaramara, proving that the industry was of more than local importance. From these remote heights of the Lake District the axeheads travelled, through trade, to distant parts of the kingdom, perhaps the clearest indication of the value placed by prehistoric man on this distinctive rock type (see pp 184 and 185).

Unlike granite, so susceptible to surface weathering, volcanic rocks usually provide ideal conditions for climbing. The knobbly surface can give excellent handholds on bare faces, while fissures provide an alternative method of ascent. The Glyder Range in Snowdonia, particularly the faces of Tryfan and the Idwal Slabs, have been much in favour in recent years. All the year, the multi-coloured tents are sprinkled over the fields below the crags by the side of Thomas Telford's great Holyhead road as it wends its way through the col towards the head of the Nant Ffrancon valley. The mushrooming of climbing-gear shops in Bethesda, Llanberis, Capel Curig and Bangor is an indication of how rapid the growth of this relatively new leisure activity has been. The Ogwen area tends to be favoured for beginners; the Llanberis valley, in contrast, has some of the hardest of the Welsh climbs, like Lliwedd in Cwm Dyli and Crib Goch buttress high above Cwm Glas. Whereas the early climbers

28

8 The volcanic area around Snowdon is becoming increasingly popular for winter climbing, especially in the vicinity of Crib Goch

tended to restrict their activities to the summer months, it has now become very much an all-the-year-round activity, for although some of the classic rock climbs are impossible in the winter owing to frozen snow and rime, the high gullies can still prove exhilarating, especially during a rare flowering of sunny, anticyclonic weather.

## Limestone scenery

With its varied succession of rocks, upland Britain is a treasure house of great scenic contrasts. Within a particular rock type, however, there is often a repetition of landform features even though the areas may be separated by the whole length of the kingdom. This is well illustrated by the limestone districts which occur in widely scattered parts of highland Britain, and the descriptive term 'mountain limestone' is often given to these thick calcareous beds of the Carboniferous Age. Because of the ease with which limestone 'swallows' surface drainage, most of the outcrops are waterless in appearance with the main flow taking place underground. As a result there is a whole new and distinctive suite of landforms associated with this subterranean world. The surface, too, has its own characteristic features, for although the area appears

29

'dry' today, this has not always been the case. Relict landforms like dry valleys, sink holes and dry waterfalls take us back in time to the period during the Ice Age when conditions were very different from those we experience today.

The area of mountain limestone stretches in a discontinuous band right across Britain. In Somerset, the Mendips, rising to over 1,000ft, have a tenuous link with similar limestone areas around the northern fringes of the South Wales coalfield. A thin strip of limestone runs through much of the length of the Welsh Marches until it finally reaches the north coast to form headlands like the Great Orme at Llandudno. Limestone beds of the same age make up one of the two dominant rock types of the Pennines and are especially prominent in the area of the White Peak and around Malham. The northern Pennines and Lake District each have their smaller limestone districts which nevertheless show up distinctly through their landforms. Everywhere the limestone is hard and massively bedded, but with a well-developed vertical jointing system. It is the combination of vertical fissures (pitches) and horizontal passages which allows the subterranean drainage system to develop. The point of access at the surface is usually marked by a conical pit, variously known as a swallow hole, swallet or shake hole in different parts of the country. Some still have surface streams entering them, but most are dry and can only have developed under the wetter conditions of the past. Once underground the water is capable of widening and extending the passage system so that, under suitable conditions, great caves have developed. Some passages have a water flow in them which is akin to that of a normal stream, only partly filling the cross-section. These are known as vadose passages. Others – phreatic passages – are more cylindrical in shape and completely filled by the underground water flow, rather like a gigantic pipe. Both types form part of the hidden limestone drainage pattern, though the phreatic pipes tend to occur only in the lower levels below the normal water table. The study of cave and drainage systems has been actively pursued during the past thirty years, and numerous groups of enthusiasts now regularly enter the underground world to explore and map. In some cases the results of exploration have been surprising. In the Mynydd Llangattock area close to the Brecon Beacons of South Wales, narrow clefts at the surface lead into a system which extends for over 9 miles underground. The entrance is by a cave, Agen Allwedd – now closed by an iron door – high up on the scarp face at the end of the old quarrymen's track. Other extensive underground cave and passage complexes exist in South Wales, as in the Mellte valley, a headwater tributary of the River Neath. The river normally flows beneath the usually dry pebbly bed for about a mile before descending into the much-explored cavern Porth Yr Ogof. On the surface the countryside around is pitted with circular depressions where the limestone has collapsed. Although not impressive at close quarters, the swallow holes, especially when arranged along linear belts, add a new dimension to the landscape when seen from the air.

Cave systems entered by small clefts, like those of South Wales, remained largely undiscovered until the recent surge of interest in speleology. The more

30

obvious and accessible caves, however, had long been frequented, first by animals seeking a natural shelter during the Ice Age and later by prehistoric man. Many of the famous show caves of today, like Wookey Hole in the Mendips or Peak Cavern in Derbyshire, provide plenty of evidence of this early occupation. The chance opening up of the Hyena Cave below Wookey Hole during the building of a canal in 1852 led Sir William Boyd Dawkins to carry out a thorough examination. In addition to hyena bones, there were remains of mammoth, rhinoceros, lion, bear and reindeer, indicating a long period of occupance spanning several changes of climate. Charcoal from fires and tools pointed to man having also used the cave at an early date. Similarly, the digging of a tunnel in Gough's Cave in Cheddar Gorge in 1903 led to the discovery of the

9  Gaping Ghyll, the largest of a number of swallow holes which fringe the lower slope of Ingleborough where surface streams enter the system of underground drainage (*C. H. Wood (Bradford) Ltd*)

skeleton of a young man belonging to the Paleolithic period. The nearby Cox's cave was rediscovered in 1832 after remaining undisturbed for centuries. Those who entered found the floor piled with bones, but unfortunately commercial rather than scientific interests prevailed and they were piled into wagons and carried off to be used as a fertilizer. For the thousands who now crowd into the Cheddar and Wookey caves, interest is centred on the natural formations which are displayed to full advantage by subtle lighting effects. A visitor to Wookey in 1681 would not have had the benefit of such splendid illumination and not surprisingly, as one complained, 'twenty-four candles barely lit up the huge cavern'.

One limestone area with a wealth of both surface and underground landforms is that of the Craven Uplands centred on Malham, now much visited by tourist and student alike. Unlike that of the Mendip Hills, the limestone here is almost horizontal and bounded on its southern and western sides by major faults. The result is a block of plateau country at a height of about 1,300ft with the major fault lines forming marginal features such as Giggleswick Scar, Malham Cove and Gordale Scar. Resting on the limestone surface the repetitive sequence of shales, grits, coals and limestones – the Yoredale Series – is responsible for upstanding massifs like Ingleborough, Pen y Ghent, Whernside and Fountains Fell. These carry surface drainage, so that when the streams reach the limestone outcrop they disappear down a succession of swallow holes. The upper margin of the limestone plateau around Ingleborough, for example, is pitted with swallow holes, including perhaps the most famous of all, Gaping Ghyll, with its 365ft drop into the expansive cavern below ground. Its great size rules out development under present-day conditions, and therefore we must look to the Ice Age, when much more surface water was available and other erosional processes were more pronounced. Today only a relatively small volume of water from Fell Beck tumbles into the chamber. Once underground, the water takes a circuitous course of about a mile before emerging at Clapham Beck Head. Some famous experiments in 1904 using water impregnated with salt showed that it could take up to eleven days to pass through the underground labyrinth. After heavy rain, however, the journey might take only a matter of hours. As with the Mendip caves, those around Ingleborough have been intensively explored, and one is open to the public, with an entrance in Clapdale, about a mile from the village of Clapham. The discovery of the Ingleborough Cave, almost 2,000ft long, dates from 1837 when a Mr Farrer, the owner of the estate, decided to break through an outer stalagmite barrier to enter the present cavern.

For many visitors to this area of the central Pennines the village of Malham has become the focal centre. The nearby 'amphitheatre' of Malham Cove, with its encircling cliffs utterly dwarfing the small stream emerging at the foot, immediately attracts attention. A break in the centre of the cove rim suggests that there was once a stream cascading down from the top, but here again no true waterfall may have existed since the Ice Age. There is no doubt that under exceptional conditions there is the occasional flow over the top, for according to Howson, a local author, a stream had twice poured over the cove during the forty years previous to 1850 when he was writing. The plateau around the top of the cove can also boast one of the finest displays of limestone pavement in Britain, with the bared and fretted rock split up as a result of solution weathering. It is uncertain when the pavement came into being, but it seems likely that the solution processes which led to the formation of the clints (columns) and grykes (fissures) were most effective when a soil cover gave rise to acidic waters. The subsequent exposing of the limestone rock is believed to have taken place during the final phase of the Ice Age, perhaps twenty thousand years ago. Even today the lowering of the upper limestone surface is still continuing at a slow pace. Some idea of the rate is provided by the evidence of the Norber boulders lying on the fell top about a mile east of Clapham. These are erratics of Silurian Grit left behind by the ice, and today they rest in rather ungainly fashion on pedestals of limestone. The latter are about a foot in height, suggesting that this amount of solution weathering of the limestone surface has taken place during the past fifteen thousand years. This may seem slow by human standards, but it indicates that the continuous cycle of change is still affecting the landscape. If we measure the amount of carbonate in the stream waters of the area a figure of about 0.04mm a year for the lowering of the

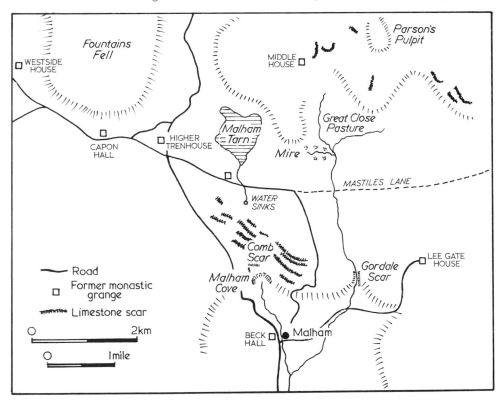

Fig 4   Features of the limestone country around Malham

33

10  One of the Norber boulders of Silurian gritstone set on a plinth of limestone. Erosion of the limestone around contrasts with the protection afforded by the boulder and this gives a measure of the amount of solution weathering since the arrival of the erratic

limestone surface is suggested, while another 0.043mm a year is estimated to be lost through underground solution. Taking these two values together gives a figure for the erosion of the limestone of the same order as that obtained from the evidence of the Norber perched boulders. In certain local areas much higher values of solution weathering prevail, especially where acidulated waters drain directly on to a bare limestone pavement. Another variant is caused by different snowfall amounts, as snow can hold more carbon dioxide than ordinary rainwater and therefore tends to increase the rate of limestone weathering. One worker in the area, Parry, has even suggested that the limestone pavements themselves may have originated as a result of snowbank solution at the end of the Ice Age, up to about 7500 BC.

Skirting Malham Cove and its limestone pavements the road across to Littondale soon leads on to Malham Moor with its tarn and clump of trees dominating the open landscape. The existence of the tarn in what should be a waterless terrain is something of a puzzle until it is realized that faulting has intervened and led to the preservation of a small parcel of older Silurian rock. As this, along with some patches of glacial drift, is impervious, the surface waters do not readily disappear underground as on the limestone outcrop.

Once the small stream leaving Malham Tarn has crossed the Silurian rocks and reached the limestone it has no option but to burrow underground, though its valley feature continues southwards in the direction of Comb Scar. Occasional flows of water still occur in the 'dry' valley and in 1962 it even cascaded over the 'dry' waterfall at Comb Scar. A more permanent flow, Gordale Beck, exists further east, draining the marshy ground of Great Close Mire. It then flows through its narrow valley before dropping over the scarp edge at Gordale Scar. The beauty of this area has long attracted both poets and artists, and there is a wealth of descriptive writing about the waterfall. An early visitor was the poet Thomas Gray, who was completely overcome by what he saw but managed to clamber up the limestone face to a vantage point from which he could view the fall, 'the principal horror of the place'. Wordsworth came with his sister about thirty years later and referred to Gordale chasm in one of his sonnets. He was clearly impressed, writing: 'I stayed there not without shuddering, a quarter of an hour, and thought my trouble richly repaid for the impression will last with life'. Later writers, such as the authors of Victorian guide books, continued to whet the appetite of any prospective visitor, though the description was now becoming less romantic and more scientific. In *Murray's Guide,* published in 1867, it is noted that

> . . . above the first waterfall a limestone ridge unites the two sides of the scar; and a hole through it, 8 feet high by 15 feet long, gives a passage to the water which, it is said, first burst through in 1730 after a violent thunderstorm but it is probable that the whole form, first produced by contraction during the consolidation of the rock, has been enlarged by the action of water at remote periods.

In addition to the swallow holes which pepper the surface of the limestone plateau, there are a number of much larger depressions. On Malham Moor they occur mainly in the vicinity of Parson's Pulpit, north-east of Malham Tarn. They can be over half a mile across and 300ft deep, recalling the dolines of the Yugoslavian karst. Their origin is uncertain, but one suggestion is that they are the end product of a long period of solution weathering under a soil cover. The once favoured belief that they arose as a result of underground collapse of limestone beds is no longer widely held. An alternative explanation places emphasis on past conditions when there were patches of shale remaining on top of the limestone surface: the depressions are thought to have arisen at the edge of the outcrop. Whatever the true explanation of their origin, they add diversity to the limestone landscape, which can, on occasions, appear rather dull and uniform, especially when seen under conditions of low stratus cloud.

Major valleys like Swaledale and Wensleydale, which come within the bounds of the Yorkshire Dales National Park, also have their full share of limestone scenery. Their sides often show marked rock scars as harder limestone bands outcrop at intervals down a hillside slope. During the Ice Age powerful ice streams moved down the valleys of the Swale, Ure and Nidd, and in doing so stripped off the weathered mantle to expose the bare scars of rock. In

11  The Buttertubs, vertical slots in the limestone which lead into an extensive underground drainage system

Littondale the projecting buttress of Kilnsey Crag was undercut by ice to leave the famous overhang, a test for every novice climber. Further north near Hawes a relatively thin bed of limestone set between two beds of shale has been responsible for the unusual Hardraw Force. The limestone, with its greater resistance to erosion, forms an overhanging ledge, while the softer shale underneath has been scooped out, making it possible to walk behind the waterfall – a prospect which delighted many of the early Victorian tourists. During flood conditions the normally small stream is swollen to the extent that it sends a vast jet shooting off the ledge and into the boiling pot below. As one visitor put it, 'the white column of water, relieved against the inky rocks, and the impending character of the precipices around, forms an imposing scene which has been worthily portrayed by the pencil of Turner'. Wordsworth, on a visit in December 1799, found the winter setting of the fall inspiring and wrote at length to Coleridge about it. Close at hand is the Buttertubs Pass, running across country from Hawes to Muker and climbing as high as 1,700ft at the summit col. Just after reaching the head of the pass and beginning the descent into Swaledale the buttertubs themselves are met – deep circular columnar fissures in the limestone. They are aptly named, for with their fluted sides and flat bottoms they recall the old slatted wooden tubs used for storing butter. The surrounding hillsides have similar but smaller features where a limestone band lies in juxtaposition with a shale outcrop.

Many of the distinctive qualities which we associate with limestone country arise not so much from the rock itself, though clearly this asserts itself, but rather from man's use of it. Where it is well bedded and jointed, the bare hillside scars make a very accessible quarry for the stone. Its natural block-like character, together with the relative ease with which it can be shaped by hammer and chisel, has meant a wide use for building purposes, from the stately home to the humble cottage. Perhaps even more striking has been the use of limestone for walling, especially after the Enclosure Acts. The central part of the Peak District, in particular, is laced with mile after mile of loose stone walls, the earliest perhaps going back to the sixteenth century, when their curvilinear forms followed the boundaries of some former open strip. Most of the nineteenth-century walling is long and straight, parcelling the land up into huge rectangular blocks.

Limestone rock was also a valuable asset to the farmer as a source of lime; carefully applied, it could improve the quality of the land. Lime-burning kilns sprang up all over the limestone outcrop, especially during the 'Age of Improvement' in the late eighteenth and early nineteenth centuries when thousands of acres of moorland were being reclaimed. In the Yorkshire Dales National Park, for example, it is estimated that there were up to seven hundred kilns functioning at one time. In their usual form they consist of a squat tower of drystone masonry which encloses a funnel-shaped lining usually built of sandstone. The lime rock, together with coal in the ratio of 4 to 1, was loaded from the top, and the whole mass allowed to burn for up to three days. After firing, the lime and ash were raked out at the base of the kiln and loaded into carts for carrying to the fields and moorland wastes. The canals later became a useful means of distributing the lime, and many kilns were built on the canal banks, especially in areas where both coal and limestone were close at hand. Today the picturesque kilns lie abandoned, gradually falling apart. Modern methods of lime making require a much more sophisticated plant and a large-scale working operation to be economic. With their voracious appetite they consume vast quantities of rock, and huge quarries dominate areas around Buxton in the Peak District or Horton-in-Ribblesdale. As both are close to the boundaries of National Parks, the inevitable disfigurement of the landscape has aroused considerable opposition, especially as the surrounding countryside is covered with a blanket of white dust. For their part, the operating companies can point to the contribution they make in providing employment in areas which would otherwise experience considerable depopulation. The limestone is being increasingly used as a road metal and a basic constituent of concrete, so the quarries are likely to grow even more rapidly over the next decade. There is fortunately a credit side: earlier limestone quarries, now abandoned, like those which border the old Midland Railway line through Millers Dale in Derbyshire, have been sealed by a profusion of vegetation, so that in time they will merge imperceptibly into the side walls of the gorge.

## Sandstone country

After limestone, sandstone is probably the most widespread of rock types in upland Britain. Because of its range of colours, from dull grey to bright red, the sandstone gives rise to a rich variety of scenery. It can be fine-grained and therefore easily eroded, but often it is coarsely speckled with quartz chippings which make it highly resistent to weathering: for this variety the name gritstone seems appropriate. Both the natural and man-made landscapes respond to these variations in the actual rock type, so that there is no single really distinctive sandstone landscape. The Brecon Beacons, for example, have little in common with the gritstone moors of Yorkshire or the coastal plateau lands of Caithness.

In South Wales the Old Red Sandstone formation encircles the coalfield in a broad band of country which takes in the Fforest Fawr of Carmarthenshire, the Black Mountains and the Brecon Beacons. Throughout its outcrop there is a variable succession of marls, sandstones, conglomerates and breccias, each with its own character. Two beds in particular have the necessary resistance to create great upstanding plateaux – the Brownstones, 1,200ft thick, and the Plateau Beds which are responsible for the distinctive table tops of the Beacons and Black Mountains. The most striking feature of the area is the scalloped north face of the Beacons with its prominent cornices of Pen y Fan and Corn Du, both of which rise to almost 3,000ft. The sharp drop from the scarp top down into the coombe-like heads of valleys draining northwards to the Usk is

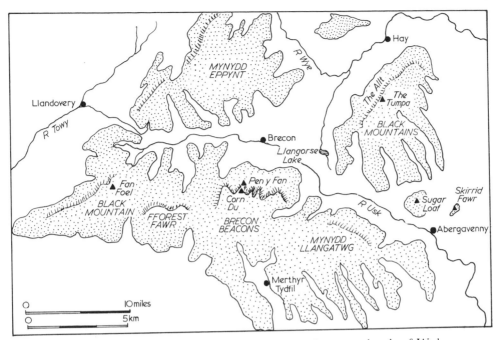

Fig 5   The Brecon Beacons together with other sandstone uplands of Wales

one of impressive proportions, particularly as it is largely bare rock, the harder sandstone and conglomerate bands standing out as strengthening ribs. Because of its height the ridge crest of the Beacons gives unparalleled views to both north and south.

Although the Brecon Beacons and the Black Mountains of Gwent have similar rock types, they are markedly different in appearance. A series of headwater streams has cut deeply into the Brownstones formation so that the once continuous plateau top of the Black Mountains is now represented only by a series of long, gently falling spurs. The crest ridge is still almost continuous and forms an imposing front overlooking the middle section of the Wye valley. Just below the crest there is a remarkable bench feature known as the Allt where a sequence of relatively hard sandstone bands has resisted erosion. As the undoubted contrasts in the scenery of the Black Mountains and Brecon Beacons cannot be explained in terms of rock type or structure, it is necessary to look elsewhere for a possible solution. At their highest point the Beacons are almost 300ft higher than the Black Mountains. They also lie more directly in the path of the westerly rain-bearing winds, thus receiving much greater amounts of precipitation. The same was probably true in the Ice Age, so that larger snowfields developed on the Beacons which in turn nurtured and sustained larger and more active valley glaciers. Much of the scalloped character of the Beacon scarp owes its origin to this fact. In contrast the Black Mountains, high as they are, were not subjected to such intense glacial effects and have remained relatively unscathed.

12   The Brecon Beacons as viewed across their north-facing escarpment in a south-easterly direction (*Aerofilms*)

Two hundred miles away across country in the Peak District of Derbyshire and the bleak upland wastes of the Yorkshire Pennines, a completely different landscape setting has been built on a sandstone base – here the coarse variety locally termed gritstone. Even though reclamation in the past has made deep inroads into the formerly extensive moorland tracts, large areas still remain. It is not a question of altitude, for nearby limestone areas at even greater heights have all been transformed into rich pastureland with even the occasional crop of oats being grown at heights of about 1,200ft. The contrast between the White Peak (limestone) and the Dark Peak (gritstone) stems largely from the poorer

40

siliceous soils derived from the underlying gritstone beds, which are reflected in the agricultural inferiority of the Dark Peak. At heights above 1,400ft there are thick beds of peat giving rise to ill-drained mosses which can be treacherous to cross at most times of the year. Anyone who has attempted to walk the final section of the Pennine Way from Kinder Scout to Edale after wet weather will know of the feeling of helplessness as the sodden peat becomes less and less able to support the weight of the human body. Certain sections of this famous and now increasingly popular upland walk, as in the area further north at Doctor's Gate, have had to be provided with duckboards and plastic matting to allow an easier passage.

The peaty acid soils of the gritstone moors are remarkable for the uniform vegetation cover they carry, with only a limited range of plant species. In the wetter mosslands cotton grass, the cross-leaved heath, the bog moss and the insectivorous sundew – trying to supplement the lack of nitrogen in the soil – form the most common plant association. In May and June the cotton grass is in full flower and its white fruiting heads in their thousands have given rise to such topographical names as Whitebed or Featherbed Moss. The peat, which on the Kinder plateau can be as much as 15ft thick, has been accumulating since about 6000 BC. We know this from Mesolithic flint implements which have been found under the lowest peat beds. It is not clear whether peat is forming under present-day conditions, for many of the sphagnum species found preserved in the peat are no longer growing on the surface of the moor. Pollution during the past two hundred years has undoubtedly contributed to the decline of the sphagnum, but whether this is the sole cause is unknown. Many moors now covered with cotton grass were formerly dominated by sphagnum, and in areas like the East Moor, close to Sheffield, pollution seems the most likely reason for the change.

Much of the forbidding appearance of the gritstone moors stems from their dark heather vegetation. Save for two months in the autumn, when the whole plateau top is a blaze of purple and mauve, the tangled mass of withered stems lacks the inviting quality of the springy turf of the limestone uplands. The dark appearance is not improved where controlled burning or swaling has taken place in the spring in order to promote the growth of fresh green shoots – an early bite both for sheep and red grouse – in the following year. Sadly, in the dry summer of 1976 thousands of acres of heather moor were burned and charred and are only now recovering.

Fortunately the monotony of the peat mosses and heather wastes on the plateau top is broken by the occasional rocky outcrops. In the Peak District they are especially prominent on Hathersage Moor where a bed of coarse pebbly sandstone, the Chatsworth Grit, has successfully resisted erosion to give rise to a series of tabular hills crowned with rock piles reminiscent of the Dartmoor tors. The parallel can be carried further, for around each knoll there are large flat boulders littering the adjacent slopes, the equivalent of the granite clitter. Freeze–thaw conditions during the period towards the close of the Ice

13   Brimham Rocks, where a bed of coarse sandstone has been fashioned into a curious collection of rock piles. Some, like the Idol, rest precariously on the smallest of pedestals

Age would seem to offer the best explanation of the shaping of the gritstone tors, often into curious forms resembling strange creatures. Mass movement of the sandstone blocks away from the tors would have taken place at the same time, as the superficial soil began to move slowly over the permanently frozen subsurface. Icy winds, perhaps armed with sharp stone fragments, would have helped in the work of fluting and reducing the upstanding rock masses. The fact that the rocks have survived to the present day points to a half-completed task on the part of the erosional agents.

One of the most fascinating collections of sandstone rock features occurs on Brimham Moor, north of Harrogate. Over an area of 50 acres, now under the care of the National Trust, pillars of Millstone Grit stand out defiantly against the elements. Over a period of several thousand years the rocks have undergone moulding so that their surfaces show evidence of fretting, cavitation and odd shaping. It was an area that fascinated the Victorian traveller, who was continually searching out the unusual. Many of the fanciful names given to individual rocks – Turtle, Oyster, the Frog, Dancing Bear and Watchdog – date from the last century. Brimham means 'high dwelling', suggesting early occupance of this rather exposed site which reaches over 900ft. The Victorian traveller was recommended to visit Brimham at dusk 'when the whole scene is more strangely fantastic than any other that can be found on this side of Saxon Switzerland. It is difficult to conceive circumstances of inanimate nature more affecting to the contemplative mind than the strange forms and unaccountable combination of these gigantic masses.'

Rivalling the tor grouping on Hathersage Moor and the Brimham Rocks as features of outstanding interest and spectacular scenery is the 'edge' country which occurs on both flanks of the Peak District. In the east the Millstone Grit outcrop is responsible for a series of rock ledges rising in steps from the floor of the Derwent valley. The hard band of rock may be only 40ft thick, but such is its resistance that it rises as a sheer wall of impressive solidity. Many sections form excellent nursery slopes for rock climbers. Where the rocks have been gently folded, as in the area known as the Roaches on the western fringes of the Peak District, the edge country becomes even more pronounced and concentrated. Here the Millstone Grit formation consists of three harder sandstone beds, the Chatsworth Grit, Roaches Grit and Five Clouds Sandstone, separated by softer shale bands. Because of its synclinal or piedish form, there is a repetition of beds on either flank, each giving rise to a prominent out-facing edge. Many of the rock outcrops have a block-like appearance due to well-developed bedding planes and vertical jointing. Weathering has also led to curious shapes and isolated pinnacles, and those of the Ramshaw Rocks must have been familiar features to the Roman soldiers who tramped the road which runs along the foot of the edge en route to Buxton.

14    Steeply dipping beds of grit give rise to a prominent escarpment along the western edge of the Roaches

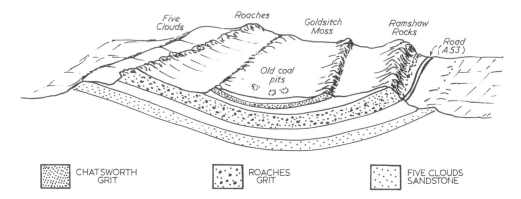

Fig 6   The basin structure of the Roaches area along the western edge of the Peak District

The sequence of hard sandstone layers and softer shale bands is repeated elsewhere in the Peak District, though its effects on the landscape are rather different. In the valley of Alport, one of the Derwent headwater streams, it has led to the creation of a fantastic assemblage of landscape features. Named Alport Castles, from their castellated form, they are entirely natural, though when seen from across the valley they could easily be mistaken for a man-made feature. Only a walk amongst the broken rock piles will finally convince the viewer that nature's own handiwork is represented. The great landslip must have taken place in the past when the underlying shale beds gave way and caused a great mass of sandstone to come away from the plateau edge. The mass movement most likely dates back to the Ice Age when landslipping was much more active than at present. Much the same explanation probably applies to yet another fantastic piece of sandstone landscape, the rocky cleft known as Lud's Church, due north of the Roaches. The feature was once named as one of the wonders of the Peak, and no Victorian traveller passed by without seeking it out on the wooded slopes of one of the tributaries of the River Dane. As a mass of the Roaches Grit moved away from the hillside it opened up a deep fissure with a dog-legged shape. To enter it is necessary to pass under a natural arch where one great slab of rock still links both sides. The name Lud's Church is intriguing: the most likely derivation seems to be the association of the cleft with Walter de Ludank, a follower of Wycliffe, who, in the fourteenth century, used the spot as a spiritual retreat.

Though man played no part in the grand design which created features like Alport Castles or Lud's Church, he modified the gritstone landscape of many parts of the Pennines once he realized the value of the rock for building and other specialized uses. The name Millstone Grit for the whole assemblage of different sandstone and shale beds clearly points to one very important use of the stone in the past. When millstones and grinding stones were in demand, many small quarries were opened up to supply this need. One can be seen close to the A265 Hathersage to Sheffield road; unfinished millstones still litter the old quarry floor. The Chatsworth Grit formation provided the best stone, especially in the area between Hathersage and Padley. More recently, pulp stones have been quarried for export to Finland. It is, however, as a building stone that the rock has been most extensively quarried. Many of the nineteenth-century industrial towns of the Pennine fringe were built of the dark grey or yellow sandstones, and today the houses still have an appearance of solidity in keeping with the attitude of their inhabitants. Unfortunately the rough surface of the stone attracted the smoke and dust of the local textile industries; public buildings also suffered, and a fine sweep like the Crescent at Buxton quickly acquired a grimy façade. Even Chatsworth House, the pride of the Peak, did not escape the polluting airs from nearby towns, although the problem has lessened considerably in recent years. Since the introduction of smokeless zones, many buildings have been cleaned, and now for the first time the real beauty of the stone can be appreciated.

## Shale and slate scenery

The muds which accumulated in the deeper waters of the various seas that existed at different times in the geological calendar have given rise to a range of rock types. In the lowlands, with their typically younger rocks, clay is the most common. In the uplands, by way of contrast, the muds have become compressed into shales. Where pressure has been great and exerted over a long period of time, the long axes of the sediment particles have developed at a steep angle to the bedding, so that the rock has acquired the property of cleavage and become a true slate. It is the cleavage which allows the rock to be split into thin layers to form the commercial roofing slate. Not all slate beds are suitable for this purpose, and the actual areas of exploitation are limited in distribution.

Extensive areas in Central and North Wales, the Lake District and in the Southern Uplands of Scotland have landforms directly attributable to the underlying shale and slate beds. As the shale does not resist erosion to the same extent as many other rock types of similar age, the landscape is best described as hilly rather than mountainous, subdued rather than severe and with few, if any, bare rock outcrops. In Central Wales the shales are responsible for great upland plateaux deeply dissected by valleys running in from the margins. It is only when other rocks like grits and flags are present that the landscape comes alive and is exciting to the eye. In the Moorfoot and Lammermuir Hills of the Southern Uplands of Scotland the scenery is again rather subdued, though here, unlike in Wales, the widespread accordant surfaces are absent. Dissection by river valleys is so complete that the intervening ridges are usually narrow and sharp-crested. Deep valleys penetrate the uplands from the south, but even here the rivers have failed to create a bare rock landscape. Instead the slopes are everywhere clothed with a liberal soil cover and above the limit of enclosure there are extensive upland grazing grounds. Glaciation has aided the smoothing process, for the shales readily succumbed to the planing effect of the ice as it passed over the hills. Only in the west, in areas like that around Hartfell, which rises to 2,551ft, does the underlying rock assert itself, but here it is the grit rather than the shale which is responsible.

The Skiddaw Slates in the northern Lake District are really largely shales in spite of their name. Their role in the landscape was appreciated at an early date by Jonathan Otley, who in 1821 produced the first account of the geology of the area, in which he noted that 'there are indeed some lofty precipices in the first division [the Skiddaw Slates] but owing to the shivery and crumbly nature of the rock they present none of the bold colossal features which are exhibited in the Borrowdale Volcanic Series'. This early appreciation of the influence of rock type on scenery is perhaps to be expected of one who lived so close to the mountains around Keswick. To the north lay the great lump of Skiddaw, where the shales had weathered to give steep but smooth slopes – a dull mountain, though almost as high as any the Lake District has to offer. In contrast the area to the south in Upper Borrowdale, reaching up to Scafell and Great Gable, has the rugged and roughened topography which we associate with volcanic rocks.

Although true slates occur within many of the older rocks of highland Britain, from Delabole in Cornwall right across the country to Ballachulish in

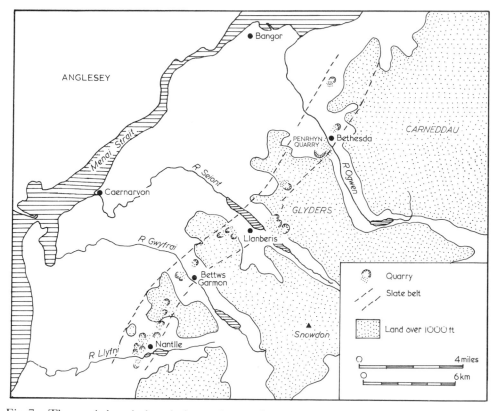

Fig 7   The peripheral slate belt on the north-western edge of Snowdonia

46

15  The use of slate for both building courses and roofing, Bethesda, North Wales

Scotland, it is in Snowdonia that their economic worth has been fully realized. The relative ease with which the slate could be prised away from the bedrock using simple tools meant that the material found a variety of uses from the earliest time. Apart from its universal function as a roofing material, the fact that it could be shaped and trimmed led to its adoption for a whole range of purposes both inside and outside the home. Many of the Welsh farm cottages had a slate floor formed of huge slabs. In the corner there would be a washing trough of slate sections carefully fitted together. Slate slabs in the pantry or as working surfaces in the kitchen were almost universal in the cottages around Snowdonia. In addition, craftsmen were able to shape the slate into clock faces, ornaments and the like, usually with intricate designs. In the outbuildings the slate would be used for cattle troughs and dividers in the cow byres, and even scooped out to form drainage channels. Long low buildings like pigsties and storage sheds would be covered with great overlapping slate slabs obtained cheaply from the nearby quarry. Boundary posts and even lengths of fencing were made from long lathes of slate, and many have survived to the present day.

Workable beds of slate occur mainly on the fringes of the mountains of Snowdonia. One belt runs from the North Wales coast near Llanfairfechan right across country to the neck of the Lleyn peninsula, forming a zone of foothills between Bangor and Caernarfon. It is along this outcrop that the famous nineteenth-century quarries at Bethesda, Llanberis and Nantlle were developed. There had been sporadic small private workings from medieval times, but after 1800 local landowning families like those of Lord Penrhyn, Assheton-Smith and others introduced a programme of rationalization and bought out the private entrepreneurs. Lord Penrhyn acted as a father-figure and after opening his great quarry near Bethesda allowed his workmen to build cottages on his vast estate and created a new village close to the quarry (see Chapter 6). The great boom in slate working coincided with the insatiable demands of the new industrial towns. Not only did it transform the landscape – the Penrhyn quarry soon became a deep hole with gallery after gallery ascending the adjacent hillside – but it also led to the growth of new quarry settlements with biblical names like Nebo, Salem and Carmel. Slate came to be used wherever it was at all suitable, for window, roof and door lintels, cladding, paving, fencing and even guttering. The great chapels which dominated the villages and originally gave the settlements their names, were also a monument to the slate industry, without which the money to build them would not have been available. The decline of the industry – only Penrhyn quarry is now operating – must bring in its wake a considerable change in the life-style of many living in the villages, and with it alterations in the landscape itself.

# 2

# A Hostile Environment

Even a casual acquaintance with the upland areas of Britain cannot fail to reveal that the weather and climate are very different from those of lowland or coastal situations. Apart from the colder feel to the air and the fact that the highest mountain tops seem to attract a cluster of clouds around their summits, there are many less obvious factors which are more difficult to define. For those living and working in the higher parts, weather characteristics play an important part in their daily habits. Because of the more extreme conditions of temperature, precipitation and humidity, frost, snow and wind, resulting from altitude, the weather is a constant focus of attention and always a force to be reckoned with. Knowledge of the weather signs can be invaluable, so that the local inhabitant need seldom be ill-equipped or ill-prepared to face the elements. With a marked variation in the seasonal weather from year to year, the calendar can only be a rough guide for the hill farmer, whether in planting his potato crop or harvesting his hay. Nevertheless, it is seldom possible to steal a march on nature by planting potatoes in April rather than early May at heights above 800ft. Similarly, at the end of the season the harvest can be a month later than for the lowland farmer. It is the weather and climate much more than the effects of topography which directly affect the uplander and give rise to the basically hostile environment which has to be faced year after year, always with a sense of the unknown and unpredictable.

## Temperature

Expressed in the simplest terms, a rise in altitude leads to a marked drop in temperature and sunshine amounts, while precipitation and windiness show a corresponding increase. The fall-off of temperature with height, known as the lapse rate, is usually taken to average about 11°F (6°C) for a 1,000ft rise in altitude, but this could well be an underestimate, for Manley has recorded values of 12·5°F (6·9°C) for the northern Pennines and values 13°F (7°C) have been suggested for Central Wales. In practical terms this means that while sunbathers on the beach at Llandudno may be basking in temperatures of 68°F

49

(20°C), anyone walking the nearby Carnedd tops above the 3,000ft contour could find it distinctly chilly, especially if it is cloudy and windy. This marked difference is partly due to the fact that lapse rates in Britain are some of the steepest in the world. If the increased cloudiness of the uplands is also taken into account, the result is an environment which is inhibiting both to animals and plants. It has also been estimated that in highland Britain the length of the growing season decreases by about one day for every 30ft increase in height. Expressed another way, a change in level of about 1,800ft will effectively halve the length of the growing season. A hill farmer near the upland limit of settlement, at about 1,600ft, will lose more than a month compared with his valley neighbour 1,000ft below. It can be the middle of May before grass begins to grow, and by the end of September the cold nights and chilly winds will bring a virtual halt. The limited availability of the upland pastures has led man from prehistoric times onwards to practise transhumance, involving seasonal migration of his animals. Many of the permanent farms which today lie above the 1,000ft contour began as summer shelters – 'shielings' – when perhaps the whole family took flight from their valley home for a brief period of three months. The *hafodau* in Wales or the 'booths' of the Peak District can look back, now in name only, to an earlier period of distinct farming practice in our uplands.

Apart from the high lapse rate found in highland Britain, the character of the annual mean temperature curve is also unfavourable to full utilization of the higher lands. Compared with similar upland areas in Europe or North America the curve is remarkably flat, so that the summer excess above 42°F (5·6°C) – the traditionally accepted value for plant growth – is relatively low. When exposure to wind is taken into account, it is not surprising that the limit of tree growth is about 1,700ft in Britain, although the occasional tree can survive above the 2,000ft contour in favourable circumstances. In the High Peak of Derbyshire about 25 per cent of possible growing time is lost in the summer months (June to September), a figure which rises to 55 per cent in October and over 80 per cent in December or April. It is not surprising, therefore, that above heights of 2,000ft, and lower in many parts, upland Britain is a treeless waste, a great empty space almost comparable to the tundra lands of polar latitudes. In an over-populated island, these untenanted acres of Wales, the northern Pennines and Scotland form a treasured preserve which will become increasingly valued as an oasis of tranquillity for future generations.

With the uplands and mountains of the country forming a gathering ground for clouds, sunshine amounts are correspondingly low. Few precise figures are available owing to the lack of measuring stations above the 1,000ft level; above 2,500ft there is a mere handful. A station was maintained on the summit of Ben Nevis at 4,406ft between 1884 and 1903, during which time it produced an invaluable and much-quoted set of data relating to the extreme conditions found at this height. Two shorter records are available from the western edge of the Pennines at Dun Fell (2,780ft) and Moor House (1,870ft). Since 1967 the

16 The automatic recording weather station on Cairn Gorm summit, set up to provide data about upland climatic conditions

Institute of Hydrology has maintained a station on the top of Pumlumon in mid-Wales. The most recently established mountain-top instrumentation is that on the Cairngorms where, after a fitful start due to recurrent trouble with the recording equipment, the station is now beginning to provide valuable results and additions to our knowledge of mountain climates. What little data we have show a remarkable decrease in sunshine amounts. Ben Nevis summit, for example, can expect only 757 hours a year, compared with over 1,100 hours at Fort William. In the Pennines only about 25 per cent of the possible total is actually achieved. Here we have one of the great limitations to which the holidaymaker is subject in highland Britain, compared with those seeking the sun along the coast. Inevitably he must accept a much higher proportion of dull days.

It would be wrong to paint too gloomy a picture of mountain weather, for in its dynamism and changes of mood we have something unique. The clear mountain air at sunset is often associated with colour tones which give a sense of unreality captured by many an artist. For a brief moment before the onset of twilight the distant slopes take on a deep purple tint. Turbulence brought about by rising mountain barriers may be the cause of violent thunderstorms with short, sharp hail showers quickly giving way to unblemished sunlight that illuminates the freshened landscape. The deep green hues of the mountain pastures and the reds and browns of the autumn bracken, especially with a low sun, are especially welcome after the inky darkness of the passing storm. The clear night air and the absence of street lighting give an opportunity to see the vast bowl of the universe in unrivalled splendour.

## Precipitation

Along with decreasing temperature, it is the marked rise in rainfall that makes the uplands stand out climatically from the rest of the country. A relief map and an annual precipitation map are almost identical. With rain-bearing winds sweeping in from the Atlantic soon encountering the main highland masses, it is not surprising that they quickly release most of their moisture as relief rain. Mountainous areas like Snowdonia, the Lake District and the Western Highlands of Scotland have annual totals in excess of 150in. For the lee slopes just below the Snowdon summit the annual average is about 170in, but in some years it can exceed 200in. It is a similar story in the Lake District, where the fells around Great Gable have a total of about 180in in an average year. This area is classic ground in upland climatic observations, for it was here that John Fletcher Miller set up a rain gauge at Seathwaite in 1844 and followed it with another at a higher level a few years later. The incredibly large amount collected during the first years caught the imagination of the Victorians, and Seathwaite was always quoted as the 'wettest place in England' in every book of records, in spite of much greater precipitation amounts recorded at Miller's own station higher up the fells at Sty Head in the shadow of Scafell and Great Gable. The tendency for the highest precipitation amounts to occur in this lee situation rather than on the mountain peaks themselves is now well established and appreciated. It is true of Snowdonia as well as the Lake District, with Glaslyn (2,500ft) to the north-east of Snowdon summit averaging 198in a year, a figure which makes it a close runner-up for the title of 'wettest place in Britain', usually accorded to the head of Glen Garry in the Western Highlands of Scotland. In each case a contributing factor to the high precipitation values is the convergence of air streams coming up valleys open to the west. This is especially true of the Lake District, with its well-known radial valley pattern converging on the central peaks. Conical-topped and isolated mountain summits like Great Gable or Ben Nevis tend to allow rain-bearing winds to flow around their summits so that precipitation amounts are lower than expected.

As with temperature records, it is the absence of a close network of rain gauges in highland areas which limits the value of such information as we have. It has also led to varying views on the character and distribution of the precipitation. One commonly expressed view is that the rainfall amounts increase linearly with altitude, so that for every 500ft rise there is a regular build-up of the rainfall. On the other hand, some meteorologists take the view that the relationship between height and precipitation total is exponential, so that the highest mountains have higher values than would be expected. Pearsall in his vegetation studies of our upland areas noted that in some of the eastern highlands the maximum rainfall total occurred at a height of about 1,500ft and thereafter decreased with altitude. It seems probable that topographic diversity is another important factor which we are only now beginning to take into account.

Perhaps the most detailed study of the rainfall characteristic of a mountainous region has been provided by Pedgley's work in Snowdonia carried out in the 1970s. The area can be likened to a dome rising to 3,500ft in the centre. Frontal troughs coming from the west are slowed down as they meet the mountain wall, and this leads to continuous and heavy rainfall over the highest parts. The peripheral areas will also experience widespread falls of the same duration, though not of the same intensity. Cwm Dyli, below Snowdon, for example, has a mean annual rainfall of 150in with a mean duration of fall approaching 1,300 hours a year. Holyhead, on the other hand, with only 40in of rain, has wet conditions lasting 713 hours. Thus Cwm Dyli experiences 2·7mm per hour while Holyhead only has 1·4mm per hour. Expressed another way, rainfall when it occurs in the highest areas is twice as heavy as on the coast. Pedgley attributes this to a type of scouring action in which raindrops falling through a thick cloud layer over the centre of the dome will tend to grow larger under these conditions. Scouring is most effective with large drizzle and small rain droplets, as these grow in size steadily as they drop through the cloud. Large initial drops will fall too quickly to increase much in size, while the smaller drizzle passes out of the mountain-top cloud in a horizontal manner owing to air flow. This model as used by Pedgley to explain the Snowdonia rainfall characteristics has to be modified to take account of local topographic effects such as the presence of deeply incised U-shaped valleys cut into the broad domal surface. When a valley faces the wind, a funnelling effect develops and this can lead to heavy precipitation at its head. If the valley lies transversely to the prevailing wind, an eddy effect is noticeable and is often the cause of great variations in rainfall amount on different slopes.

Although much of the rainfall in Snowdonia is due to frontal systems subjected to an orographic effect because of the mountain barrier, on sunny days in summer the latter can act as a high-level heat source. Convection clouds will tend to develop preferentially over the mountain tops and under these conditions can give rise to immense thunderheads towering to great heights. From Anglesey, basking in unbroken sunshine, the build-up of the towering clouds can be clearly seen across the Menai Strait. The occasional lightning flash and the distant rumbling of thunder announces that a severe storm is in progress of which the Anglesey resident is no more than an interested spectator. Some of the heaviest recorded rainfalls in mountainous country have occurred under the combined effects of an almost stationary front, the orographic influence and the high-level heat source. Even modest uplands can give rise to similar effects. Perhaps the best-known example of this was the concentrated rainfall experienced over the western part of Exmoor on 15 and 16 August 1952, when over 9in fell in twenty-four hours. The heaviest fall occurred at heights above 1,500ft in the area known as the Chains. The first half of the month had been wetter than usual and under unsettled weather conditions a depression began to develop over the western English Channel. Frontal rainfall associated with this depression and subject to orographic influences as air had to rise over the western end of Exmoor was not the only cause of the heavy fall. The situation was complicated by thunderstorms occurring throughout the area and a tendency for the front to be elongated in an east – west direction so that as the depression moved eastwards the front stayed over Exmoor. Northerly and north-westerly winds blowing off the Bristol Channel brought in a moist and unstable air stream which was forced to ascend the steep north-facing slopes. Between 7pm and midnight on 15 August no less than 6in of rain fell, and as the water poured off the plateau top into the headwater valleys of the Lyn, it gave rise to a raging torrent which dropped over 1,500ft in only 4 miles. Huge boulders acted as battering-rams and wrought great destruction in Lynmouth.

Much of the winter precipitation in the more mountainous parts of Britain falls as snow, though owing to the nearness of the sea to our western mountains it does not have the same impact as on the Continent, where colder conditions persist throughout the winter months. Snowdonia belies its name, for the landscape, certainly below the habitable levels, is seldom blanketed in snow. As the mountain peaks are normally covered in cloud and seldom display their snow cappings, the normal winter scene is painted in green and brown rather than white. There are occasions, as in the severe winters of 1947 and 1962, when uplands like Dartmoor feel the full effects of a heavy snowfall and residents can be virtually cut off for weeks. Many upland railways, like the line from Ashbourne to Buxton, were originally saved from closure so that they could act as a lifeline in such an emergency. A succession of mild winters throughout the 1960s and 1970s led to a feeling that there was little danger from winter snowfall and roads could be kept open using modern clearing techniques. Not surprisingly, the severe winter of 1979, when parts of the Peak were isolated for long periods, proved this faith misplaced. Many living in upland areas had been lulled into a false sense of security and a dependence on the local authority gritting lorry. It is true that air-drops from helicopters can help those marooned in isolated farms, but even in 1978 trains on the Highland line through Caithness were blocked and motorists on the A9 road were stranded and left to die – a stark reminder of the effects of heavy snowfall in our upland areas.

If height were to be ignored, it is clear that the eastern side of Britain would suffer most from winter snowfall. Cold polar air spreading across the North Sea from the Continent as a biting north-easter, or brought directly from the Arctic by northerly winds, can act as a snowmaker if it comes into contact with rising ground. Thus the Cairngorms, the Lammermuir Hills or the Cleveland Hills of north-east Yorkshire are particularly susceptible to heavy snowfalls. Warmer rain-bearing winds in the southern half of the country will often give rise to a period of snow when they come into contact with the much colder air farther north. Considering their height, the western mountains do not have as much snow as might be expected; this is due to the ameliorating effects of warmer bordering seas and the lesser effectiveness of easterly weather. In Snowdonia it is often the easterly ranges of the Carneddau that carry the greatest amount of snow. The same is true of the Lake District fells around Shap which, though lower than the highest central peaks, can be more prone to heavy snowfall. It would be misleading, however, to give the impression that the highest mountain systems of the west do not have their fair share of snow. During the twenty-year period when continuous meteorological observations were carried out on the top of Ben Nevis, snowfall was recorded on an average of 169 days a year. Comparable figures no doubt apply to other high mountains of Wales, the Lake District and the Western Highlands. It is the lack of continuous accumulation in the western mountains that is most noticeable during the winter months. Milder air streams from the Atlantic, especially if accompanied by heavy rainfall, will quickly clear away snow from all but the highest slopes. It is this fact which poses a problem in running ski resorts in the Highlands. Apart from the need for suitable slopes free from outcropping rock or isolated boulders, the lack of continuity in the snow cover throughout the winter on the better runs has prevented a full development of this sport in Britain. Only in the Scottish Highlands around Glencoe, and more particularly in the Cairngorms near Aviemore and at Glenshee, has it been thought worthwhile to invest in ski lifts and costly access roads. The Cairngorms, because of their easterly situation and height above 4,000ft, seem to offer the best possibilities, but even here the succession of mild winters in the 1960s and 1970s proved disappointing to those who had a vision of turning Aviemore into another St Moritz. Snow falls on about 90 days a year at the Ptarmigan Restaurant at the top of the chair lift, but this is generally insufficient to give more than modest conditions for skiing.

The recording of the persistent snow in mountain areas well into the summer months has long proved a popular pastime for local observers. The scientist John Dalton regularly climbed Helvellyn in early July for scientific observations, and as he needed to cool a small vessel to determine the humidity of the air, any convenient snow patch would claim his attention. For almost twenty years, between 1805 and 1823, he noted lingering snow in a sheltered gully close to the summit. William Wordsworth and his sister Dorothy, on their walks close to their home at Grasmere, probably saw the same patches, and he perhaps had them in mind when he referred to the 'lingering summer snow' in one of his poems. Snow had an unusual fascination for poets, and Keats remarked on the snowbed which he found high up on the slopes of Ben Nevis in August. Snowdonia also has its late-surviving snowbed in a gully close to the summit of Carnedd Llewelyn. In 1879 the snow persisted until the middle of August, and in other years it was early July before it finally melted. Gethin Jones, in his study of the subject, went so far as to claim that it was the latest surviving snowbed in England and Wales. Given a combination of adverse conditions, he suggested it might be possible for the bed to persist throughout the year. However, at a height of 3,500ft and in a relatively southerly latitude it is unlikely that it could possibly survive from one year to the next. That distinction must belong to two locations in Scotland, one on Ben Nevis and the other on Braerich in the Cairngorms, both situated above 4,000ft and with a north-easterly aspect. Even these snowbeds, lying in deeply sheltered gulleys, are not permanent, and disappear completely in certain years. For consistent accumulation to give rise to incipient glaciers, there would have to be a lowering of the summer minimum temperature by about 3·6°F (2°C). Expressed another way, none of our mountains are high enough to attract a permanent snowbed, though Ben Nevis reaches within 800ft of the critical level of a present-day snowline.

The semi-permanent snowbed in Observatory Gully on Ben Nevis has been studied by Professor Manley over a period of years. After winter snow it can be as much as 15ft thick and measure 120ft by 150ft in total area. Summer warmth is not the only factor which determines whether the snow will persist through the critical period of late September. Of great significance is a late fall of snow in the spring and an absence of heavy rain in the summer. In the last century it was firmly believed that the Ben Nevis snow was permanent, for it had been known to persist each year since 1840. In 1933, however, it did melt, and so put an end to the speculation that here was a glacier in the making which, given a slight shift of temperature, would be the first sign of another glacial period affecting Britain.

## Wind

Wind plays a greater part in the upland environment than is generally recognized. Not only are wind speeds much higher than elsewhere, especially in winter, but their chilling effects can cause discomfort and hardship. They limit the growth of vegetation so that trees find difficulty in surviving above about 1,600ft save in especially sheltered areas. The result is that the uplands of the British Isles are unusually bleak and open compared with areas of similar height on the Continent of Europe. Even where conifer plantations have been successfully established at heights above the 1,000ft contour, there is a marked diminution in the growth rate and size of trees as the upper limit is approached. It would be wrong to assume that wind is the sole factor inhibiting tree growth at higher altitudes, for animals, particularly sheep, can prevent regeneration of young seedlings by eating the growing shoots. This can, of course, also occur at lower levels, but with slower natural growth rates in the higher parts the damage seems much greater.

The exposed summits of many of the highest mountains feel the full effect of strong winds. Within a year of the establishment of an anemograph on the uppermost pylon of the Coire Glas chair lift in the Cairngorms it measured a gust of 125 knots – the highest value recorded on an instrument in Britain. It seems probable that wind speeds have exceeded this value elsewhere, to judge by the damage done to some of the coniferous woodlands during past storms, but as with other meteorological data, few records have been kept of wind gusts on mountain tops. The best set of observations again comes from the observatory on Ben Nevis at the end of last century. On average there were 261 gales a year recorded with wind speeds in excess of 50mph. This is a much higher figure than is experienced on an open coast, the only other comparable area where wind speeds of similar magnitude are likely to occur. On Cross Fell (2,930ft), the highest part of the northern Pennines, the average wind speed is approximately twice that found in the adjacent Vale of Eden. Even at lower altitudes open plateau areas experience high winds throughout the year. On Rannoch Moor, for example, at a height of 900ft, wind speeds of Force 4 or more were recorded for about 40 per cent of the year.

Local topography can play an important part in determining the wind speeds likely to be experienced. Many upland farms sought out natural features for shelter, and this, along with water supply and aspect, often determined the choice of site. Winds from the north and west quarters often proved the most troublesome, so that any natural rock obstacle giving protection from these directions was looked on with favour. But even with the most carefully chosen site there is no absolute guarantee of complete freedom from excessive winds. In Snowdonia the funnelling effects of a valley like Nant Ffrancon can mean that south-easterly winds are often more destructive than the more common westerly gales. Flimsy corrugated roofs of modern barns provide easy targets of destruction for upland winds which at an earlier date could make little impression on low stone cottages with heavy slate roofs. Wherever possible, shelter belts or even clumps of trees round a cottage can reduce the exposure felt in an isolated position, with birch and ash being the most favoured deciduous trees as they are more likely to withstand a gale than the oak or beech.

The distinctive features of the topography of upland regions are often responsible for the creation of local patterns of air flow. Towards the end of a clear day the loss of heat by radiation from the surface of the plateau top leads to

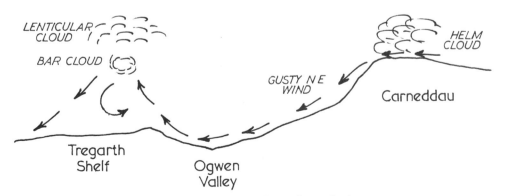

Fig 8   Features of the helm wind over northern Snowdonia

a cooling of the adjacent layer of air to below the temperature of that found at the same level over a nearby valley. The result is that the cooler and therefore denser air slips down the valley side and forms a distinct air flow. This katabatic wind, as it is termed, frequently occurs near the time of sunset in most of our upland areas. Cooler winds from the Carneddau, for example, often develop over the adjacent Ogwen valley at the close of a clear day when the setting sun is bathing the valley sides in an orange and purple light. Prominent escarpments can give rise to even more noticeable winds under certain meteorological conditions. The best-known is the helm wind which occurs in the Eden valley below the scarp edge of Cross Fell. When the wind is in an easterly quarter and gathering strength as it moves over the top of Cross Fell, the escarpment acts like a gigantic submerged weir and in doing so generates a considerable turbulent air flow down the treeless slopes towards the vale floor. Under these conditions some of the isolated foothills like Dufton Pike are almost impossible to climb owing to the strong downdraught of the helm wind. A few miles away, in the valley bottom at Appleby, conditions are much calmer as the air has become less turbulent. Anyone living in the area cannot fail to be aware of these unusual wind conditions which occur from time to time. As early as 1837 the Reverend William Walton, in a paper read to the Royal Society, related that

on the western declivity of a range of mountains, extending from Brampton in Cumbria to Brough in Westmorland, a distance of forty miles, a remarkable violent wind occasionally prevails, blowing with tremendous violence down the western slopes of the mountains, extending two or three miles over the plain at the base, often overturning horses with carriages, and producing much damage, especially during the period when ripe corn is standing. It is accompanied by a loud noise, like the roaring of distant thunder; and is carefully avoided by travellers in that district, as being fraught with considerable danger. It is termed the *helm wind:* and its presence is indicated by a belt of clouds, denominated the *helm bar,* which rests in front of the mountain, three or four miles west of its summit, and apparently at an equal elevation, remaining immovable during twenty-four or even thirty-six hours, and collecting to itself all the light clouds which approach it. As long as this bar continues unbroken, the wind blows with unceasing fury, not in gusts, like other storms, but with continued pressure.

This clear and precise statement of the Reverend Walton sums up the features of the helm wind which anyone can experience today under the right conditions. Similar topographically generated winds occur elsewhere under different names. Again the diagnostic features are the line of stationary cloud over the scarp top and the consistent strength of the wind as it rushes down the hill slopes towards the valley bottom. In the Carneddau of Snowdonia the helm cloud sits immovable on the ridge connecting Carnedd Dafydd and Llewelyn while the floor of the Ogwen valley and the slopes around Tregarth bask in unbroken sunshine. Easterly weather in this corner of Snowdonia is welcome in that the drying winds and high sunshine amounts allow the farmer to burn his gorse and bracken before the stipulated date of the end of March.

The same area from time to time also experiences another local weather phenomenon which is associated with its upland setting. In January 1971 Llandudno on the North Wales coast experienced the highest January temperature ever recorded in Britain, when on a day of unbroken sunshine the thermometer reached 65°F. The cause was a gentle southerly breeze descending the lee slopes of the mountains and warming as a result of compression. The parallel is with the well-known *Föhn* winds of the Alps or the Chinook (snow-eater) of the Rockies. The movement downhill is brought about by a high-altitude inversion which commonly occurs when a pressure rise heralds the beginning of anticyclonic conditions. Similar high temperatures (64°F) were recorded that same day at Machynlleth where the mountain barrier of the Cader Idris range and the Arans acted together to give the *Föhn* effect. The record British December temperature, also 65°F, is probably due to the same cause and belongs to Achnashellach in Ross-shire – a most unlikely place but nevertheless serving as a reminder of the unusual and unpredictable nature of the British weather.

The *Föhn* effect, for all its enticement and unseasonality, is somewhat rare in Britain. Much more common is the biting north-easter importing sub-zero air from distant Siberia. Although low temperatures in themselves can cause an increase in the degree of stress felt by animals and plant life, it is the combination of strong winds and heavy rain which is most damaging. Each year mountain rescue teams are called upon to deal with climbers and walkers suffering from exposure, when body temperatures are reduced to dangerously low levels. Because of the ever-increasing number of people visiting mountain areas in winter, often with little knowledge of the dangers they face, more and more attention has been devoted to the effects of windchill. This is usually defined as the cooling effect of air movement and low temperatures. Calculation of an index of windchill, which expresses the cooling powers of the wind for various combinations of temperature and wind speed, is a better indicator of hostile upland conditions than simple readings of low temperature. A wind at 45mph and at 20°F has about the same feeling as one of only 5mph at –20°F. In mountain areas it is the mountain tops, with their low temperatures and high wind speeds, that experience the highest indices of windchill. Exposure rather than low temperature is the usual cause of death for anyone caught unprepared on the high tops. From calculations of heat transfer between the clothed body and the atmosphere it is possible to derive minimum values of clothing thickness required to withstand the adverse conditions of winter in our upland regions. For average December conditions on Ben Nevis a clothing thickness of 0·6in (16mm) seems necessary to give adequate protection against exposure. For the more extreme conditions which occur from time to time, it is probable that a value twice as great is more applicable to maintain the body in thermal equilibrium with its surroundings.

## Plant and animal life

Upland Britain, with its climatic extremes, is a region where the natural vegetation and man's utilization of the landscape show a clear response to the conditions encountered. It is now almost thirty years since Professor W.H. Pearsall wrote his classic *Mountains and Moorland* in the New Naturalist Series and brought together, for the first time, the whole assemblage of elements which make up this habitat for plants and animals covering perhaps a third of the total area of the country. Even the most casual visitor cannot be unaware of the interplay of rock, soil, climate and natural vegetation, which seems to be expressed with a much greater clarity than in lowland Britain. It was this aspect, above all else, that Professor Pearsall stressed in his study of the upland environment amongst the high hills, plateaux and moorlands of the north and west of the country. The drop in temperature with altitude, for example, has a marked effect on the rate of biological processes. Pearsall instanced the case of the moth, the northern egger, which takes two years over its larval stage compared with only one in the case of the oak egger living in a more favourable lowland environment. Some have argued that the difference is due to nutritional factors rather than lower temperatures. What is more certain is that as temperature approaches freezing point in certain plants there is a conversion of insoluble food reserves like starches into soluble sugars. This in turn gives the plant greater protection from frost damage. Common plants of upland areas like the moor rush are able to withstand the hostile environment though some of their normal functions are affected by the greater height. Growth rates are much lower, so that a plant at 2,500ft will have a flower stalk only half the length of one growing at 500ft. There is a similar reduction in the number of flowers pollinated, so that above 2,500ft there is virtually no chance of the rush producing viable seed. The fact that the rush does grow at and above that level is probably due to dispersal of seed brought by animals from a lower altitude. Also, an exceptional summer like that of 1976, when in July and August the temperature on the Cairngorm tops exceeded 70°F for a long period, would allow seed production to take place above the critical level of 2,500ft.

The number of plants that can survive in the highest areas is extremely limited. In the Cairngorms, with a large area above the 4,000ft contour, the only really successful colonizer is the prostrate woolly hair moss. This is able to form a grey-green mat on the surface among the stones and boulders of granite. With the minimum temperature above freezing point for only five months of the year, conditions resemble those experienced in the coastal areas of the Arctic. The Scottish mountains were the last area in Britain to be freed from the enveloping ice sheet, and are still a last refuge for both plants and animals more commonly associated with the Arctic and High Alps. This is the only place in Britain where the short-winged and flightless Alpine sawfly is found. As it is incapable of extensive migration it seems that it must have survived in its mountain fastness around Braerich since the end of the Ice Age.

The Cairngorms, lying on the east side of the country, have a climate more influenced by Continental conditions than that experienced by the mountainous areas of the Western Highlands. Easterly weather in winter can bring considerable snowfalls which are more likely to persist throughout the January to March period at levels above 2,000ft than they would be further west where the maritime influence is much greater. Summer conditions are also different, and with higher sunshine totals and lower rainfall, the land utilization potential is enhanced. The Cairngorm forests, remnants of the much more extensive Caledonian Forest, have stands of Scots pine and birch well represented. At the present time the tree line is approximately 1,600ft, though on the western flanks of Creag Fhiaclach at 2,100ft, gnarled and twisted pines have survived in a prostrate form. In such an area, exposure is of prime importance, and therefore it is something of a surprise for even stunted trees to survive. The lower level of 1,600ft, which approximates to the true tree line, is not a natural one, for in areas like the Rothiemurchus Forest the past exploitation of the timber resources and uncontrolled grazing did untold damage to the natural woodland. As in other parts of the country, forest once destroyed is difficult to re-establish naturally. Tree seedlings, even if protected from nibbling by sheep, find it hard to recolonize the higher levels. Wind action is often a potent factor, subjecting even young saplings to considerable mechanical stress. The more windward branches tend to have slower growth rates and soon give the young tree a lop-sided appearance. Desiccation in late winter and early spring owing to frozen soils can also do considerable damage. The large areas of bare ground where the former woodland has been cut down can provide the wind with loose particles that become the abrasive tool with which to blast the young seedlings. When these and other factors are taken into account, it will be seen that any natural regeneration must invariably be very slow, if not impossible. Under present-day conditions there seems little likelihood of the Rothiemurchus Forest reaching levels much in excess of the natural tree-line limit of 1,600ft, still less the 2,600ft level attained during the Boreal Period. Even in the nearby Glen More Forest which is now being planted, the upper limit has been set at 1,500ft. Although trees will grow above this height, the economic return is much less and hardly justifies the effort. Studies by R. W. Golspie on wind effects in upland areas have shown that even where coniferous plantations have been successfully established above the 1,000ft contour there are significant differences in growth rates recorded by trees near the lower and upper limits. Even trees with a fair measure of protection show retarded growth rates, suggesting that other factors such as soil, drainage and temperature must be taken into account, along with wind, before any decision is made about tree-planting schemes for our bare uplands.

Some indication of what is possible is provided by relict woodlands which have survived from the past in many of our upland regions. Their survival is not always closely connected with natural conditions but often the result of historical accident. Perhaps the most famous is Wistman's Wood on Dartmoor, which stands at a height of between 1,330 and 1,400ft. The low stunted pedunculate oak trees lie amidst the wilderness of granite boulders of a clitter slope on the eastern side of an open valley running northwards from the main A384 road at Two Bridges. At this height the rainfall is over 80in a year and the trunks and branches of the trees are covered with mosses or hung with rich epiphytes. Much of the Dartmoor plateau must have carried similar woodland at one time, but exploitation of the timber by tinners and others reduced the 'natural' woodland to a few sites like Wistman's Wood. That trees can still flourish on Dartmoor at heights well in excess of 1,000ft is shown by the success of Fernworthy Forest, whose conifers grow at 1,650ft on White Ridge, 4 miles south-west of Chagford. Along with other similar plantations, Fernworthy Forest points the way to a more economic use of some of our upland areas. Competing interests for land use, like sheep farming or tourism, have so far resisted the wholesale taking over of these areas for timber growing, though future needs will probably necessitate a compromise solution.

In certain upland situations aspect plays an important role in creating conditions more favourable than would at first appear likely. Where a valley runs in an east–west direction, the south-facing slope will obviously receive more sunshine than the opposite side. In the summer months the difference may be relatively unimportant, but with the low sun of winter and early spring heavy shadows on the north-facing slopes can lead to considerable differences of temperature between the two valley sides. This *ubac* (sunny) and *adret* (shadow) effect is best seen in the Alpine valleys where it is of great significance in determining the siting of settlements. In Britain, aspect plays a lesser role, though its human and biological significance can still be important in certain local situations. In the Peak District the Hope valley has marked differences due to the favoured situation enjoyed by the south-facing slopes. It is often said that living in Aston is a topcoat warmer than in the shadows of the opposing north-facing slope. Further south, in the nature reserve established in Lathkill Dale, Ian Rorison has made measurements to study the influence of climate and topography on plant growth. On a north-facing slope with less insolation, ground water flow and hence soil movement is much less developed than on the warmer south-facing slope. This is especially so in winter when the north-facing side of the valley may be permanently frozen throughout the day, whereas the more favoured side experiences a thaw. Over a long period of time this leads to the soils of the north-facing slope having more organic matter, greater depth and lower pH values than those on the opposite slope. Less predictable perhaps was Rorison's finding that the north-facing slope was more favourable to plant growth, partly because it was less subject to extreme climatic conditions in both winter and summer. The south-facing slope in winter was certainly more subject to alternate freezing and thawing. In summer the surface soil was liable to dry out much more quickly, and again this limited plant growth. Another interesting fact discovered by Rorison was that different varieties of plant occupy each slope, those on the south-facing side being fairly

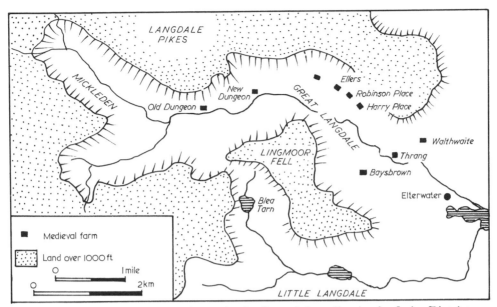

Fig 9   The siting of the early farms in the Langdale valley in the Lake District

characteristic of southern England, while those on the north-facing side are more typical of the northern uplands. Whether Lathkill is typical of other east–west trending valleys is not known, and further work seems desirable to see if the results found by Rorison are of wider application.

The well-known Great Langdale in the Lake District displays clearly the contrast which can occur between opposing valley sides and its effect on the pattern of settlement and human activity. Settlement in the east–west trending valley goes back at least to the Norse colonization of the tenth century, when farms were being carved out of the waste and upland pastures utilized, perhaps for the first time – hence the place-name designations like Rossett Gill, which is pure Scandinavian. The narrow road which today wends its way to the head of the valley at Dungeon Gill keeps to the north side and connects a string of statesman's farms like Harry Place, Robinson Place and Ellers, all of medieval date. These were not the first farms in the valley, for that distinction belongs to Baysbrown (meaning Bruni's cowshed) away across the valley and often in complete shadow during the short winter days. The initial siting of the farm at Baysbrown dates back to the time of the Norse colonization, and clearly other factors than aspect were uppermost in the minds of these early farmers. Subsequent centuries were to establish the superior position of sites on the south-facing slopes, and it is no coincidence that the statesman's farms sought out the more favourable position. Does the original Norse choice mean that conditions changed over the centuries, possibly due to a worsening of the climate? In the case of Great Langdale this seems unlikely to have been a major influencing factor, but elsewhere in upland Britain there is increasing evidence of climatic change which has materially altered the settlement possibilities of

17   Middlefell Place, the uppermost of a string of farms in Great Langdale sited to take advantage of maximum insolation

what has always been looked upon as marginal land.

The most detailed study of the influence of climatic change on the utilization of upland grazing grounds has been made by M.T. Parry in his analysis of the farm settlements of the Lammermuir Hills in the Southern Uplands of Scotland. During the past thousand years there have been a number of minor climatic fluctuations, perhaps only hiccups in the post-glacial record. Where farming is marginal in character, which is often the case towards the limit of cultivation in many of our upland areas, even slight changes in temperature, precipitation and wind speed can have a far-reaching impact. From his work in the Lammermuir Hills Parry has argued that while climatic deterioration may not have been the sole reason behind the abandonment of the land – the decay of monastic farming, soil exhaustion and a fluctuating demand were other influencing factors – it could have acted as a catalyst and quickened the pace of change in land use in the uplands. Since the middle of the thirteenth century a pulsating deterioration in the climate has steadily reduced the possibilities of successful cultivation of oats at levels above 800ft. While one bad harvest would not necessarily lead to the total abandonment of oat cultivation at a high level, a succession of failures would soon convince the farmer of its unprofitability. A small yield might hardly produce sufficient seed for next year's sowing, let alone provide a margin for his own use.

In order to match up the historical evidence of land abandonment, harvest delays and crop failures with a pattern of changing climate since about AD 1300, Parry used a combined isopleth made up of temperature and precipitation parameters. The most effective measure of warmth is one of accumulated temperature calculated over a base of 4·4°C (40°F), the latter figure being the satisfactory base temperature for cereal growth. This parameter was calculated in terms of a total of degrees Centigrade above the base for each day over the period of a year. The other factor connected with plant growth, precipitation, was best measured by the end-of-summer water surplus as an index of wetness. For the Lammermuir Hills the 1,050 day degrees Centigrade (1,922 day degrees Fahrenheit) total and the 60mm (2·4in) potential water surplus were found to be applicable and were used by Parry for his delimiting isopleth. As the accompanying map shows the isopleth was initially restricted to the Lammermuir tops above the 1,200ft contour at the beginning of the fourteenth century, gradually moved downhill to a level of 850-900ft by the end of the fifteenth century. When most of the land was initially

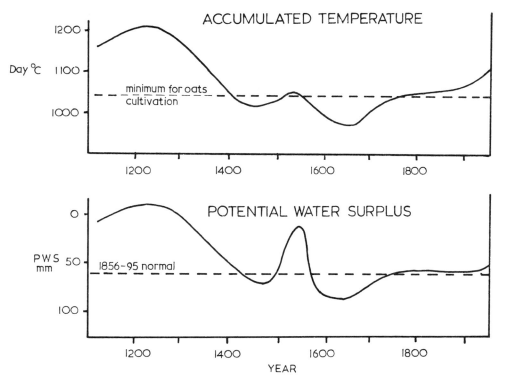

Fig 10  Accumulated temperature and potential water surplus curves for the period from AD 1100 to 1950 relating to the Lammermuir Hills in Scotland (*after Parry*)

65

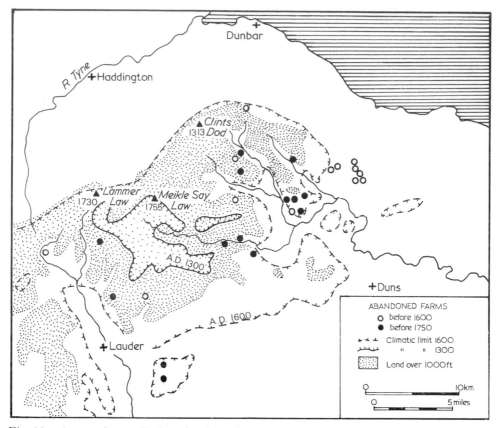

Fig 11   Approximate limits of cultivation on the Lammermuir Hills AD 1300 and 1600 together with abandoned farms (*after Parry*)

reclaimed from the waste, through the effort of abbeys like Melrose and Kelso between 1150 and 1250, high-level cultivation at 1,200ft was possible because of the exceptionally favourable climatic conditions existing at the time. Professor Lamb's work in central England using residual minimum temperature and precipitation data was considered as a reliable guide to conditions prevailing in the Southern Uplands in medieval times and was used for this purpose by Parry. He went on to show that the gradual abandonment of the cultivated fields at over 1,000ft in the Lammermuirs from 1300 onwards was closely influenced, if not caused, by a deteriorating climate. The climatic optimum (1150-1250), the medieval climatic deterioration (1250-1550), the cold epoch or Little Ice Age (1550-1700) and a more recent amelioration all had a part to play in the changing fortune of farming in the marginal lands of the Lammermuirs. Although these broad-backed hills are not particularly high, rising to a maximum of 1,755ft on Meikle Say Law, the area today is one of bare, open moorland on the highest part and enclosed pastureland at a lower level. Although there are some farms remaining in the shelter of the interior valleys, there are a large number of abandoned 'grange' or 'shiel' sites. Some

66

represent a withdrawal which has taken place in the last century, but many date from the earlier response to the steadily worsening climate. Fifteen settlements with their fields were deserted before 1600, while a further twelve disappeared in the period up to 1750. Most of these lay on the upper side of the isopleth determined for the period 1856–95, which is considered the limit for successful cultivation of cereal crops like oats. The critical isopleth has been moving steadily towards lower levels over the centuries so that today, even with improved techniques of land reclamation, there is little natural incentive to take in land last managed in the twelfth century by the monks of Melrose and Kelso.

What happened in the Southern Uplands in medieval times probably had its parallel in other parts of the country. In North Wales, Professor Glanville Jones has shown that a period of high-level cultivation occurred from about 1070 to 1300, and this was then followed by a recession, brought about partly by climatic deterioration. In Gwynedd, the golden age of farming in the lower mountain lands of Snowdonia was ushered in during the latter part of the reign of Gruffyd ap Cynan, who died in 1137. There was regularly cropped land at heights of over 1,000ft in the Denbighshire Moors at Llaethwryd near Cerrig y Druidion. Even the exposed plateau tops around Trawsfynydd furnish evidence of arable cultivation at high altitudes at this time. When the climatic deterioration set in from about 1300 onwards it was these lands that lost their crop growing. Fortunately, as arable cultivation decreased, prospects for pastoral farming increased owing to the development of the cattle trade with England. The number of cattle grazed at the upland *hafodau* around Dolwyddelan increased twofold between 1353 and 1568. There is the intriguing possibility that some *hafodau* might have started as upland farms with arable cultivation. With the steadily worsening climate from the beginning of the fourteenth century onwards they were abandoned as permanent habitations in favour of summer dwellings where animal husbandry could take advantage of the already cleared lands. This transhumance became an established routine in many of our upland areas and played a vital role in the lives and livelihood of the farming community. A succession of wet summers, such as occurred between 1789 and 1802, led to crop failure even in lowland situations and meant greater dependence on the pastoral economy of the distant *hafodau*. Fortunately the nineteenth century saw a slight improvement in climatic conditions – accumulated temperature increased from 1,050 to 1,125 day degrees Centigrade (1,922 to 2,057 day degrees Fahrenheit) – and marginal lands were once again taken in up to about 1870. Now, a century later, there is little incentive to re-occupy former cultivated lands, as present economic circumstances dictate that better returns are available from increased productivity in the more favourable lowland farms. Even wartime ploughing campaigns seldom led to the re-tilling of the medieval fields at heights of 1,200ft.

There are some areas, however, where crops are regularly grown at what might be considered unfavourable altitudes, but in each case there are special circumstances prevailing. Crops of oats are harvested each year on the limestone plateau lands of the Peak District where the well-drained soils are particularly suitable. The soils are also fertile, having been derived from wind-blown loess deposits which accumulated in the Peak District during the closing stages of the Ice Age. Natural basins in the limestone plateau provide ideal sites for the loess accumulation, and surprisingly rich farmland at altitudes of 1,200ft results. Similarly on Exmoor and on the Long Mountain of Shropshire the presence of a thick cover of 'head', a rubbly soil derived from alternate freeze–thaw conditions prevalent at the end of the Ice Age, is the basis of a very successful farming economy. But these areas represent only small oases in what is still a basically hostile upland environment.

# 3

# The Ancient Landscapes of Upland Britain

In the development of the British Isles since the end of the Ice Age, the time span of prehistory is immensely longer than the fifteen hundred years of recorded history. The last extensive glaciers retreated from northern Britain in the centuries about 12000 BC. These islands, then only the westernmost fringe of Europe's continental shelf, remained for several thousand more years an unattractive wilderness of Arctic tundra. It was only after 8000 BC that the spread of birch and pine forest began to mark the slowly increasing warmth of the post-glacial period. Between 6000 and 5500 BC the climatic improvement in western Europe heralded the epoch that is known as Atlantic times, an epoch of warmth and abundant rainfall in which the mean annual temperature of these islands stood higher than ever since. In the climatic optimum of the Atlantic millennia an almost unbroken forest, composed of oak and elm, lime, hazel and alder, covered Britain from the chalk downs of southern England to the Orkneys.

After 3000 BC, with the first Neolithic farmers long established in the British Isles, it is possible to chart in greater detail the activities of prehistoric man. Burial places, huge and mysterious earthworks, monuments in stone such as Avebury and Stonehenge, the faint foundations of huts on Cornish moors that tell of clustered settlements and some kind of communal life, and the scarcely discernible outlines of ancient, long-abandoned field systems, all are evidence of the three thousand years before the Roman Conquest in which prehistoric man was engaged in shaping the landscape of Britain. The greatest achievement of this epoch, a task that encompasses the main divisions of archaeological time, the Neolithic, the Bronze Age and the Iron Age, was the clearance of many thousand square miles of primeval forest at the hand of man. The decimation of the forest cover of upland Britain and its succession by vast tracts of bare moorland, the work of many centuries of burning and grazing hastened by the deteriorating climate of the Iron Age that favoured a thick growth of blanket bog, created the most characteristic element in the landscapes of our highland west. The bare shapes of the mountains of Cumbria, the long skylines of the Millstone Grit 'edges' of the Peak District and the seemingly endless prospects across the high plateau of Central Wales are all the result of the long, unconscious task of forest clearance that began in the prehistoric centuries.

## The changing physical landscape

During the twelve thousand years that have elapsed since the waning of the last Quaternary ice sheets the very shape of Britain and the position of its coastline have been subject to dramatic changes. The most striking event of all, but one that influenced only indirectly the upland regions of Britain, was the creation of the Straits of Dover as a result of the rising sea level in early Atlantic times, soon after 5500 BC. Britain ceased to be a remote extension of Europe that could be reached across the marshes and rivers that occupied the southern arm of the North Sea basin. The flooding of valleys on the site of the Straits of Dover, valleys that had been carved out in an earlier interglacial phase of the Ice Age, accounted for only a small part of the immense area of land that was lost around the British Isles as a result of the rising sea levels. Off our eastern coast a tract of lowland equal to the present area of England was lost as the North Sea took on its present shape. A much smaller area of land was lost in western Britain by the post-glacial submergence. An extensive plain vanished under the advancing seas of Mesolithic times in Cardigan Bay. Today the only hint of this long-lost landscape of western Wales appears in the stumps of pine trees exposed at low spring tides on the sands of the Dyfi estuary. The same submergence caused the loss of a considerable amount of land around the Isles of Scilly. Today broken, battered lines of stones run out below tide marks in sandy bays to tell of ancient prehistoric fields that have been lost to farming for three thousand years and more.

Recent speculation about the character of the environments in which Mesolithic hunting communities flourished has raised the thought that the lost coastal plains of the highland west were of immense value as a source of food to those peoples and to the wildlife on which they depended. It is believed that aurochs, possibly the wild forerunners of domesticated cattle, grazed for most of the winter months in the mild Atlantic environment of the coastal plains between the western uplands and the sea. As J.G. Evans has written in a recent paper contributed to a research report on *The Effect of Man on the Landscape in the Highland Zone*, 'the west coast in Atlantic times supported floral communities directly comparable with those which in the seventeenth century AD fattened the best beef in Britain by the thousand head'.

But if the land losses of the sixth millennium removed many of the richest and most fruitful of the environments of the upland west, perhaps a slight compensation was provided by the calm shores of the extended estuaries, in the rias or drowned valleys of south Cornwall, the branching arms of Milford Haven, along the banks of the rivers that empty into Morecambe Bay, and

18  A complex of sand dunes covered this late Neolithic settlement in the Bay of Skaill, Orkney. A great gale in the last century revealed the buried buildings, since when Skara Brae has been thoroughly excavated and has become one of the most instructive displays of our prehistoric past to be seen in the whole of Britain

among the wide sheltered waters of the Solway Firth that glisten in the sunlight of late summer afternoons. Here, at the right season of the year, was to be had the immense wealth of the Atlantic salmon fisheries. In faraway British Columbia, along a narrow coastal belt of the Pacific Ocean, rich primitive cultures of North American Indian tribes that rested primarily on the harvest of salmon and the resources of the forest survived unchanged until the closing years of the nineteenth century. The environment that nurtured the Mesolithic communities of the Atlantic west in Britain for some five thousand years must have had characteristics similar to the forested mountainous rim between the coastal ranges of the Rockies and the ocean in western Canada.

Another important change of the post-glacial centuries that affected the environment of prehistoric man was the growth of extensive belts of sand dunes in parts of the Atlantic coastline. At the time of the rising post-glacial seas it seems likely that stronger winds from the ocean, associated with the depressions of the wet Atlantic period, carried blown sand a considerable distance inland. Dune complexes occupy several parts of the Atlantic and Irish Sea coasts from St Ives Bay in Cornwall to the Bay of Skaill in Orkney. Dunes moving under the force of Atlantic gales have buried, preserved and yielded much important evidence of early man in western Britain. Stone tools and

71

pottery, together with the evidence from kitchen middens, suggest that the growth of the dune complexes began only in Neolithic times. For instance, a site in Benbecula, one of the islands of the Outer Hebrides, has shown with the aid of radio-carbon dating that wood from a peat deposit lying beneath a system of sand dunes dates from between 3800 and 3600 BC. This exact date for an object that formed part of the landscape of Benbecula before the start of dune formation agrees with the abundant evidence of archaeology from other places in western Britain that the formation of the massive systems of sandhills in some parts of our coastline did not begin until Neolithic times.

It seems too that a degree of deforestation was a necessary preliminary to the accumulation of sand. The buried soils exposed in the cliff edge of the Penhale Sands to the north of Perranporth, in Cornwall, have given proof that this was an open landscape before the deposition of a massive dune complex that in later centuries was to overwhelm the little Dark Age chapel dedicated to St Piran. The question of great importance that remains to be answered is – what caused the destruction of woodland in these coastal regions? The plainest answer seems to lie with prehistoric men, burning and clearing land for grazing animals in the earliest Neolithic centuries, combined with a minor environmental change of more frequent salt-laden gales from the ocean that inhibited the growth of woodland.

The most striking and universal image of upland Britain at the present time is the nakedness of its landscapes. From the tors of Dartmoor outlined against a darkening sunset sky to the huge, bare mountains that rise from the platform of Lewisian gneiss in the North-West Highlands of Scotland, the lasting impression of the British hill country is a sense of shapes carved by ice and running water and hewn out of many rocks of different qualities – granites and slates, sandstones, limestones, conglomerates and an immense range of materials of volcanic origin. But the elemental forms of our mountains have been revealed only as a result of the efforts of mankind in shaping the landscape to his needs over the five thousand years and more that have passed since the earliest Neolithic farming communities established themselves. It is the work of botanists analysing fossil pollen from peat bogs and the muds accumulated on the floors of mountain tarns that has shown beyond doubt that until the close of Mesolithic times the mountains of Britain were almost completely clothed in forest.

There has been much debate about the highest levels reached by the tree-line – the contour at which a pine and birch scrubland faded into an open, rock-strewn tundra. In the warm, moist Atlantic times the forests on the mountains of the Lake District reached to between 2,000 and 2,500ft above sea level. Five thousand years ago the familiar shapes of the Cumbrian landscape as we know it today were lost beneath a cover of woodland. Sheila Hicks has used the techniques of pollen analysis to reconstruct the prehistoric environment of the gritstone country on the eastern flank of the Peak District. Working from evidence gathered on East Moor she concluded that in late

Atlantic times, before 3000 BC, a forest dominated by oak and alder had flourished on this tract of high moorland that dips gently eastward from a rocky escarpment above the Derwent valley. The only break in the forest mantle came with the exposed rock outcrops along the gritstone edges. In his work on 'Environment and early man on Dartmoor' Professor Ian Simmons arrived at similar conclusions about the extent of the natural climax forest before man appeared on the scene as a major influence in the shaping of the landscape. Although it is hard to determine the position of the upper limit of prehistoric woodland from the pollen preserved in a handful of scattered peat-bog sites that have been subject to analysis, nevertheless Ian Simmons believes that 'forest probably covered all the present moorland except the very exposed summits that were bare or had birch or oak-hazel scrub'.

If, as seems most likely, there were no important and lasting clearances in the deep woodlands that covered the whole of lowland Britain in the millennia of the Mesolithic, perhaps the most striking feature of the landscape of prehistoric Britain in these times was the lack of any marked differences between our upland and lowland regions. The long history of forest clearance that began between 4000 and 3000  BC was to define in ever-greater clarity the two major zones of these islands. Man was a major agent in this long task.

The most striking feature in the evolution of the forests of north-west Europe that has been revealed by the study of tree pollen in peat bogs and lake muds is the sudden decline in the elm that took place about five thousand years ago. At a critical date, about 3100 BC, there was a catastrophic fall in the annual rate of deposition of elm pollen to between one-fifth and one-tenth of the quantity that had accumulated in the undisturbed woodlands of Atlantic times. Detailed analysis of the pollen from a succession of mountain tarns in the Lake District has revealed this change in the character of the forest cover. There was a parallel fall in the deposition rates of birch and pine, and a rising percentage of the pollen of grasses, heather, and the sunlight-loving weeds that are believed to have accompanied the clearance of land for farming. From many other parts of upland Britain proof has been obtained of a marked decline in the mantle of deep enveloping woodland at the time of this sudden falling-off of the rain of elm pollen. On the gritstone moorland of the Peak District, at Totley Moss above Sheffield, the same pattern in a pollen diagram is closely dated by a radio-carbon measurement to the years about 3000 BC. The same basic story is told by the researches of palaeobotanists in the bogs of County Antrim, Northern Ireland. However, there it has been shown that the woodland clearances of the early Neolithic period stretched over a longer period of time than was originally suspected. Here the meaning of the pollen diagrams is unmistakable: tree pollen drops sharply and the evidence for the ribwort plantain, nettles, bracken, bluebells and garlic rises abruptly. The time of the earliest clearances in Northern Ireland seems to date back to 3700 BC, and it has been reckoned that the forest-clearance stage marked by the 'elm decline' may have lasted for as long as four or five centuries.

G.F. Mitchell, one of the pioneers of palaeobotanical studies in Ireland, has described the landscape as he imagines it to have been at the time of the 'elm decline', when the first great inroads seem to have been made into the forests: 'The countryside became a mosaic, with areas of virgin forest, tillage patches, rough pastures, and areas of secondary forest in various stages of regeneration.' The ultimate causes and the methods of woodland clearance in Neolithic times still remain far from certain. There seems little doubt, wherever the pollen evidence has been forthcoming, that the sharp recession of the elm and the opening up of the woodland was the work of little groups of Neolithic farmers, but the methods and means of the clearances are still unsure. Charcoal layers among the peat suggest burning at some sites, but it has also been proposed that of culling of green shoots and branches for fodder did irreparable damage to forest trees. A modification of this view suggests that severe damage was done to elms by cattle tearing off long strips of bark in the winter months as a source of fodder.

In recent years, however, refined work in the analysis of pollen diagrams from upland Britain has shown the complex character of the processes that produced the bare landscapes of the Atlantic north and west. The Neolithic clearances revealed by the 'elm decline' were not a beginning to a continuous and final decimation of the forests. From many sites in the Lake District, among the mountains of Northern Ireland and the great bog at Tregaron in Central Wales it has been shown that the rents made by Neolithic farmers in the woodlands were of a temporary kind; the forest returned after little more than a generation. From her work at Tregaron Bog, Judith Turner has suggested that the temporary clearings lasted for a time span of some fifty years. Pollen evidence gathered in Ulster shows that in late Neolithic times the primitive woodland recovered almost completely. In the Lake District, sediments gathered from Ennerdale Water point to temporary Neolithic clearings in the oak woods of the valley floor between 3200 and 2700 BC. It is clear that soon after 2800 BC the Neolithic episodes of forest degeneration in this part of the western Lake District were over. A major extensive clearance of the upland forests that was to have a lasting effect on the landscape and the quality of the soils in our mountain regions was postponed for more than a thousand years until the Bronze Age.

The effectiveness of man's interference with the forest cover of the Bronze Age and the reduction of large tracts to moorland is attested by the work of botanists in several parts of upland Britain. In Northern Ireland pollen studies in the Sperrin Mountains show that woodland clearance was under way about 2000 BC: the tree cover was already very much reduced, and a blanket of peat occupied the higher and flatter surfaces, formerly the sites of woodland. By the late Bronze Age, according to A.G. Smith writing on 'Neolithic and Bronze Age landscape changes in Northern Ireland', 'large areas of upland were supporting heath or blanket bog', while 'woodland probably persisted on steeper slopes'. The same story of a drastic reduction of the primitive forests in Bronze Age times comes from other parts of Britain. The eastern gritstone moors of the Peak District bear an abundant and silent testimony to the presence of Bronze Age communities. On Ramsley Moor alone there are four stone circles and scores of burial mounds. Another Bronze Age circle on Totley Moor contained two urns that were associated with burials. This latter site has been dated to between the twelfth and tenth centuries BC through the application of radio-carbon dating methods. Sheila Hicks in her study of the evolution of East Moor finds a reflection in her pollen diagrams of the appearance of Bronze Age man and his monuments on the gritstone hills. A major phase of forest clearance over the whole of the upland is indicated in the latter part of the Bronze Age. A steep rise in the pollen of heather points to an extending area of moorland on the gently undulating sandstone plateaux above the valley of the Derbyshire Derwent. Dr Hicks believes that this decimation of the upland forests of the eastern Peak District was associated with pastoralism and, as she writes, this major phase of forest clearance over the whole upland 'must be a reflection of the people who left the collared urns'. The objects found in the burial mounds are related, for the first time, through the techniques of pollen analysis developed in the twentieth century, to a revolutionary change in the history of the natural landscape.

The South-West Peninsula and the Lake District yield similar proof of a drastic reduction of the area of forest during the Bronze Age. From his work with pollen taken from several sites on Dartmoor, Professor Ian Simmons has been able to draw a detailed sketch of the changing landscape of the region through the prehistoric centuries. Here the evidence of the peat bogs for the drastic diminution of woodland on the higher flanks of Dartmoor is supplemented by the abundant evidence of man in the form of clusters of hut circles and the faint outlines of field systems. By the centuries of the middle and late Bronze Age, between 1400 and 500 BC, two somewhat different patterns of economic life had emerged among the communities that were exploiting the environment of Dartmoor. In the upper valleys and on the wetter flanks of the moor the inhabitants of the clustered groups of hut circles were probably largely engaged in pastoral activities. To the east of the granite upland and in the lower Plym valley it seems likely that cereal growing played an important part in the Bronze Age way of life. Dartmoor has produced some striking proof of active woodland clearance as early as the transition period from late Neolithic times to the early Bronze Age. Soil from beneath a row of standing stones at Cholwichtown, on the southern edge of the upland at more than 1,000ft above sea level, has been analysed for its pollen content. The results show a flora characteristic of an agricultural clearing within an oak wood where cereals were being grown. By the close of the Bronze Age a thousand years of farming had reduced the forests of Dartmoor to a thin, discontinuous belt of woodland above the 1,000ft contour. Much open grassland and heath had evolved around the numerous settlements, represented today by the faint marks of hut circles and former field boundaries. In contrast to the earlier woodland clearances of the Neolithic period, this time the forests failed to regenerate in many places; on the high ground the blanket bog grew deeper and began to spread its insidious, sterile mantle of peat. Closer to the settlements the good brown earths that had developed under the cover of deciduous woodland began to degrade into the poor podzols – grey, leached impoverished soils – known there today.

The vital epoch in the making of our moorlands and the baring of our mountains was the thousand years of the middle and late Bronze Age. The ensuing centuries of the Iron Age, after 500 BC, only served to complete the picture. But now the impoverishment of the uplands that had started with man's interference with the high forests was accelerated by a notable deterioration in climate that had set in after 900 BC and was to dominate the Iron Age. Sub-Atlantic times, as this period is known in the succession of prehistoric climates, saw a deterioration to cooler and wetter conditions. More depressions probably moved across Britain from the Atlantic and the occasions of anticyclonic calm might have been less frequent. Any attempt to express the changing factors of the British climate of the Iron Age in statistical terms can be little more than guesswork. The most striking piece of indirect evidence is the immense growth of blanket bog in the uplands of every part of highland Britain that can be attributed to sub-Atlantic times. It has been suggested that in some years the rainfall may have ranged between 25 and 50 per cent higher than the precipitation for an average twelve months in the twentieth century. Something at least is discernible across two thousand years of this climatic fluctuation whose sole evidence now lies in the record of the peat bogs and the accelerated deposition of sediment in the mountain tarns of the Lake District. The upland plateaux of Central Wales that seem to spread into an infinite distance when viewed from the high summit ridge of Cader Idris were a less pleasant place than they had been for the Bronze Age settler in sub-Boreal times. Now, after about 500 BC, they were wetter and colder. The contrasts between temperatures in the sheltered wooded valleys and on the exposed, treeless spurs and the long, peat-covered slopes that crept to the higher summits were far sharper. Wind velocities too had been increased by the removal of the forest cover from the higher hill country.

One of the more drastic results of man's first effective interference with one of the major elements of his natural environment, combined with the climatic change of sub-Atlantic times, was the influence of forest clearance on soils and the run-off from the heavy precipitation of highland Britain. Flooding in those long spells of heavy, continuous rain that visit the mountains facing the Atlantic became more frequent. The steepest slopes of the bared hillsides of the Lake District were scarred with deep, boulder-choked ravines. Even more serious was the widespread transformation of the upland soils through the last thousand years BC, when the brown earths that flourished under the former forest cover were degraded into pale podzols leached of nutrients, a process that was hastened by the rising rainfall of sub-Atlantic times.

The wilderness of blanket bog that replaced the forests has been described as 'the black legacy of the impact of several thousand years of upland climate directly on the ground and its heath vegetation'. The new environment of the wastes of peat was probably far less valuable to prehistoric farmers than the landscape of open woodland and heath that had been widespread in the uplands during the Bronze Age. Forage for grazing animals was reduced and a probable consequence was the making of even greater inroads into the remaining woodland. Professor Ian Simmons's pollen diagrams from Dartmoor show that still greater reductions of forest occurred in the Iron Age times. He believes that the remnants of woodland between the settlements around the higher fringes of the moor were cleared in these centuries after 500 BC. As he has written, 'to a large degree the upland assumed its present landscape, although the vegetation pattern and composition would have differed because of variform intensities of burning and grazing'. The only compensation that the vast tracts of blanket bog could provide for the Iron Age farmer was a new source of fuel – peat – to replace the ever-diminishing store of firewood in the declining forests.

During the Iron Age large tracts of upland Britain, on Bodmin Moor and Dartmoor and on the fringes of the Lake District, were abandoned by settlers and they were never effectively occupied again. No simple answer is forthcoming to explain the later concentration of settlement at lower levels, within the valleys of Britain's uplands. An obvious solution is that the worsening climate of the Iron Age made the higher tracts of upland uninhabitable; man was defeated by excessive rainfall, lowered temperatures and blanket bog. Alternatively, as Professor Simmons has suggested, perhaps the distribution of the Iron Age communities on lower ground to the east, in the lee of the moor, was determined by 'some unknown cultural appraisal'. We can never know all the motives that determined these movements and settlements.

## The works of prehistoric man

Scattered across the face of highland Britain from Cornwall to the remote northern isles we discover the evidence of man and his works from the four thousand years of prehistory before the Roman Conquest. The everyday tasks of wresting a living from the land are recorded in the faint patterns of fields that have lain largely unused since the later centuries of the Bronze Age in the higher and remoter parts of Bodmin Moor and Dartmoor. Farther afield, in Northern Ireland, the cultivation strips of Neolithic farming, a primitive ridge-and-furrow pattern, have been revealed beneath the heavy cover of blanket bog that gathered through the centuries of worsening climate in the Iron Age. The evidence of the need for shelter in the prehistoric centuries can be read in the thousands of hut circles – faint rings of tumbled stones on heather moors – that form one of the most frequent elements of the upland landscape from the Cornish hills to remotest Sutherland.

19 Callanish, the Stonehenge of northern Britain. This 'henge' monument in western Lewis, Outer Hebrides, remained unknown, almost completely buried in the growth of blanket bog, until the last century. It was raised at some time between 1800 and 1300 BC

But the most impressive works of early man seem to have come into existence through the satisfaction of demands that lay beyond the elementary needs of food and shelter. Among the communities of Neolithic farmers the burial of the dead demanded the raising of monuments of huge stones, each weighing several tons. These structures – chambered tombs – date from the centuries before 3000 BC and are found widely in the Atlantic west of Britain. On the high places of the Penwith peninsula in Cornwall their sites embrace wide views across the open sea. In Pembrokeshire, the Lleyn peninsula, Anglesey, the Isle of Man and Arran, the same natural element – the far horizon of the open sea – seems to have been a factor in the siting of these communal burial places.

The numerous circles of standing stones and massive 'henge' monuments from the later centuries of Neolithic times and the early Bronze Age are also thought to have served the non-material needs of prehistoric society. From the earliest descriptions and speculations about Stonehenge it was claimed that similar though simpler layouts of big stones, such as Long Meg and her Daughters in the Vale of Eden, or Callanish, beside a lonely sea loch of the

Outer Hebrides, must have been raised for ceremonial gatherings and functions of a ritual kind. Recently, and largely as a result of the research of Professor Alexander Thom, it has been convincingly argued that these monuments of long-lost prehistoric societies were raised for the purpose of recording important astronomical events such as the midsummer and midwinter solstices and the complex cycle of lunar risings and settings. Their construction, it has been argued, involved a deep knowledge of astronomy, the application of geometric principles in the laying out of circles and ellipses, and a uniform unit of measurement – the 'megalithic yard', as it has been called – that was applied at sites in every part of highland Britain.

## Settlements and fields

Our countryside is unfortunately, in both the hill-lands and the lowlands, largely lacking in the direct evidence of the villages and hamlets where the pioneer farmers of the Neolithic and Bronze Age lived, and of the fields and pastures that came to take the place of the woodland. Settlements from the two thousand years of the remote Neolithic period are scarce indeed. Their precise location and the character of their buildings have only been brought to light by the application of recent and more refined techniques of archaeological investigation. The sand dunes along the shores of Luce Bay in south-west Scotland have given up an abundance of Neolithic pottery as well as axes that had been brought from Great Langdale in the Lake District and Tievebulliagh in Northern Ireland, another source of hard rock that could produce sharp cutting edges. These artefacts are all that remain to betray the location of settlements that must have been important to engage in trade with other communities around the Clyde, in Northern Ireland and along the shores of Solway Firth and the Cumbrian coastal plain.

In western Cornwall at Carn Brea, a shapely granite outcrop of three summits that rises to more than 700ft above sea level on the outskirts of Redruth, a detailed excavation in 1970 uncovered much precise evidence about a Neolithic settlement that must have been in existence already before 3000 BC. The difficulties in unravelling the occupation history of Carn Brea are multiplied by the long succession of peoples that have inhabited its slopes. Early finds there before the age of scientific archaeology included a hoard of Bronze Age axes, dating back to the years between 800 and 650 BC, as well as a considerable number of gold coins from Gaul. Both of these eighteenth-century finds suggest the trade links with Brittany of this exposed summit whose view embraces the Land's End peninsula in the west, much of the northern Cornish coast, and the moorlands around Brown Willy and Rough Tor in the east. Within the saddle to the east of the central summit of Carn Brea the relics of fifteen and more hut circles bear witness to a settlement in Iron Age times, the time when it is believed that the rampart joining the central and eastern summit outcrops was constructed. Since the prehistoric centuries man and his works have left ever-deeper traces on the landscape of Carn Brea. On the most easterly of the three summits, a bare hilltop strewn with granite boulders, a medieval castle was raised that later served as a hunting lodge. Later still, in the early nineteenth century, mining damaged the southern and eastern flanks of the prehistoric site.

The evidence yielded by the most recent excavation at Carn Brea may be used to draw one of the most detailed pictures of a Neolithic settlement that has yet been achieved in the British Isles. Large quantities of Neolithic pottery, of flint implements – scrapers, arrowheads and knives – as well as many stake-holes and the sites of several storage pits suggested the former presence of a Neolithic settlement on the eastern slopes of Carn Brea. An enormous wall of massive stones that throws a ring around the eastern slope of the hill enclosed the settlement and has proved to be a construction entirely of the Neolithic age. Ten houses, occupying small terraces within the walled area, sheltered the five-thousand-year-old community of farmers. Around the village rough piles of stones were discovered that seem to be the relics of the first clearance of land before the spade was used to break up and cultivate the narrow patches of soil between.

Until now the most striking evidence of the settlements and field systems of the two thousand and more years of the Neolithic and Bronze Ages has come

20  Grimspound, one of the many long-abandoned prehistoric sites of Dartmoor. Recent research, using the techniques of pollen analysis, has shown that this was a forested upland until the Bronze Age

from the uplands of the South-West Peninsula and remote sites in the northern isles of Orkney and Shetland. The slopes of Dartmoor and Bodmin Moor above the 1,000ft contour abound with evidence of long-forgotten settlements. Ring banks, between 20ft and 30ft in diameter, mark the foundations of huts. Ancient field systems accompany the clusters of hut circles on exposed and windy moorland. Only at a few places, up to the present time, has a thorough excavation uncovered some of the basic facts about the origins and economy of these settlements. In Cornwall Roger Mercer, whose research has revolutionized our views upon the prehistory of Carn Brea, has also conducted a thorough investigation of a Bronze Age settlement at Stannon Down on the westernmost edge of Bodmin Moor. Here on 'stony down' eleven hut circles were recognized, as well as an associated field system and a number of boundary walls. Finds of pottery from the site showed two distinct phases of occupation separated by several centuries of prehistoric time. The first belonged to late Neolithic times in the centuries between 2000 and 1500 BC; the second, seemingly the date of the hut circles, lay in the middle of the Bronze Age between the twelfth and tenth centuries BC. The two main phases in the settlement history of Stannon Down are reflected in the evolution of the adjacent system of fields. The fields of the Bronze Age hut cluster were laid out in long strips separated by boundaries composed of stone gathered in the clearance of the land for cultivation. In addition three walled enclosures were related to the Bronze Age settlement. Unlike the field walls, which are mere lines of stones or clearance heaps, the walls of the enclosures were carefully constructed of small rubble bonded with large flat stones. The enclosures, it is believed, were used for the penning of livestock that supplemented the precarious grain harvest gathered from the strip fields. Beneath the Bronze Age fields Roger Mercer recognized a still earlier soil layer that seems to represent an older phase of cultivation before the laying-out of the settlement of huts. Pottery from this layer suggested that the cultivation was related to the first farmers on the flanks of Bodmin Moor in late Neolithic times. There are signs of a strip system in this faint and very ancient field pattern, and the discovery of a greenstone axe in the depths of the Neolithic soil layer perhaps provides proof of the first clearance of the land or else its primitive cropping by some system of hoe cultivation.

The excavation at Stannon Down presents one of the most complete pictures of the layout of a prehistoric settlement before 1000 BC in upland Britain. Details of the interior layout of the huts have emerged from the excavation, extending the study of vernacular architecture, back over a period of more than two thousand years from the Middle Ages into the realms of prehistory. The entrances to the huts all face towards the south – to the sun and the most clement aspect of Bodmin Moor's climate. A central post in each hut supported a conical roof that rested on the ring of stone blocks. A system of stone-covered drains curved beneath the earthen floors of the huts and a series of post-holes suggest that the interiors were divided in a radial fashion with wattle screens.

Other patterns of post-holes may once have contained the supports for wooden dressers or arrangements of shelves. More traces of post-holes, outside the huts, point to the equipment of a farming settlement – drying racks, tethering rails for livestock and wooden shelters raised off the ground for storing food. In his general conclusions Roger Mercer suggests that the Bronze Age settlement at Stannon Down nourished a population of about a hundred. There are many other such sites of clustered prehistoric dwellings and field systems on the flanks of Bodmin Moor and Dartmoor. All the evidence points to the abandonment of Stannon Down shortly before 900 BC, most likely in response to the climatic change in the uplands.

During the Iron Age, in the second half of the first millennium BC, the rural settlement patterns of upland Britain became adjusted to a worsening climate. On Dartmoor as the blanket bog spread across most of the higher land above 1,600ft, settlements were confined to the lower ground. Further north and west, in Central Wales, there is similar evidence that the extensive plateau around the summit of Plynlimmon – a favoured tract in the Bronze Age – was abandoned for lower, more sheltered and wooded ground in the valleys during the middle centuries of the Iron Age. Proof of this movement of Iron Age farmers to the lower ground is suggested by a band of charcoal discovered at a depth of some 2ft below the ground surface on a wooded slope in the Ystwyth valley. Radio-carbon analysis has yielded a date for its formation of 233 - 110 BC, in the middle Iron Age. The suggestion is that this lowland site, at only 450ft above sea level, was cleared at that time, by burning, for the purposes of agriculture.

The imprint of Iron Age farming communities is widespread on the landscape of the Pennines. The Peak District's heart of Carboniferous limestone ranks among the earliest settled tracts of upland in northern Britain. The sites of nine chambered tombs within the limited area of the White Peak between Buxton and Ashbourne speak of the first farmer settlers more than five thousand years ago. The earliest surviving visible traces of agriculture in the region are the faint outlines of lynchets – cultivation terraces – that occupy some steeper slopes. At Taddington they may be discerned enmeshed in the pattern of stone-walled enclosures that represent the site of a former medieval open field. A careful survey in the late 1960s of the Manifold valley between Hulme End and Ilam, where that river now follows an underground course for several miles across the limestone plateau, revealed twenty-six groups of lynchets. The flights of long-abandoned cultivation terraces occupy the higher slopes and spurs above the deep, winding trench of the Manifold or the steep slopes of the bowl-shaped hollows at the heads of dry tributary valleys.

Lynchets are among the oldest surviving features of farming in the Pennine landscape. But there is no agreement among archaeologists and local historians about the time when the land was first cleared for the making of strip lynchets. It has been a long-held opinion that they came into existence with the settlement of the Pennines by the Anglo-Saxons, an event that may not have

21   Malham, North Yorkshire. Here in the Carboniferous Limestone country of the northern Pennines the rectangular stone-walled enclosures contain the lynchets – terraced cultivation plots – of an older system of farming

taken place in the Peak District until the opening decades of the seventh century AD. The recent detailed surveying of lynchets in the Manifold valley has done nothing to settle the question of their date of origin, but it does seem more than likely that some of these steep, terraced cultivation strips were the work of Iron Age farmers.

On the limestone hills of the northern Pennines, in the Craven district of the West Riding, numerous places preserve evidence of field systems of Iron Age times and the centuries of the Roman occupation. At Grassington, in Wharfedale, a complex of square and rectangular Celtic fields covers an area of 90 acres. This is evidently an Iron Age settlement because the foundations of huts, in reality prehistoric farms, have been found within the fields. From this austere limestone country of West Yorkshire comes evidence of profound environmental changes since the time when those Iron Age farmers laid down a regular pattern of fields. In some places – at Colt Park, for instance, at the head of Ribblesdale beneath the sheltering mass of Ingleborough – some of the field boundaries run across stretches of bare limestone pavement. The same feature is met once more in the stern limestone scenery of the country above Malham Cove. Here the boundaries, sinuous lines of stones, suggest that cultivated

83

strips once existed in a landscape of which more than half the area is now taken up by bare outcrops of limestone. Such faint clues in the contemporary countryside suggest that much erosion of fertile soils has taken place on these hills over the past two thousand years. It seems that the area of limestone pavement has extended considerably since Roman times.

Further north, in the hill country of Northumberland and southern Scotland beyond the Tyne gap, archaeological research has revealed abundant evidence of settlements that were in active occupation during the last millennium of prehistory. Between the Tyne and the Forth many such sites, composed of a number of round huts surrounded by wooden palisades, have been discovered since World War II. The remains of charcoal recovered from two of these sites, at Craigmarloch Wood in Renfrewshire and Huckoe in Northumberland, have been subjected to the radio-carbon dating technique and the results show that these wooden settlements reach back to at least the seventh century BC. In size these early settlements, now only faint marks on the ground identified through aerial photography and careful fieldwork, range from single homesteads to clusters of dwellings that may be described as villages. Hartburn, for instance, in Northumberland, had thirty-six houses and was occupied without interruption from the middle of the first millennium BC until the second century AD. Excavation there has shown that the buildings of the village had to be reconstructed on several occasions, and at least twelve phases of renewal have been recognized. The importance of the Iron Age as a period of settlement in the uplands of northern Britain – settlement of land that has often been little used in the succeeding centuries – is evident from the number of hamlets, farms and villages surrounded by palisades or ramparts that have come to light in recent years. Fifteen hundred sites are now known in Scotland, and of these almost twelve hundred have been discovered in the territory between the Tyne and the Forth.

In the northernmost parts of Britain, however, beyond Scotland's Great Glen, there is a lack of detailed archaeological investigation of the kind that has revealed a coherent picture of these remote centuries on Dartmoor. That the lower lands of the North-West Highlands were occupied by farming communities, however tiny and scattered, is shown by the number of hut circles that have been recognized in the lonely, depopulated wilderness of Sutherland, where two thousand and more are known. In addition, on hundreds of acres of land between the Moray Firth and the grey kyles of Scotland's northern coastline the presence of ancient fields, 'cultivation plots' to be more exact, has been recognized. For instance, at Loch Laide, between Drumnadrochit above the northern shore of Loch Ness and Inverness, the surviving fragment – some 7 acres – of a larger field system has been investigated. The site lies at 1,000ft above sea level and a large proportion of the ancient fields has been lost through peat digging in historic times and as a result of recent afforestation. Nevertheless, a closer investigation of the long-abandoned cultivation plots at Loch Laide, over a sample area of 10 acres, revealed a hundred cairns – heaps of stones resulting from the original clearance of the land for farming. In addition, eleven platforms were discovered that probably provided the foundations for buildings, and these were integrated with the cultivation plots. The evidence found at Loch Laide may appear faint and fragmentary to us today, but this is only one among many places in the country north of the Great Glen that bear witness to the presence of farming communities after 1000 BC. They suggest a far more extensive use of land up to the 1,000ft contour by settled groups of farmers than the landscape knows today.

But much still awaits investigation in this remote corner of Britain. The long-established and now less certain frontiers of prehistoric time, separating the Bronze Age and the Iron Age, seem far less well defined in these northern territories. The hard and fast divisions of archaeological time are replaced by a sense of cultural continuity that extends over a thousand years into the post-Roman centuries. One fact that seems to be established with some certainty is the extensive abandonment of land in the northern regions of upland Britain in the latter half of the first millennium BC. It has been argued by R.W. Feacham in a paper entitled 'Ancient agriculture in the highlands of Britain' that until the early Iron Age there was 'no noticeable difference in quality between lowland and highland areas'. Then followed a serious falling-off of material culture in the uplands as compared with lowland Britain. Except in the South-West Peninsula, the cultivation of crops was abandoned or drastically reduced. In response to the worsening climate of sub-Atlantic times, highland Britain – the parts of these islands that centuries later were to become synonymous with Celtic Britain – came to rely on stock raising at the expense of crop cultivation.

## The hill-forts

In many parts of the British Isles, and especially in the lowlands, two thousand years of land use since the end of the Iron Age has obliterated all evidence of prehistoric man from the visible landscape. The most long-lasting and impressive objects that have descended to us from the Iron Age are without doubt the ramparted earthworks, enclosures defined by weathered banks and ditches, that are known to us under the collective label of 'hill-forts'. Recent intensive archaeological research at some of these sites – primarily in North Wales, Herefordshire and Somerset – has shown that the term 'fort' is hardly an accurate descriptive label. Some were certainly considerable settlements occupied over many centuries whose functions may well have been concerned not only with agriculture but also with trade and the tasks of regional government. The 'hill' element in the name has also been exposed as a misnomer with the realization that several of these foci occupy valley and lowland sites, places lacking in any strategic significance.

Detailed investigation at a handful of important sites, together with the use of radio-carbon dating methods, has shown that some of the ramparts and material from early wooden buildings inside the forts predates, often by several centuries, the conventional beginning of the Iron Age early in the fifth century BC. Firm proof from two of the hill-forts of North Wales, Moel y Gaer and Dinorben, on limestone hills that flank the plain of Clwyd, shows that these places were occupied as early as the eighth century BC. At Moel y Gaer radio-carbon analysis suggests a time in the eighth and seventh centuries BC for the construction of the earliest wooden buildings on the site. The evidence from Dinorben carries the age of settlement on the site of this typical Iron Age fort even further back, into the centuries of the late Bronze Age. Here the radio-carbon date from charcoal found in the timbers of the oldest rampart comes from the year 980 BC, and the evidence from the settlement that preceded the building of the rampart has yielded a date of 1032 BC. The long-lasting features of the Iron Age forts that have survived as part of the present landscape – the deep, grass-grown trenches, the weathered ramparts that conceal facings of laid stones and elaborate timbered frameworks, the complex embanked corridors that led to the protected inner space – represent an obscure history of settlement and organization of the regional environment that stretches, at some places, from the Bronze Age into the Roman period.

Throughout Britain there are more than three thousand such features of the landscape, embanked and ditched enclosures, that may be called hill-forts. According to their size, and as excavation uncovers a wealth of telling detail at a handful of scattered sites, it is possible to see that these places served varying functions in the life and economy of the inhabitants of Britain during the last millennium BC. More than half of the enclosures – and there must be many more that are still unnoticed or else lost to the visible landscape – served as defended homesteads or sheltered a tiny cluster of huts. Generally the 'forts' of this category contained less than 3 acres of enclosed ground within the limit of their ramparts, and their siting shows no predilection for places of high strategic value. In highland Britain such places occur in abundance. They are the 'rounds' of the South-West Peninsula, while in South Wales and Ireland such tiny enclosures, hemmed in by a green circular embankment, are known as 'raths'. In Cornwall the 'rounds' lie thick upon the ground on the broad platforms that rise gently inland from the sea. Detailed fieldwork in the west of the Cornish peninsulas during the 1960s revealed the presence of a 'round' for an average of every square mile of the countryside. Scarcely any of these banked and ditched enclosures has been excavated, but one that has been explored with the tools of archaeology, at Trevisker, has revealed Iron Age occupation in the second or early first century BC. The evidence from Trevisker hints too at the use of this same site in an earlier period of prehistory, with the suggestion of a Bronze Age settlement in the second millennium BC.

A similar story of the evolution of open, undefended settlements, tiny clusters of huts of the Bronze Age, into earthwork-enclosed homesteads has also been revealed by research among the many small Iron Age forts in Northumberland and south-eastern Scotland. More than a thousand such sites, rampart-enclosed settlements that have the appearance of hill-forts, are known in the region between the Tyne and the Forth. Most of them take up an area of less than 3 acres and, like their counterparts in south-western Britain, they seem to have been associated with a pastoral, stock-raising economy among the hills and valleys that lie inland from the coastal plains.

The large hill-forts, landscape features to which the name is applied with greater meaning, range between 10 and 60 acres in extent. Although such hill-forts are numerous in lowland south-eastern England – so much so that in such areas as the South Downs of Sussex their distribution pattern seems to provide the clues to a regional organization of society in the Iron Age – they form much rarer objects in the landscape of highland Britain. The large hill-forts of the lowlands – at least in the chalk country, east Devon and the Cotswolds – seem to dominate limited tracts where scattered farms relied heavily on arable production. In the uplands, only in North Wales and among the hills of the Welsh Marches do such large structures form a regular element among the surviving remnants of the prehistoric landscape. In north-east Wales, along the range of hills that forms a barrier between the Vale of Clwyd and the Dee estuary, a line of large rampart-ringed earthworks occupies the more prominent spurs and summits. Five hill-forts occur along an 8-mile stretch of the Clwydian Hills. Three of them, Moel Fenlli, Moel Hiraddug and Pen-y-Cloddiau, must rank among the greatest in the British Isles. Pen-y-Cloddiau stands at 1,400ft above sea level and its earthworks of four ramparts and three ditches enclose an area of 65 acres. No excavations have yet been undertaken at this mysterious relic of the Iron Age landscape, brooding from its height over the lush pastures of the Vale of Clwyd. The huge enclosed space within the ramparts contains no superficial evidence of a settlement in the shape of platforms or hut circles. It seems most likely that this largest of hill-forts was designed primarily as a shelter for livestock that grazed the high hill pastures above the permanent settlements in the Vale of Clwyd. In his all-embracing study of *Iron Age Communities in Britain,* Professor Barry Cunliffe has proposed that elsewhere in these islands the largest of the forts, 'massive straggling structures of 60 acres and more', were probably built for the protection of cattle.

The hill-forts of the Clwydian range possess a lonely, mysterious quality, partly no doubt because of the lack of detailed knowledge about their purpose and history, and also perhaps because of their remote sites on windy hilltops far above the world of everyday affairs. Further west, in Snowdonia, where the dark, brooding cloud-capped hills reach out towards the sea between Conway Mountain and the little isolated summits of the Lleyn peninsula, a succession of large hill-forts has yielded firm proof that they formed permanent settlements in the society of the Iron Age, perhaps extending their active functions into the centuries of the Roman occupation. Castell Odo, lying at the remote western tip of the Lleyn peninsula, has revealed a development sequence that stretches through several centuries, beginning with an open settlement of several circular timber houses. The most striking of these large hill-top settlements in Caernarvonshire are Garn Boduan, Tre'r Ceiri and the ramparted enclosure

87

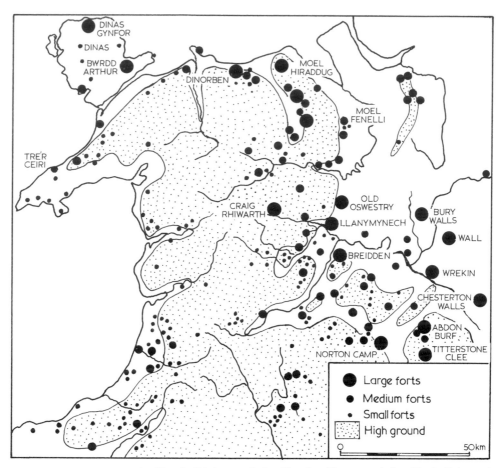

Fig 12   Hill-fort sites in North Wales and the Border Country (*after Forde-Johnston*)

with its numerous hut foundations that crowns the summit of Conway Mountain. They are all notable for the use of drystone wall structures and the large communities that they seem to have sheltered – populations that probably ranged between a hundred and four hundred people. At times, the late prehistoric settlement on the summit of Conway Mountain could have sheltered as many people as the medieval walls of the town that was planted at its feet some fifteen centuries later. But the most exciting of the ramparted hilltop enclosures in North Wales is undoubtedly Tre'r Ceiri, 'the town of the giants'. This 'fortified hilltop town' glowers down on the surrounding lowland of the Lleyn peninsula from the most easterly peak of Yr Eifl, whose rough screes of igneous rock were able to provide ready building materials for the Iron Age founders of this remote mountain settlement. Within the encircling drystone rampart of Tre'r Ceiri more than 150 hut circles have been counted – the stone foundations of flimsy structures of peat and wood and wattle. A.H.A. Hogg, an authority on the archaeology of the innumerable long-abandoned settlements of late prehistoric times and the Dark Age centuries in North

Wales, has excavated some sixty of the hut circles of Tre'r Ceiri. Most of the finds were of Roman pottery, suggesting that this hilltop settlement was inhabited for the greater part of the centuries between AD 150 and AD 400.

The life and economic purposes of this community that continued to occupy an Iron Age fort when so many similar places in the rest of Britain had been abandoned can only be dimly perceived through the evidence available to the archaeologist today. Tre'r Ceiri's carefully built stone ramparts and narrow, inturned entrances with passages that must have been closed by heavy wooden gates suggest that this was a refuge, a place to be defended. Some have seen Tre'r Ceiri as one of the last and strongest defences of the Ordovices against the Romans in the later decades of the first century. But that was before the discovery of abundant evidence of life on this lonely mountain summit through the Roman centuries. An alternative hypothesis, put forward by Sir Mortimer Wheeler, proposed that the main purpose of Tre'r Ceiri was defence against the Irish raiders who plagued the coasts of Wales in the later Roman centuries. Certainly, in clear weather, this hilltop in Lleyn provides a wide sweep westward across many miles of the Irish Sea. But the true character of the life of this community, which seems to have equalled in numbers the population of a small medieval town, eludes an all-embracing explanation. Defence may have played an intermittent role in the life of Tre'r Ceiri, but the pottery and the large number of hut circles suggest that other purposes are involved in a complete explanation. One telling piece of the archaeological evidence, though of a negative kind, is the complete absence of querns or anything suggestive of arable farming from the scores of huts that have been investigated. Tre'r Ceiri, it seems, was concerned only with pastoralism. Was this perhaps a large summer settlement where folk from the surrounding coastal lowlands gathered their flocks and herds for safety through the dark hours of the short night? If this view is correct, Tre'r Ceiri provides evidence that transhumance, the movement of livestock to the high mountain pastures between May and September, was already a part of the way of rural life in upland Britain during the prehistoric centuries.

As we survey the pattern of large hill-forts in the high country of northern England, the problems surrounding the interpretation of their functions and purposes are no easier to solve. The Pennines and the Lake District both lack the abundance of ditched and ramparted enclosures that characterizes the landscape of the Welsh Border country from the Dee to the Severn. Consequently the rare Iron Age earthworks of the north seem all the more impressive. Mam Tor, one of the finest Iron Age sites of the southern Pennines, surveys an incomparable landscape. Westward lies the limestone plateau of the Peak District, a grey-green pattern of thin pastures and stone walls seamed by the shallow canyons of dry valleys. To the north and east the prospect from Mam Tor is closed by the ever-frowning, shapeless mass of Kinder Scout, a dark wilderness of crumbling sandstone cliffs and treacherously deep mires of brown blanket bog. Repeated landslips in the unstable shales of the precipitous southern face of Mam Tor have swept away part of the fort's encircling rampart. On the north-eastern slope, above Edale, where the earthwork is still finely preserved, the imagination can reach back through two thousand years to glimpse the organization and labour that must have been involved in enclosing the 16-acre summit of this mountain with a rampart that still stands some 30ft above the encircling ditch. Until a few years ago the purpose and origins of this earthwork astride the summit of a Pennine mountain were as obscure as that other relic of the Iron Age, Pen-y-Cloddiau in the Clwydian Hills. But over the past decade, the Department of Archaeology at Manchester University has used Mam Tor's hill-fort as a regular training site for its students. It is already evident that the ramparts enclose a space that was something more than a place for the corralling of livestock grazing the high summer pastures above Edale. The evidence of post-holes, hearths and finds of pottery as well as platforms cut into the steep hillside to the east of the mountain summit show that there was a settlement of some kind on this bleak, windswept hilltop. The pottery belongs to a simple native type manufactured by the Brigantes – the Celtic tribe that

22   The huge ditch and rampart – almost two thousand years old – that marks the limits of the Derbyshire hill-fort of Mam Tor

ruled the greater part of northern England at the time of the Roman Conquest. From this limited evidence it has been concluded that the earthworks of the hill-fort were constructed at a late date, most likely between AD 50 and AD 70. But the mystery surrounding Mam Tor's purpose and origin is by no means dispelled. Was this a summer settlement of Iron Age farmers, or is Mam Tor a military earthwork thrown up by the Brigantes as the Romans made their way into northern Britain in the second half of the first century?

Major hill-forts are rare in the northern Pennines and the Lake District. Two of them, Ingleborough and Carrock Fell, occupy wild mountain summits that even today are hard to reach. The gently sloping 'table mountain' of Ingleborough, at a height of more than 2,300ft, dominates the stony limestone pastures of the Craven district in the northern Pennines. A stone wall – a 14ft-thick rampart faced with coarse gritstones – encloses the 16-acre summit plateau, a cold, forbidding place on all but the hottest and haziest days of high summer. There are traces of hut foundations within the enclosure that seem to be contemporary with the rampart wall whose crumbling stones still outline the precipitous edge of the mountain's top. The only pottery that has been found that may help to date the prehistoric occupation of Ingleborough is a sherd dating from late Roman time, in the third or fourth century. Carrock Fell lies on the eastern fringe of the Lake District, surveying from a height of more than 2,000ft the lowland of the Eamont valley around Penrith and the limestone hills that lead southwards towards Shap – an important region of Celtic settlement in the centuries that led up to the Roman occupation and, in these latter times, part of the extensive territories of the Brigantes. More than forty years ago, R.G. Collingwood surveyed Carrock Fell hill-fort inside a single July day. He mapped the line of the crumbling broken wall, but found no trace of hut circles or other superficial evidence of occupation within the 5-acre enclosure. It is tempting to place Ingleborough and Carrock Fell alongside the other exposed hill-forts in the Clwydian range of North Wales, both as places where livestock were gathered in the summer months, and also as refugee strongholds for the Brigantes in the first century.

The absence of a close network of hill-forts in the uplands of northern England suggests a sparse population in these parts. Nevertheless, it is puzzling that most of the major forts are in the most inhospitable sites. Professor Cunliffe in his wide-ranging survey has suggested that an explanation for the 'general absence of hill-forts in the northern Pennines' may be found in 'the pastoral nature of the economy that prevented the development of politically cohesive tribes requiring defended foci'.

Further north, in southern Scotland and the eastern foothills of the Cheviot, the prehistoric role of the larger hill-forts appears to be much clearer. Here, fourteen sites with ramparts and ditches enclosing areas of up to 40 acres have been described as *oppida* – clustered settlements that by the late Iron Age had developed some of the functions of towns. Yeavering Bell, Northumberland, has 130 huts gathered within the space of 13 acres. Its Iron Age population has

23   The Eildon Hills. The late Iron Age settlements (*oppida*) of Central Scotland occupy the summits of prominent volcanic hills. This was probably the tribal capital of the Selgovae, and on Eildon Hill North the foundations of 500 houses have been recognized

been estimated at about five hundred. On Eildon Hill North, Roxburgh, the foundations of 500 houses have been counted on its 40-acre site. R.W. Feacham has estimated that Eildon Hill North sheltered a population of between two and three thousand. It is most likely that this was the tribal capital of the Selgovae, the Iron Age tribe that dominated the central Southern Uplands of Scotland. With one outstanding exception, the scattered *oppida* of Scotland seem to have been abandoned soon after the Roman occupation of the north. One hill-fort, Traprain Law, was still actively occupied at the time of the Saxon settlement of the coastal plain of the Firth of Forth. The ramparts and foundations of the timber-framed buildings on Traprain Law cover an area of some 40 acres. The summit of this whaleback-shaped hill that controlled the eastern approach to the Lothian lowland was the site of the capital of the Votadini, the northern neighbours of the Selgovae. Traprain Law has yielded evidence of a period of occupation that stretches through many hundreds of years from the late Bronze Age until the beginning of the Saxon period. Several sets of defences were raised and destroyed through these centuries of occupation; the last, a turf wall faced with stone, is 3,500ft long and 4yd in thickness. It sheltered a town in the late fourth century AD whose industries of metalworking and textile manufacture, trading and administrative functions served an extensive tract of the Lothian plain. Eildon Hill and Traprain Law have been described as 'cities upon hills', the largest hill-forts of Scotland and permanent centres over long periods of time of organized tribal territories.

Elsewhere in the central lowlands of Scotland, between Forth and Clyde, and in the uplands of the south and west, certain commanding hilltops seem to have been the locations of powerful tribal centres. Burnswark, a conspicuous table mountain that dominates Annandale in Dumfriesshire, was probably the tribal centre or *oppidum* of the Novantae, the Iron Age tribe whose territories focused on the peninsulas that project into Solway Firth. Burnswark provides clues to the social changes that took place with the Roman occupation of northern Britain. On opposite flanks of the hill crowned by the rampart of the fort are the sites of two Roman siege camps, and at the southern camp the outlines of three catapult emplacements have been recognized. Archaeology has shown that after the Roman entry into south-west Scotland, Burnswark was abandoned as an inhabited site; nearby the Roman fort of Birrens was raised as a sign of a new and alien control in the territory of the Novantae. The outlines of the relations between the Iron Age peoples of Scotland and the Roman invader remain in a deep obscurity at the two remaining sites of suspected *oppida*. Dumbarton Rock, girdled by the tall cranes of a Lower Clyde shipyard, looks itself like some huge abandoned artefact of prehistory. Although no remains of a prehistoric fort can now be traced on the summit or across the steep flanks of the rock, it is believed that this was the tribal capital of the Damnonii, the people whose territories embraced the western part of Scotland's central valley. Arthur's Seat, an equally striking fragment of upland Britain in the townscape of Edinburgh, still preserves some evidence of its role among the *oppida* of North Britain. The surviving ruins of prehistoric stone walls suggest that a space of some 20 acres was contained by the former ramparts and the precipitous flanks of the hill. Down the centuries all traces of dwellings, whether timber-framed or stone-built, have been erased from the site, largely, it is believed, as a result of ploughing over the whole of the interior of this suspected *oppidum*.

The surviving objects of late prehistory in the Highlands and the north-west of Scotland reflect the character of the landscape, the societies and the economies that evolved in those regions. In the west, the Atlantic thrusts long fingers of sea lochs between the forbidding mountains. Patches of lowland fit for permanent settlement are extremely restricted; tiny communities were isolated from their neighbours by the intractable wilderness. Only towards the North Sea's coastline does one find evidence of more strongly co-ordinated communities in prehistory: communities that controlled areas of lowland, in the lee of the Grampians or around the Moray Firth, as extensive as the coastal plains of south-eastern Scotland.

24   Arthur's Seat. The Iron Age forerunner of Edinburgh occupied this defensive site

The rocky headland of Burghead that guards the wide mouth of the Moray
Firth is the site of one of the most impressive and elaborate fortifications of the
Iron Age and later centuries in northern Scotland. Unfortunately, the fort at
Burghead today is only a remnant of the complex structure that was still
surviving at the beginning of the nineteenth century. Until 1808, when 'certain
improvements' were made under the direction of a Mr James Young, three
huge ramparts, each about 800ft in length, ran across the neck of the headland.
Their combined width was almost 200ft. Nothing remains of these massive
earthworks, and our detailed knowledge of the topography of Burghead today
depends upon a plan of the fort that was made, at the request of the Duke of
Cumberland, by General W. Roy in the 1740s. Most of what remains of
prehistoric Burghead consists of the ruins of walls within the enclosure. But
there is little doubt that this place ranks among the most important prehistoric
sites of the north. As Feacham has written, 'the fort at Burghead must have had
a status at the nature of which it is now only possible to guess'. The
interpretation of the finds at Burghead takes the mind out of the realms of
prehistory into the dark centuries of post-Roman Scotland. Several carved
stone slabs have been found bearing Pictish and Viking motifs. Recently, from
an excavation of the fragment of the surviving inner wall, a Carbon 14 date has
been obtained for timbers that formed part of the building. A construction date

in the fourth or fifth century AD is suggested. Burghead seems to have had a long and active life extending from the Iron Age across the Roman centuries into the obscure history of Pictish Scotland. Was this place at the entrance to the Moray Firth with access across the sea to the whole of the north-eastern coastline of Scotland a Pictish *oppidum,* the central capital of this far-flung territory of northern Britain? Did the Roman armies reach Burghead in their effort to subdue the remotest parts of these islands in the first century? Was this the place where Columba visited Bruide, the ruler of the Picts, when he came with the news of Christianity to the pagan north in the sixth century?

The archaeology of northern and western Scotland is still in need of extensive and detailed exploration before a full picture of the settlement geography of the Iron Age peoples can be drawn. For instance, a promontory fort overlooks the wild waters of Pentland Firth at St John's Point: a stony rampart and ditch cross the headland for about 600ft, ending abruptly above the cliffs and the boiling seas. Nothing is known about the date and purpose of the enclosed headland behind this rampart, except that it has the claim to be the most northerly promontory fort of the British mainland. But similar sites, out of reach of the record of history and all of them as yet unexplored by archaeology, occur along the whole length of the stormy coastline of northern Scotland as far west as Durness. Like the Cornish cliff castles they may well have been constructed in the Iron Age, later to be taken over by the Vikings who, elsewhere in the Northern Isles and the Hebrides, took over the structures of a remoter past during their tenth-century settlement of the British Seas.

The Scotland of the western sea lochs and of the high mountains with their sub-Arctic climates must have been one of the most thinly peopled parts of Britain in the prehistoric centuries. Here the largest cores of settlement lay in the islands, on the windy lowland of Caithness, or in such a rare and favoured tract as the neck of the Kintyre peninsula in Argyll where the high mountains lie back from the coast and a more benign landscape of broken hills, wide straths and low rocky peninsulas faces the Atlantic. Here, in this favoured region of the west, are a number of 'forts', thick-walled enclosures that date back to the Iron Age and the post-Roman centuries. Most of them are modest structures that served restricted local communities, the focal point for the inhabitants of a single glen, but Dunadd on a small, isolated rocky hill some 4 miles to the north-west of Lochgilphead seems to hold a more important place in the development of Scotland. At several different levels the natural outcrops of rock on the hillock at Dunadd have been edged with walls to strengthen the natural defences of the fort. This work, it is believed, dates to the early Iron Age, but, close to the entrance, slabs of the living rock bear carvings that undoubtedly belong to the school of Pictish art. The most striking among them is an illustration of a boar, and experts in the primitive art of the north date this work to the late seventh or early eighth century AD. The fort at Dunadd is also one of those rare objects of the prehistoric landscape that are mentioned in the record of history. The *Annals of Ulster* report the siege of Dunadd by the Picts in

AD 683 and again in AD 736. In those times the fort lay in a critical region of conflict between Dalriada, the advancing kingdom of the Scots, and the Pictish lands to the north and east beyond the formidable mountain barrier of the Grampians. Dunadd shows evidence of occupation from the Iron Age until the time of the extinction of Pictish power and the making of medieval Scotland. The geography of upland Britain in prehistoric times is characterized by a number of favoured focal tracts, tracts that have been endowed by nature with qualities above the average. In the South-West Peninsula we recognize the value of the median levels around the high moorlands of Bodmin and Dartmoor – areas whose latitudinal position has endowed them with the most favourable climates of the upland regions of these islands. The narrow plains of Caernarvonshire and Anglesey that border the Menai Strait and the varied landscapes of the Lleyn peninsula provided an area of attraction from Neolithic times onwards, in contrast with the forbidding wilderness of Snowdonia. The Peak District's heartland, the central plateau of Carboniferous limestone with its skin or rich soils accumulated through the closing period of the Ice Age, has attracted man over the past six thousand years. Even today the conquest of the encircling rim of repulsive gritstone moorland is hardly complete. The pre-eminence of the limestone lands of Derbyshire and north Staffordshire as a primary core of settlement in prehistoric times is emphasized by the abundance of relics surviving in the landscape from all phases of prehistory – rock shelters where Mesolithic implements were shaped, nine chambered tombs from Neolithic times and countless burial mounds of the Bronze Age. But the importance of the limestone plateau in the settlement geography of the past is summarized in the great stone circle at Arbor Low, the Stonehenge of the southern Pennines, whose layout and location suggest that this was one of the hubs of social organization among the scattered communities of highland Britain. As we consider the role of the uplands in the centuries after the Roman Conquest, it will be noticed that the same focal tracts lie at the centre of man's interest in these landscapes of mountains, deep, constricted valleys and boundless, open plateaux that turn their face to the west and the Atlantic over a span of almost 1,000 miles between Land's End and Cape Wrath.

# 4

# The Cultural Remoteness of Highland Britain

Upland Britain turns its back to the lowland south and east. Even in the South-West Peninsula, the deep trench of the Tamar has always acted as a frontier beyond which the land rises towards the upland mass of Bodmin Moor. The mountains of the Lake District, if seen across Morecambe Bay from the green lowland of the Fylde, represent another world, a distant, blue, remote place. And from Edinburgh Castle on a clear winter's day the far rampart of the Highlands, a ghostly barrier of snowy peaks, stands out as a frontier between two worlds that has prevailed down the centuries. Upland Britain, through the long centuries of prehistory and after, has looked to the west, to the Atlantic coastlands, the sea passages of the Irish Sea, its island-sheltered straits and kyles and the long, quiet lochs and estuaries, for the means of communication between its different parts.

The social differences between highland and lowland Britain were first imprinted on the geography of these islands during the four Roman centuries. The lowlands acquired most of the elements of a Mediterranean civilization – towns, an effective network of made roads, busy harbours along the Channel coast swarming with naval vessels and engaged in trade with the Continent, and a countryside in which extensive tracts were organized as villa estates practising Roman systems of management and land use. The historians of Roman Britain, writing at the beginning of this century, called the south-eastern parts of the country the 'Civil Zone' – a region where a Roman way of life with Latin as an everyday language became firmly implanted. In the uplands of the west and north the Roman found himself in another world – the Atlantic fringe of Europe that was never totally incorporated within the domain of this Mediterranean imperialism. The same historians chose to call this the 'Military Zone' because the chief objects of the landscape of the uplands in Roman times were military roads, signal stations and fortresses. Two such fortresses were Segontium, a forerunner of Edward I's planned town at Caernarfon, and Trimontium, the great stronghold at Newstead-on-Tweed, named after the triple-peaked summit of Eildon Hill crowned by its *oppidum*, an

25   Hadrian's Wall, raised early in the second century AD between the Tyne and the Solway Firth to mark the limits of Roman power in Britain. This is one of the great monuments of Europe, with sections remaining remarkably well preserved despite centuries of pillage for farm buildings and field boundaries

embryonic town and tribal centre of an Iron Age people. The political insecurity of highland Britain in Roman times is shown in the massive linear defences of Hadrian's Wall that join the Tyne to the Solway, and in the Antonine Wall, built largely of turves, that runs for 37 miles between the Forth and the Clyde, with its closely spaced forts at intervals of 2 miles.

The Roman impression on the far-flung territory of the Military Zone varied immensely. Cornish tin and the seaways that led across the Channel to Gaul secured a firm hold over the native peoples of the South-West Peninsula. The sources of lead and silver in the Mendips, among the hills of west Shropshire, in the Peak District and the northern Pennines ensured a Roman interest in these parts of upland Britain. In Wales, too, the easily accessible copper reserves of Parys Mountain in Anglesey and the gold-bearing veins of Dolaucothy led to a permanent interest in the lands of the Silures and the Ordovices. But the remoter parts of northern and western Britain always lay beyond the sphere of

Roman control. Ireland, from the scarce and scattered evidence of coins and pottery, felt only the occasional contacts of trade with Roman Britain. For the most part, Highland Scotland lay beyond the fringe of the Roman world. The Antonine Wall, a line bristling with forts, defined the southern boundary of the vast wild territory of the Picts for only a few years of the second century. It was built and defended between the years AD 142 and AD 158. After a short period of reoccupation during the last two decades of the century, it was finally destroyed in about the year 207.

As the influence of Roman civilization faded from the life of Britain in the first part of the fifth century, so the old ways and customs of Iron Age society were revived. At Lydney, overlooking the widening estuary of the Severn on the fringe of the Forest of Dean, an elaborate temple was founded in the closing years of the Roman period. Dedicated to the god Nodens, it was raised within the enclosure of an Iron Age camp. If the Lydney temple suggests the survival of pagan Celtic religious practices and beliefs, there are several other pointers to the resuscitation of an older Iron Age way of life in the west and north. Most striking perhaps is the gathering evidence for a reoccupation of the hill-forts. Dinas Powys and Coygan Camp in South Wales, and Castle Dore and Chun Castle in Cornwall, are among several ramparted Iron Age sites that were inhabited during the early Christian period of the fifth and sixth centuries. Most impressive among the sites in Wales, Dinas Powys has yielded proof of occupation, albeit not continuous, from the early Iron Age to the time of the Norman Conquest – a time span of more than a thousand years. A hall-house and a barn, built of timbers, were raised within the camp in the fifth and sixth centuries. Finds of glass and pottery as well as the fragments of an Anglo-Saxon bucket date the buildings, known only by the evidence of post-holes, to the Dark Age centuries before the Saxons extended their frontier of settlement across the Cotswolds into the valley of the Severn. Dinas Powys played an active role on the stage of history again in the eleventh century when more earthworks were thrown up, this time in the form of a substantial ringwork that is believed to represent the reaction of Celtic Britain to the westward advance of Norman power. South-western Scotland – the present counties of Galloway and Dumfriesshire – was one of the more favoured regions of upland Britain. Like South Wales and the lower, more attractive lands that separate Dartmoor and Bodmin moor from the sea, this was a wealthier tract with a considerable population. Here too archaeology has shown that the ancient hill-forts were reoccupied. The Mote of Mark, the most famous site in Kirkcudbright, was an active settlement from the fifth until the close of the seventh century. Bronze and iron working went on there. Archaeologists have uncovered abundant evidence of such industry in clay moulds for the shaping of metal objects, scrap bronze and the slag of iron as well as the foundations of a furnace. Mote of Mark has been described as a princely stronghold, perhaps part of that shadowy kingdom of Rheged that once stretched from the northern Pennines to the lands around the Solway Firth.

Western Britain presents many tantalizing problems in the long period between the Roman abandonment of these islands and the conquest of the greater part of England by the Normans at the close of the eleventh century. These times, often known as the Dark Ages, have left far less identifiable evidence in the form of settlements, burial places, rough-hewn monuments of stone, pottery, objects of metal and the relics of agriculture in the form of field systems than have the earlier epochs of prehistory. In Wales, for instance, so little is known about the settlements – even their very whereabouts – for the latter part of this period, between the seventh and eleventh centuries, that it is impossible to create a coherent picture of the distribution of population in that country. Only in recent years, as a result of the evidence from a handful of sites such as Dinas Powys that have been archaeologically explored and from an examination of scattered references in medieval documents, has it been possible to obtain a clearer picture of the rural economy of Wales in the Dark Ages. Once it was believed that the peoples of the early Welsh kingdoms followed a nomadic way of life; now it is known that settled forms of agriculture – the growing of arable crops with a land-use system that involved open fields – were widespread in the larger vales and strips of coastal lowland beneath the mountains of the principality. The geography of upland Britain in the Dark Ages can only be discerned, and then without any semblance of completeness, through the use of widely different types of evidence – lists of kings that seem to reach back to Roman times, heroic tales handed down through the poetry of the Middle Ages, stones inscribed with the grooves and notches of the Ogham alphabet, the lives of the great saints of the Atlantic world written down many centuries later, and the church dedications to these men who preached and established churches and monasteries from Cornwall to the furthest northern isles.

## The lost kingdoms of highland Britain

It is possible to discern a series of distinct territories, dating back to the fifth century, between the South-West Peninsula and the harsh, extensive, thinly populated lands of the Picts that occupied the greater part of Scotland beyond the line of the Antonine Wall. These kingdoms, Celtic-speaking by language, and looking back to the Iron Age in the structure and organization of their societies, owe much to the native tribal territories that the Romans found when they set foot in these islands. The Romans knew the inhabitants of the South-West Peninsula as the Dumnonii. The most westerly part of Dumnonia beyond the Tamar was to keep its independence until the tenth century when Aethelstan of Wessex received the submission of the king of Cornwall in AD 926.

The most potent factor in the shaping of the kingdoms of upland Britain in the fifth century was a constant threat from outside. The Anglo-Saxon pressures against the whole length of the frontiers of the British kingdoms still lay in the womb of time, in the seventh and eighth centuries. When Roman interests in Britain became extinct it was the Irish who threatened from the west and the Picts from their remote strongholds in the Highlands. Irish raiders had already seriously threatened South Wales before the end of the third century. In 367 a combination of the Irish, Picts and Saxons in an onslaught upon Roman Britain, the *Conspiratio barbarica* as it became known, foreshadowed one of the patterns of Dark Age history – migrating war-bands and the tribal settlement of alien territories. In Wales and southern Scotland the new political orders of the fifth century emerged from the need to counter the incursions of the Irish and the Picts, peoples of the furthest parts of western and northern Britain who had always lived beyond the ambit of Roman civilization. In the closing years of the Roman occupation, the solution for the perpetual threat to western Britain was found in a devolution of power. The Roman troops who defended the frontier territories were replaced by a native militia, and government was placed in the hands of native princes whose descendants make up the royal dynasties that figure in the genealogies surviving to us from later centuries.

The evolution of Dark Age political geography under the influence of Irish raids and tribal migrations as well as the policies of the closing years of the Roman epoch is clearly illustrated in the emergence of a mosaic of little kingdoms in Wales, each ruled by its own dynasty. The Irish settlements have had a profound effect on the history and geography of south-west Wales. Before the end of the fourth century, probably about AD 380, a major settlement of the Irish had been established in Dyfed, in the seaward-extending, recently extinguished county of Pembrokeshire. This early tribal migration from Ireland to Wales is recorded in legend, in the story of the expulsion of the Desi that tells how 'Eochaid, son of Artchorp, went over the sea with his descendants into the territory of Demed [Dyfed] and it is there that his sons and grandsons died'. Centuries later the compilers of the genealogies of the kingdom of Dyfed looked back to the migration period in tracing their dynasty to an Irish prince Eochaid Allmuir, Eochaid from overseas. But the importance of a tribal migration across the Irish Sea for the shaping of Wales is evident not only in the carefully handed-down traditions of the rulers of Dyfed, but in elements of the landscape as well. The greater number of stones inscribed with the Ogham alphabet, of which there are about fifty in the whole of Wales, have been found in the south-west. Most of the stones, memorials often raised near ancient trackways into the interior of the country, bear the names of Irishmen. Stones with Ogham inscriptions were being raised until the middle years of the sixth century; such a date, almost two centuries after the tribe of the Desi had been forced to migrate from its Irish homeland, implies the continuity and distinctiveness of these alien settlers in South Wales through several generations.

The Irish settlement of the western peninsulas of Wales and its coastal lowland is further borne out by a scattering of place-name elements. Some of

101

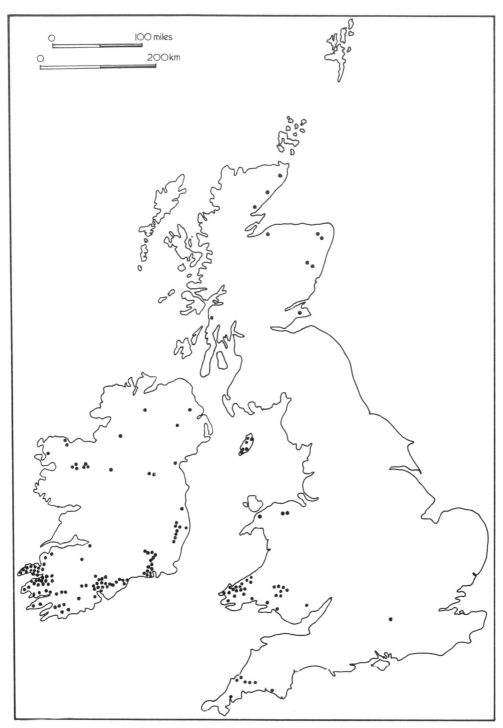

Fig 13   The distribution of Ogham stones in Britain (*after Macalister*)

the names of rivers, brooks and hills – as a rule among the oldest of a region's place names – preserve Irish elements and traces of the Goidelic branch of the Celtic language from which Irish evolved. The Irish suffix *-ach* is found in some river names, while the element *cnwc,* derived from the Irish *cnoc,* a hill, is found among the Welsh topographical names. The distribution pattern of the *cnwc* names is especially important in locating the major area of Irish settlement in the south-west. This element is practically restricted to the country south of the River Ystwyth in Cardiganshire and Pembrokeshire; eastward it is found reaching out to Carmarthen and in the Tywi and Teifi valleys. The area thus marked out seems to correspond with the extent of the early kingdom of Dyfed in the fifth and sixth centuries. The problem in uncovering the extent and importance of the Irish settlements in Wales is the almost complete absence of archaeological evidence of a different people and a separate culture. Scarcely anything attests to the presence of the Irish apart from the memorial stones. But one feature of the present landscape, an earth rampart and ditch known as the Clawdd Mawr, that crosses the high ground between the valleys of the Teifi and Tywi, may belong to a time when Dyfed was still a distinct political entity with a cultural and social framework grounded in the much earlier Irish settlement of the tribe of the Desi. Clawdd Mawr has been compared to the great linear earthworks of the Welsh borderland, Wat's Dyke and Offa's Dyke – frontiers marked on the ground that separated the North Welsh territories of Powys and Gwynedd from the advancing Anglo-Saxon state of Mercia. It is thought that the peoples of Dyfed raised the Clawdd Mawr in the eighth century – which is also when Offa's Dyke was constructed – at a time when the Welsh-speaking peoples of the north were pressing southwards to settle the Vale of Tywi.

The major core of settlement in North Wales had occupied the lowlands of Anglesey and the coastal plain of Caernarvonshire from the remote Neolithic centuries. The impact of the Irish raids and settlements in late Roman times induced a different reaction in this region from that of South Wales. A Roman fort, Caer Gybi, was built at Holyhead, largely to protect the trade in copper from Anglesey, and it is believed that late in the fourth century the Roman fortress at Caernarvon was rebuilt on lower ground at the mouth of the river with the same purpose of securing the traffic through the Menai Strait to Anglesey. The most persistent tradition concerning the beginning of the Dark Age kingdoms of North Wales tells of the inviting of a chieftain, Cunedag or Cunedda, from south-east Scotland, to settle in North Wales as a counter-force to the threat of the Irish from the west. The story goes that he arrived in Wales with eight of his sons and one grandson and their followers from Manau Gotodin – the northern frontier territory that overlooked the lands of the Picts from the banks of the Forth – and that 'they expelled the Irish forever from those lands'. It has been argued that the settlement of Cunedda's people in Wales was at the instigation of Magnus Maximus, a Roman official in late-fourth-century Britain who was acclaimed emperor by his troops when they crossed with him to Gaul in the year 383. Whatever the true facts of the story of Cunedda – and there is no evidence of where he settled, of what numbers of North Britons migrated to Wales, or of the relations in war and peace that existed between them and the Irish – there is little doubt that his name is associated with the foundation of the kingdom of Gwynedd and the rise of the most powerful dynasty in Wales. By the middle of the ninth century, when Rhodri Mawr succeeded to power in Gwynedd, that kingdom, securely rooted in the cornfields of Anglesey and protected by the natural stronghold of Snowdonia, had gained control over the greater part of Wales. It is possible that Cunedda's exploits against the Irish are little more than heroic propaganda to glorify the beginnings of the dynasty of Gwynedd. But at least there is important place-name evidence for the presence of Irish settlers in parts of North Wales. The names of the Lleyn peninsula have preserved a distinct Irish element in Dinllaen, Nefyn and Abersoch. Not only individual places but the major regional names reveal an Irish connection. Lleyn suggests a connection with Leinster and may point to the source of an Irish migration into this westernmost, sea-bound region of Gwynedd, and it has also been argued that the name Gwynedd itself is derived from the Irish *Feni*, the name of a group of people whose expansion lay behind much tribal displacement and migration in the fourth and fifth centuries.

A similar pattern of political development may be observed in the evolution of the kingdoms of central and southern Scotland after the end of the fourth century. Military and administrative power devolved on to local princes and the frontiers of their kingdoms, often defined by vague boundary zones across intractable empty upland, once more outlined the ancient tribal divisions of the Iron Age. The Dark Age states, if such a term may be applied to a concept of tribal social organization that became rapidly more and more remote from the modes of Roman government, developed under the pressures of conflict along three frontiers in central and southern Scotland. The Picts and Irish threatened from the north and west; after the sixth century the advance of the Angles from Bernicia, and later the powerful Northumbria, made inroads into the south-eastern flank of the British kingdoms.

Three major groups emerged among the North Britons. Manau Gododdin, remembering in its name the older tribal name of the Votadini, focused on the lowland that flanks the southern shoreline of the Forth. Strathclyde was centred on the sheltered, branching estuary of the Clyde, the counterpart of Gododdin at the western end of the line of the Antonine Wall. The stronghold of this British state was Dumbarton Rock – Dún Breatann, the strongly fortified place that Bede mentions in the Ecclesiastical History as *munissima civitas* – most fortified of cities. Another important core of settlement of the North British was focused on Carlisle and the sheltered peninsulas that project into the Solway Firth. This was Cymry, the country of the Cumbroges or 'fellow countrymen' – a name that has lived down the centuries in Cumbria, an ancient regional description of the English Lake District, and now resuscitated as one of the new counties that emerged from the reorganization of local government in 1974.

The kingdom of Strathclyde remained independent for centuries; the political unit that formed the core of Cymry, the mysterious Rheged whose existence is sensed mainly through the heroic poems and legends of Dark Age Wales, survived only until 638 when it was absorbed under the pressure of the expanding Anglian state of Northumbria. Although so little firm knowledge has been handed down to us about Rheged, a few scraps of evidence suggest that this was one of the successor states that came into existence at the time of the Roman retreat from Britain. As fresh archaeological evidence accumulates there is a strong belief that Carlisle survived as a settlement, perhaps even with some of the attributes of an urban society, long after the Romans. It is equally likely that this was the capital of the kingdom of Rheged, though claims have been put forward for several other places as the seat of power. They include Iron Age forts in southern Scotland and long-deserted settlements in the limestone hills at the headwaters of the Lyvennet, one of the tributaries of the River Eden.

Highland Scotland formed a distinct element in the human geography of Dark Age Britain. This was the land of the Picts, a country whose remoteness from the rest of the British Isles was emphasized by the fact that the Romans made only the briefest incursions into these territories and left scarcely any cultural impression there. The Pictish language too was different, though not completely alien from the tongues of the rest of upland Britain. Pictland survived as an independent political entity until the ruling dynasty of Dálriada, the kingdom of the Scots, achieved dominance in northern Britain in the ninth century. It is astonishing that so little survives, apart from art objects and a handful of inscribed stones, and that the reconstruction of the Pictish language has defied scholarly research. The language contained two elements – a form of Celtic akin to the Brythonic branch of the language spoken in Dark Age Wales and Cumbria, and a much older stratum of vocabulary, a non-Indo-European tongue, that was probably current in Atlantic Europe in the Bronze Age.

Of the geography of Pictland it is possible to sketch an outline with the help of a scattering of place-name elements, of earthworks such as Craig Phadraig, which crowns a wooded hilltop on the outskirts of Inverness and is known as a Pictish stronghold, and of the distribution of stones inscribed with the characteristic forms of Pictish art. The kingdom of the Picts focused on two zones separated by the high, empty wilderness of the Grampians. The northern Picts were centred on the Moray Firth and its rim of lowland. Burghead and its complex of earthworks has long been suspected as the capital of the northern Picts, a people whose ruling dynasty was briefly caught by the limelight of history when, in the sixth century, Bride mac Maelcon – better known as King Brude — was converted to Christianity by St Columba and a mission from the monastery on Iona. But the topography of northern Pictland is as obscure as its language, because strong claims have been put forward for the location of Brude's court at Craig Phadraig. The geographical limits of Pictland to the north are equally hard to define. At its full extent the kingdom included the Hebrides and reached out to the Isles of Orkney.

Four nuclei are distinguishable in southern Pictland whose ancient provincial names are Athfotla (Atholl), occupying the valleys of the Tay and Earn, Circinn in the lower part of the Tay valley, Forthriu based on the upper waters of the Forth and Earn, commanding an important route to the west, and Fib in the Fife peninsula. It has been argued that the Tay valley with its line of great hill-forts guarding the northern mountain flank must have been the heart of southern Pictland.

The struggles of the Dark Age centuries between the separate kingdoms in Scotland ultimately destroyed the Picts. The southern tribes of Pictland were particularly exposed. On the southern flank across the Forth they were open to the aggressive expanding Northumbria in the seventh century; northwards, where the vital Drumochter Pass led into the territories of the northern Picts, warfare smouldered; and from the west the emerging kingdom of Dálriada was the source of an even more dangerous threat. By the year 850 Pictland ceased as an independent power with the annexation of all these lands from the Forth to the Pentland Firth to the overlordship of Kenneth mac Alpin of Dálriada, but the memory of this forgotten state has not been completely erased from the history and countryside of Scotland. The element *pit* among the place names of Scotland derives from the Pictish centuries; and it is noteworthy that it does not occur to the south of the Forth–Clyde line. Some other elements among Scottish place names, Brythonic in their linguistic derivation, seem to hark back to this remote past. Words containing the terms *carden*, *lanerc*, *pert*, *pevr* and *aber* belong to this category. Some places that have been important in later centuries were also centres of power in Pictland. For instance, Scone was the capital of Athfotla in the later centuries of Pictish history, while the place on the coast of Fife that became St Andrews, once known as Kilrymont, 'the cell of the royal hill', was the centre of the province of Fib.

The migrations of the Irish that colour the history of western Britain from Cornwall to the Solway Firth in the fifth century had a much more profound effect upon the evolution of Pictland in the Dark Ages. During that period bands of migrant Irish, known as the Scotti, occupied the coastlands of Argyll between the Firth of Lorne and the neck of the Kintyre peninsula. An account of the settlement of this part of Scotland, Dálriada, has survived from the seventh century. It tells how three brothers, Fergus, Loarn and Aengus, sailed from Ireland with a fleet carrying 150 men. The family of Aengus took over the island of Islay. Cenél Loairn or the Kindred of Loarn took over the southern shore of the Firth of Lorne, establishing a base on the site of Dunolly Castle at Oban. Fergus and his descendants possessed themselves of Kintyre and Knapdale, where their chief stronghold was established in the Iron Age fort on the rock of Dunadd that rose from the wastes of Crinan Moss. It was the kindred of Fergus, Cenél n'Gabráin, that rose to pre-eminence in Dálriada. In later centuries, when the lists of the Scots kings were drawn up, the line of the royal dynasty of Dálriada was traced back to the fifth century and its founder, Fergus mac Erc.

Argyll must have been a thinly populated region at the time of the Irish

106

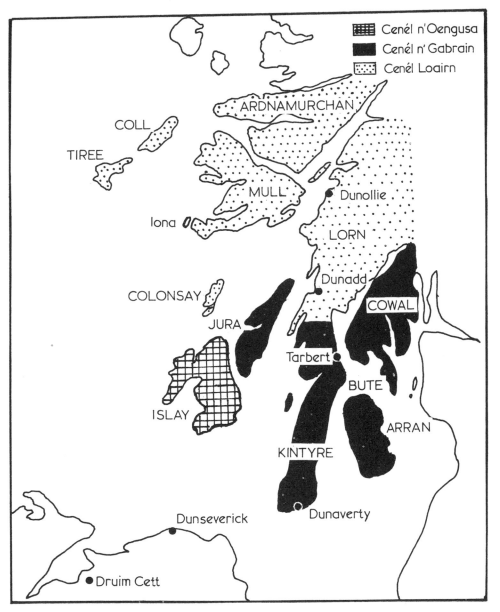

Fig 14   Dálriada in the seventh century (*after Menzies*)

settlements, for there is no tradition of conflict with a native population. The chief source of conflict for this kingdom of the Scots lay towards the east, across the great mountain barrier that screens the coastlands of Argyll, with the southern and northern Picts. Warfare between Dálriada and the Picts has passed into history's record of the Dark Age centuries in the form of two references to sieges at the fortress settlement of Dunadd – the capital of Dálriada, if a place so reminiscent of the Iron Age be worthy of that title. A reference to the year 683 mentions a besieged Dunadd; again the *Annals of*

107

26  Dunadd, one of the most important prehistoric and Dark Age sites of Scotland. On this upstanding crag in western Argyll an Iron Age fort was later taken over by settlers from Ireland to become the focal point of Dálriada

*Tigernach* report the capture of this defended place in Crinan Moss by Oengus mac Fergus, ruler of the Picts. Although warfare must have played its part in the relations between the Scotti of the west and the older and more extensive territories of Pictland, there is little doubt that cultural movements between the two parts of Scotland led towards the unity under the dynasty of Dálriada that was achieved in the ninth century. The Picts had already borrowed the techniques of the Ogham alphabet in the sixth century in the making of inscribed stones.

An even more important part in securing the pre-eminence of Dálriada was played by the missionary activities of Iona. This tiny grey island washed by the translucent green seas off western Mull was the religious capital of the Irish settlements in Argyll – a place of far greater meaning in the history of the north than the forgotten rock of Dunadd. St Columba founded his monastic outpost of the Celtic church on Iona in 567, more than a century after the pioneering Irish had colonized the western shores of Argyll. Columba took Christianity to the Moray Firth and the capital of the northern Picts; by the year 575 his follower Cormac was engaged in the conversion of the furthest limits of Pictland in his mission to the Northern Isles. To the south and east the influence of Iona spread to the Anglian kingdom of Northumbria. Columba's role in the sixth-century evolution of Dálriada was not confined to the spread of the gospel and the founding of churches. He has been described by a modern historian of Celtic Britain as 'the chief man in the power politics of the sixth century'. Within Dálriada the families of Loarn and Gabráin, with their castles at Dunolly and Dunadd, were locked in a long struggle for power. It was the 'political sagacity' of Columba that secured the dominance of the Cenél n'Gabráin. Two centuries later the dynasty that ruled the dominant clan in Dálriada was to achieve the union of the Scots and the Picts under one crown. The centre of government shifted from the west to the east, with the administration of royal power from Scone, where the traditional dwelling of the Pictish kings is found in a mound behind the royal palace.

But if the political glories of Dálriada were to fade in the emergence of the new kingdom of Scotland, the cultural imprint of the Irish in Argyll and the influence of the Celtic Church was secured as the Gaelic tongue, evolving from the Goidelic branch of the Celtic languages, spread far and wide across the greater part of northern Britain as a living means of communication. The culture of the Picts fell into an obscurity after the tenth century that has placed it largely beyond the recall of even the most meticulous scholarly research.

## Upland Britain and the seaways

When we view the upland parts of Britain through the eyes of the Roman, the Anglo-Saxon or the Norman overlord of the twelfth century, the mountainous regions of the Atlantic west seem remote and isolated. Their conquest and settlement presented an arduous, prolonged and never completed task to powers based in the lowland of south-eastern England. Hadrian's Wall between the Tyne and Solway firth, and the earthwork that was raised across the hills of the Welsh Marches in the eighth century and attributed to Offa, have inscribed upon the landscape a permanent reminder of the limits of lowland power at two very different periods of history. The mountains of highland Britain and their adjoining tracts of coastal lowland that face the Atlantic and the Irish Sea have been linked with each other, down the centuries, by the seaways of the west. On the clearest of days the prospect from the high summits of western Britain reveals the unity that is given by the sea. On a still, clear, cloudless morning the view from Cader Idris embraces the greater part of upland Wales, while to the west the far-reaching peninsulas of Pembrokeshire and Lleyn enfold the lowlands and valleys that reach down to Cardigan Bay. Further north the high peaks of the western Lake District take into view the mountains of Snowdonia as well as the hills of Galloway across the Solway Firth. From northern Arran, that clutch of granite mountains in the wide estuary of the Clyde, the eye looks northward across the tumbled uplands of Argyll to the peaks of Mull, and all around are the grey-blue fingers of sea lochs opening towards the Atlantic – the ways that guided traders, saints and settlers

27   Offa's Dyke, the late eighth-century earthwork that formed the western frontier of Mercia. In conception and planning this linear boundary that connects the Dee with the mouth of the Severn is as daring as the running frontier of Roman Britain, Hadrian's Wall

of the early Christian centuries into this northern wilderness. Further north again, the unity that the sea and its communications have given to a discordant, hostile land may be glimpsed in the prospect from the Cuillin Hills of Skye where a clear day uncovers a seemingly endless wall of mountains stretched out on the eastern horizon towards remote Cape Wrath. During the centuries of the early Christian era the seaways of western Britain helped in shaping the individuality of the zone of upland that extends, with only a few important breaks, over 1,000 miles between the reefs of Scilly and the clustered islands of Orkney. The sea allowed an ease of movement that was not to be had by land.

    We have already discussed the profound influence of the migrations of tribal groups from Ireland on the societies and settlements of south-west Wales and Scotland in the post-Roman centuries. Irish settlers also left their mark on Devon and Cornwall through secondary migrations from South Wales as well as directly from southern Ireland. Here, in the South-West Peninsula, the evidence of several distinct movements of the Irish ranging over a wide time-span from the latter decades of the Roman occupation to the seventh century is contained in the church dedications to Irish saints and the distribution of stones with Ogham inscriptions. An even more striking proof of the freedom of movement that the seaways gave to the peoples of western Britain is shown by the colonization of Brittany that took place from Cornwall and south-east Wales in the early Christian centuries. These migrants from highland Britain, founding what a modern historian of Celtic Britain has described as 'our first colony', left an impression on the social geography of France that fifteen hundred years of history have failed to eradicate. The causes of the migrations that led to the creation of Brittany have remained obscure. The sixth-century monk Gildas, writing close to these events in his *De Excidio Britanniae*, ascribed the movement of peoples from the south-west to the advance of the Saxons. Modern research believes that the pressure of the Irish across the sea from the west provides a more cogent explanation of the displacement of population from Cornwall and south-east Wales.

For a long time scholars have recognized the part played by the western sea routes in the spread of Christianity through upland Britain between the fifth and the eighth centuries. One of the most important, though controversial, of clues is provided by the vast number of dedications of churches to the many saints of this period. The most striking feature of the dedications, and one starkly revealed through the research of Professor Emrys Bowen, is the concentration of certain saints' names in strictly defined territories within highland Britain. For instance, the present map of church dedications to St Petroc shows a high concentration in Devon and north Cornwall. There is a

28   The Cuillin Hills look southward across the Sea of the Hebrides to the distant mainland mountains of Ardnamurchan

Fig 15   Churches dedicated to St Petroc in Wales, the South-West Peninsula and Brittany (*after Bowen*)

handful of dedications to this sixth-century saint in Wales – the most northerly in the British Isles occurring in the Lleyn peninsula at Llanbedrog – and another scattering of churches and chapels, eight altogether, in Brittany. St Kentigern, also known as Mungo and believed to be the founder of the first Christian church at Glasgow, is clearly associated with northern Britain. His dedications are focused on Carlisle, particularly on the northern fringe of the Lake District, and in the coastal lowlands of the Forth to the east of Edinburgh. The territory where St Maelrubha was known, if one is to judge from the present pattern of distribution of his dedications, stretched from the Kintyre peninsula through the whole of Scotland's western fringe of sea lochs and mountains. Little is known about St Maelrubha apart from the fact that he lived in the second half of the seventh century. He came from Ireland and tradition has claimed his descent from a king of that country, Niall of the Nine Hostages. He seems to have been trained in the great monastery of Bangor, County Down, before taking up missionary work in the country of the northern Picts. St Maelrubha is credited with the founding of a monastery at Applecross, a lonely patch of coastal plain hemmed in by the gaunt mountains of Wester Ross that looks across to the islands of the Inner Hebrides. It is noteworthy that among the islands off the west coast of Scotland, Skye has the only cluster of dedications to St Maelrubha, suggesting that the Sound of Raasay and its shores may have marked out a 'culture area' of the Christian Church in Dark Age Scotland.

The distribution patterns and regional concentration of the dedications to the several different saints of the early Church in the Celtic West has given rise to much speculation about the missionary journeys of these legendary figures. An attractive but extreme view would regard the dedications as the result of the founding of a new church by this or that missionary as he travelled from one pagan community to another in upland Britain. Thus, for instance, the string of dedications to St Kentigern in the northern Lake District would trace the route followed by this leader among the Christians of Strathclyde on a mission that took him from Carlisle along the south-eastern flank of the Skiddaw massif towards Derwentwater and Bassenthwaite. But the difficulty in wholly accepting this line of thought lies in the absence of any firm proof that the majority of church dedications reach back to the time between the fifth and seventh centuries when these leaders of the early Church lived and worked. Many dedications to local saints date back only to the years after the Norman Conquest when a great rebuilding of churches, a building in stone that replaced many simple wooden churches, took place. Often at a time of re-dedication the name of a fresh patron saint would be introduced. Nevertheless, although the local relationship between a church and the journeyings of a particular saint may be called into doubt, the map of dedications in highland Britain speaks of the importance of the seaways in joining the chief cores of population. That some saints belong entirely to North Britain and others to Wales and the south-west suggests the different and separate communities of the Atlantic façade.

Fig 16   The cult of St Maelrubha in north and west Scotland (*after Bowen*)

The most striking feature in the life and organization of the early Church in upland Britain was the foundation of monasteries whose communities became the focus of missionary activity. Tiny islands lying close to the mainland were favoured places for the establishment of monastic communities – places that lay on the sea routes that joined together the scattered communities of Atlantic Britain. On the western flank of Scotland two islands are outstanding in the history of the spread of Christianity through North Britain: Iona and Lismore, where Columba and Moluag are associated with the founding of monasteries in the sixth century. Lismore, in its site and history, epitomizes the geography of the Church of highland Britain in the early Christian centuries. The island, a spine of limestone 10 miles in length, rises to almost 500ft above the sea in the wide mouth of Loch Linnhe. The very name Lismore, meaning 'the great garden', seems to hark back to the time of St Moluag, when the monastery and its garden were enclosed within an oval-shaped *vallum* or rampart at Kilmoluaig. Even then, Lismore must have looked like a fragment of paradise in the wilderness of the north. We can still sense that wilderness if we climb to the rocky ridge that makes the backbone of the island; there on a clear day a prospect of the great mountains of northern Argyll opens up before one. Eastward the narrowing dark blue channel of Loch Linnhe leads the eye towards Ben Nevis; to the north and west the mountains of Morvern and Mull flank the seaway that points to Ireland, the source of the Christian communities that planted their monasteries in western Scotland. The premier role of Lismore in the geography of the Church in the north-west found its only rival in the more famous community of Iona. The sanctity of both places – and perhaps their important locations in relation to the sea routes of those past centuries – gave the islands continuing prestige in the later Middle Ages. Early in the thirteenth century a cathedral was established at Kilmoluaig on Lismore, and in 1500 the abbey church of Iona became the centre of a bishopric of the Isles.

The evidence of the earliest centuries of Christianity in upland Britain is not easy to come by in the landscape. In Scotland the ravages of time and four centuries of a Puritanism that showed a deep disdain for the thousand years of Catholic Christianity have done much to erase the evidence of the Dark Age Church and its monasteries. At Kilmoluaig, where the clean salt air of summer days is perfumed with the scent of meadowsweet and honeysuckle, the medieval cathedral was burnt to the ground at the time of the Reformation. The present building, a plain parish church, was restored out of the ruins of the choir when a roof was put over it in 1749. Iona is the great exception since its resurrection as a powerhouse of Christianity with the founding of the Iona Community by Lord MacLeod of Fuinary in the twentieth century. The ruins of the medieval abbey church and its monastic buildings were splendidly restored between 1902 and 1965. On bright summer days, when the clear light of Iona makes the heaviest heart feel one step nearer heaven, the motor launches ply a non-stop traffic across the narrow strait from Mull, and twentieth-century tourism disturbs briefly the quiet of Iona. Even so, one may quickly leave the crowded lane that

29   Iona, the sacred isle of western Scotland, where Columba founded a monastic community in the sixth century that was to influence the greater part of northern Britain. The first half of the twentieth century has seen the restoration of the medieval cathedral and the founding of the Iona Community (*Peter Baker*)

leads from the quay to the cathedral, past the ruins of the nunnery built in the thirteenth century by Somerled, King of the Isles, to climb the slopes of Dun I. From there one of the widest views in the British Isles opens out, a seascape that embraces more than 100 miles of the mountains and islands of western Scotland between Skye and Islay. Below, on the edge of the monastic site, swarming with the transient tourist crowd, one can make out a much older piece of Iona's landscape. There a curving grassy bank and ditch may well represent the boundary of that first community sketched out by St Columba.

Monasteries from the early centuries of Christianity that were as important as Iona have vanished from the landscape almost without trace. Of the community that St Maelrubha founded at Applecross in 673 only the trace of the *vallum* that enclosed the monastic huts and church on the north bank of the Crossan River may with difficulty be discerned. The destruction of the northern monasteries is believed to have been largely the work of Viking raiders in the ninth and tenth centuries, but there is little doubt that other hands have also played their part. For instance, an ancient carved cross that was said to mark the burial place of St Maelrubha was broken up and incorporated in the walls of a new manse in the nineteenth century.

The great monasteries of early Wales have suffered a similar fate to those of northern Britain. Of the two Bangors, Bangor-Is-Coed on the River Dee and Bangor Fawr beside the Menai Strait, nothing at all survives. Camden in his great account of the topography of Britain at the close of the sixteenth century mentioned the ruins of the monastery on the Dee; today its very site is a mystery. In Caernarvonshire recent building work at the University College in Bangor has uncovered a rough, rectangular building, constructed of rubble and bonded with clay, that seems to date from before AD 1000. It is surrounded by a cemetery that suggests a religious or monastic site, but until now no firm evidence has emerged to connect this discovery with the original foundation that was made here by St Deiniol in the sixth century. The rest of the early monasteries of Wales are just as unrewarding. Bardsey, a lonely deserted island separated from mainland Wales by a dangerous narrow strait, is described as possessing 'a monastic complex too disturbed by later burials to repay excavation'. In South Wales the great monastery of St Illtud at Llantwit Major, Glamorganshire, has vanished without trace and in Pembroke the early religious community at St David's is now known only through the discovery of a few sculptured stones.

The character of the monasticism that was so important in the organization of the Church during the early Christian centuries in western Britain is best appreciated at Tintagel, a rocky exposed promontory on the north Cornish coast whose very name conjures up the dark, romantic legendary past of the highland parts of Britain. But for the precarious rocky spine that joins it to the mainland, Tintagel would be an island hedged in by cliffs that rise sheer for almost 200ft from the Atlantic. The dominant object of the site for the casual traveller is the crumbling ruin of a medieval castle, but this represents almost the latest stage of Tintagel's history. A monastery was founded there early in the sixth century, probably by Julian or Juliot, one of the many saints who taught and enriched the life of the early Christian Church in Cornwall. Life continued in the monastery at Tintagel for more than three hundred years before it was deserted in the ninth century, and archaeologists have shown that in its history it passed through four different phases of rebuilding. Today the remains there consist of the foundations, walling of stone and clay, of tiny rectangular huts that cling to rock-bound ledges on the summit and upper slopes of the headland. The main complex is gathered around a Norman chapel, a place of worship that must have been built over the original consecrated site that formed the focus of the monastic community.

If time and the changing fortunes of history have all but wiped out the memory of many of the earliest monasteries of the Celtic Church in highland Britain, the influence of the first centuries of Christianity is still evident in the landscape, in the siting and layout of hundreds of parish churches. The creation of the original primary parishes looks back to the centuries before AD 1000.

117

30   The deserted island of Bardsey, off the Lleyn peninsula, was the site of one of the most important of Welsh monasteries

The least destructible feature from these remote centuries long before the Norman Conquest of England has been the make-up of the place names. The elements *lan* and *llan* in Cornwall and Wales refer to the beginnings of a place as a church site. There is perhaps no more descriptive term for these original units of social organization than the Cornish term 'churchtown'. In North Britain the prefix *kil-*, a chapel, takes the place of the Brythonic *llan* in the description of church sites, the cores of the earliest parishes.

   The early churches of the South-West Peninsula and Wales are recognized not only through their place names but also, in many places, by the shape and layout of their churchyards. The elements *lan* and *llan,* in their primitive meaning, refer to an enclosure, usually circular or oval in shape, within which a simple chapel, built largely of timber, was raised. Today we can still recognize these early enclosures in churchyards of circular or oval shape. Often they have been extended in later centuries and now we may find only a section of a wall or bounding hedge tracing out the original circular plan. Elsewhere the primitive

118

nucleus, the original enclosure, can be followed in a ring of gnarled, time-honoured yew trees. The history of the primary church sites goes back to the prehistoric centuries, before Christianity. In many places it seems that Bronze Age stone circles and later ringworks of the Iron Age centuries were taken over by the expanding Christian Church, perhaps even as early as the third century AD. In a few places a standing stone still survives in a churchyard, a mute relic of a remoter pagan past.

The beginnings of the early Christian Church in highland Britain are lost to us now. The personalities of the Celtic saints, their dates and deeds, belong more to the realm of legend than to the plain daylight world of the carefully documented and chronologically arranged facts of history. But one account that has survived into the modern world throws a brief beam of light into the history of the Celtic Church in Cornwall in the early years of the sixth century. St Samson, a Christian leader from South Wales who lived between AD 480 and 560, played an important part in the migration of settlers from south-west Britain across the Channel to Brittany. He founded a monastery at Dol, and it was there, in the early years of the seventh century, that *The Life of St Samson of Dol* was compiled. This early record contains an account of his journey from Wales to Brittany. It tells how he used the transpeninsular route from the north coast of Cornwall, near Padstow, to the deep, sheltered estuary of the Fowey River from which he embarked for Brittany. The place from which he sailed away has not been recognized with any certainty. Perhaps the site of Fowey was already in use as a regular port, but the dedication of the church at Golant to St Samson suggests that this tiny upstream settlement was the place of embarkation on the journey to the new settlements of the Britons across the Channel.

The account of St Samson's journey to Brittany shows that tracks across the peninsulas formed an essential link in the sea communications of western Britain in the Dark Ages. But in its story of the journey between Padstow and the Fowey River, the *Life* preserves some valuable evidence about the working of the early Church and its missionaries. It tells how Samson travelled overland with a waggon loaded with sacred books and holy vessels – the necessary equipment of a pioneer who was bound for new territory, there to found a monastery. The *Life* also makes it clear that pagan cults had still not been completely extinguished in Cornwall in the early years of the sixth century. In a district that was called Tricurium, now Trigg Major, St Samson saw pagan acts of worship around a standing stone. It is told that the saint protested against such unchristian practices and that he inscribed the pagan monument with the sign of the cross. The vivid detail of this incident suggests its authenticity, and demonstrates how the expanding Church of the post-Roman centuries in highland Britain took to itself the ritual sites of the pagan world.

Of the extent of the Christian Church in Wales and the south-west before the time of the Norman Conquest there is little doubt. This fact is established by the innumerable dedications to the saints of the Dark Age centuries as well as the hundreds of place names in *lan* and *llan* that refer to the original sacred enclosures. Cornwall alone contains the sites of seven hundred churches and chapels, and many of these were places of worship before the year 1000. But the material remains from the foundation centuries of Christianity are scarce today. An intense period of church rebuilding in stone began with the twelfth century and has erased most of the visible evidence of the early churches. Only at a few places can one obtain a direct insight into the past, as at St Piran's chapel, Perranporth, in north Cornwall, where the landward-moving front of a belt of sand dunes engulfed a tiny Dark Age chapel. At Burry Holms in South Wales an archaeological excavation of the 1960s revealed a sequence of church buildings developing through several centuries. Beneath a stone chapel dating from the twelfth century, D.B. Hague found the four corner-posts of a timber chapel, a tiny building measuring only 11ft by 10ft that was standing at the time when the rebuilding in stone began. The church site, oval in shape, was enclosed by a bank composed of a double line of large standing stones. The pattern of evolution of the church buildings at Burry Holms must have been repeated at scores of other places where, in their turn, the simple stone chapels of the twelfth century have been succeeded by later rebuildings of the high Middle Ages. But the shape of the original enclosure, the oval *llan*, and occasionally a length of the ancient walling composed of a double line of upright stones, still remains to draw the imagination back to the remote centuries when the first timbered churches were raised.

## The imprint of the north

The sea routes that provided the links between the scattered parts of upland Britain, bringing merchants with wine and oil from the Mediterranean lands and leading missionaries to the remote islands of the North Atlantic, were also the means of contact with the pagan, little-known territories of Scandinavia. From the early years of the ninth century, Viking ships with their organized war-bands and their companies of colonists began to appear in increasing numbers off the coasts of Britain. They were to establish strong bases in the Northern Isles and the Hebrides, and their influence reached southwards through the Irish Sea to the Severn estuary. Today we recognize the connection of upland Britain with Scandinavia through the numerous Norse place names, which convey in their very sounds something of the austerity of Europe's northernmost regions when they are encountered in the English Lake District. Dialects and the timeless traditions of the countryside, now almost completely obliterated by our urban culture, have preserved memories of this northern society that evolved before AD 1000 beyond the traditions of European civilization. The Viking society of Scandinavia represented the survival of an Iron Age mode of life in those remote parts of Continental Europe that escaped the influences of Mediterranean cultures. The period of the migrations that brought the Viking raiders to most parts of Atlantic Europe and even into the

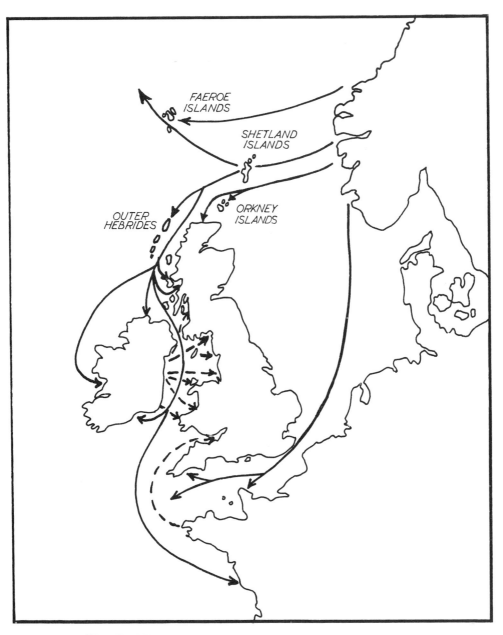

Fig 17  Viking raids along Western sea routes (*after Bowen*)

Mediterranean Sea itself may be regarded as the time of the last of the great prehistoric folk movements.

The earliest Viking raids are recorded in the closing decade of the eighth century. Lindisfarne, a holy island and the site of a great monastery, was sacked in the year 793. In 794 the Viking raiders fell on Jarrow, the religious centre of Anglo-Saxon Northumbria where Bede had composed his *History of the English Church and People* in the early years of the same century. The first recorded

121

appearance of the Viking longships off Ireland came in 795 when the church on Rathlin island was burned. Before the middle of the next century a Viking trading settlement had been established on the Liffey; it was one of the first urban communities in Ireland, and was to evolve into the city of Dublin. In the same period, between 790 and 810, the first Norse settlements were coming into being in the Northern Isles and the Hebrides. After this period of preliminary settlement, what has been described as a 'wholesale invasion' of Orkney and Shetland took place in the years between 860 and 870, an invasion that stamped the life, language and culture of the Northern Isles with a character that has survived until the present time.

Towards the end of the ninth century, Orkney became the source of a secondary movement of Scandinavians that led to the founding of settlements in mainland Britain. The impact of this later wave of colonization was felt most strongly in the north-east of Scotland close to the focus of political power centred in Orkney. By the eleventh century the power of Earl Thorfinn the Mighty reached out from Orkney to Shetland and embraced the Western Isles as well as the whole of the northern and eastern mainland of Scotland. As far south as the long peninsula of Kintyre it is believed that the greater part of the western fringe of Scotland and the Hebrides was largely Norse-speaking.

The chief clues to the understanding of the Viking settlement of northern Britain in the ninth and tenth centuries now rest in the survival of place names of Scandinavian origin. Among the earliest of the place-name elements is the term *stadir*, the nominative plural of the Norse *stadr*, meaning 'dwelling place'. Names derived from this source are common in the islands – in Orkney, Shetland and the Hebrides – and we find the term concealed in such names as Grimeston, Hourston and Berston, as well as in Mangersta, Tolsta and Mealsta in the Outer Hebridean island of Lewis, where the subsequent influence of Gaelic has distorted the original Scandinavian form. But on the mainland of northern Scotland the *stadir* place names are all but absent. There is one example alone in Caithness. These places seem to stand for the primary phase of the Viking colonization in the early years of the ninth century.

The key element among the Norse place names of a later generation is the term *bolstadr*, a term that was used to describe a farm or a family estate. It remained in use for a considerable time as an element in the making of place names and, as W.H.F. Nicolaisen has written in his paper on 'Norse settlements in the Northern and Western Isles', 'it was used wherever permanent settlements were created by Norsemen'. In Caithness we can recognize this term that points to the original cores of Scandinavian settlers in the lands of the northern Picts through the modern names of Lybster, Scrabster, Camster, Rumster, Thrumster and several others. The *bolstadr* element also appears in the *boll* and *poll* names of Sutherland remembering the presence of the Norsemen at Ullapool, Unapool, Eriboll, Arboll, Embo, Skelbo and Skibo. Again, as these names of the west have evolved under the influence of Gaelic in the later Middle Ages so the *-er* ending of the original Scandinavian

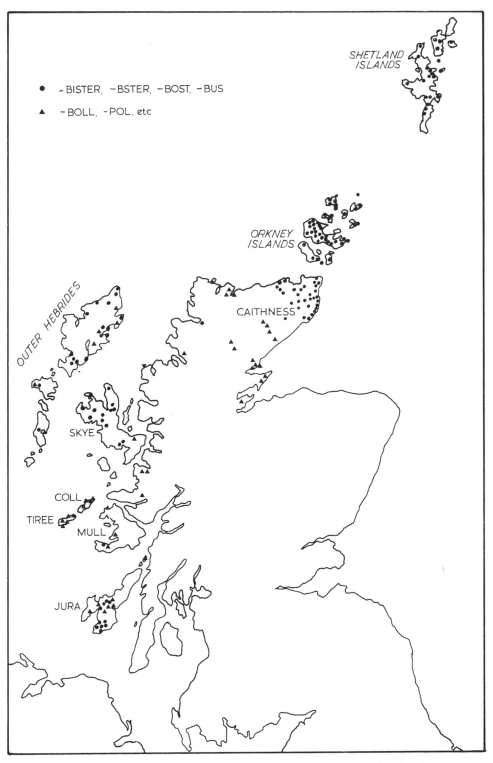

Fig 18   The distribution of Scandinavian place-name elements in Scotland

has come to be dropped. The *bolstadr* names probably coincide with the great expansion of settlement in the last quarter of the ninth century. Another Norse element, *setr*, provides a further clue to the years about 900 and the extent at that time of the Scandinavian settlements in northern and western Scotland. In Caithness we recognize this element in such names as Seater, Syster, Wester and Thurster. To the west in Sutherland it appears as *side* in names such as Linside, Sandside, Loch Coulside and Fallside. Uncertainty exists about the root of the *setr* names in Scotland. Some are derived from the Norse *setr*, meaning simply 'a dwelling'; others stem from the word *saetr*, a shieling or summer farm. If the two roots could be clearly distinguished in the modern place names, a valuable clue would be provided for the identification of settlements that began as places temporarily occupied in the months of high summer, places remote from the permanent farms to which cattle were driven to find pasture.

Together the *bolstadr* and *setr* names mark out the main areas of Scandinavian settlement in Scotland in the early years of the tenth century. The chief core of Viking influence lies in the north-east of the country, in Caithness and south-east Sutherland. No doubt access to the sea as well as the string of safe harbours along this coastline that receives the full force of winter gales from the north played a part in attracting this seafaring people. The tiny sheltered creeks that puncture the cliff-bound coast between the Ord of Caithness and Wick convey the sound of Scandinavia in their names. Further south the Scandinavian element in the place names around the firths of Dornoch and Cromarty suggests that these long sheltered estuaries provided the bases for Viking fleets as well as fertile lands for settlement along their shores. The close proximity of the Viking earldom of Orkney doubtless triggered off the secondary settlement of Caithness in the closing years of the ninth century, but it has also been argued that an inexplicable shift in the shoals of summer herring from the coasts of Norway to northern Scotland was also a factor in the Scandinavian settlement of this region. Further south, in the lands focused on the Moray Firth, there is a notable absence of a Scandinavian influence in the place names. It seems as if the wave of Viking settlement from the north came to an abrupt stop at the peninsula of the Black Isle. One can only conclude that the Inverness region and the Moray Firth, for centuries the focus of power of the northern Picts, was still able to assert its political individuality at the time of the Viking expansion. Certainly none of the clumsy rules of geographical determinism can be invoked to explain the absence of Scandinavian settlements from the shores of the Moray Firth where the same elements of the environment – safe harbourage, access to sea fisheries and the Viking homelands in Norway and the Northern Isles, attractive farmland and accessible upland pastures – are found, perhaps even more favourably disposed than further north in Caithness.

One other relic of the languages of Scandinavia that remains among the place names of Scotland is the term *dalr,* a valley. It appears widespread in the northern and western parts of the country far beyond the cores of settlement.

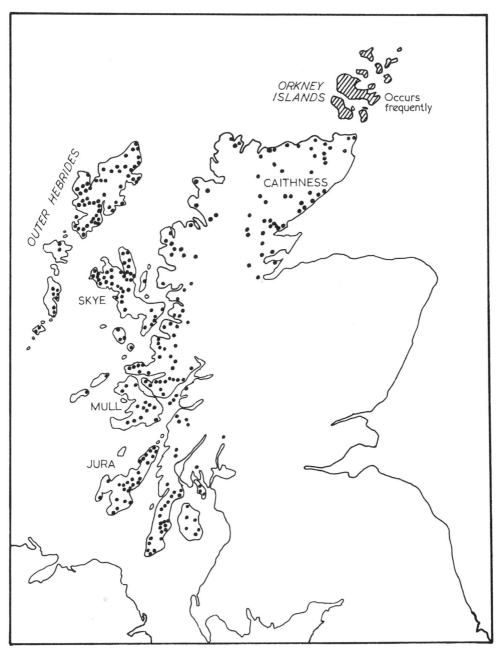

Fig 19　The occurrence of the Scandinavian element *dalr* in the place names of north and west Scotland

The presence of 'dale', usually in the naming of a major topographical feature, is considered to represent the sphere of Scandinavian influence at its greatest extent – places that were touched perhaps only by the trade that the Vikings organized and conducted along the western coast of Argyll and into the wide, branching estuary of the Clyde.

The Scandinavian interlude in the history of the highland parts of western Britain follows a different pattern in south-west Scotland, the Lake District and Wales. In Wales, apart from a long record of raids during the ninth century, the Vikings made little lasting impression on the history of the country. A scattering of place names around the Welsh coast tells of their presence. For instance, the two headlands that make dramatic stops to the long curve of Llandudno Bay, Great and Little Orme, commemorate the leader of a Viking war-band who was killed in a raid on Anglesey in 855; similar clues are found in South Wales, and there is little doubt that trade plied by Viking merchants around the coasts of Britain led to the development of Cardiff, Swansea and the port of Chester in the tenth century. The dismal record of the tenth-century incursions of the Norsemen preserved in the cathedral at St David's in Pembrokeshire is enough to remind one of the Vikings' power over the lines of trade in the Irish Sea. Wales was ever threatened from the bases of Viking sea power in Dublin, Wicklow, Wexford, Waterford and Cork. The lack of any strong Scandinavian impression on the country was probably the result of the political unity and coherence established among the tribes and petty Dark Age kingdoms of Wales by the rulers of Gwynedd in the previous century. Rhodri Mawr, Prince of Gwynedd between 844 and 878, had repelled the raids on Anglesey in which Orm had been killed.

But from North Wales northwards through the Wirral peninsula and west Lancashire into the Lake District there is abundant evidence in the place names of the presence of farmer-settlers of Scandinavian origin. In fact, among the deep valleys of the Lake District where so many facets of the environment of dark, rainy, mountainous western Norway seem to be repeated, the Scandinavian settlements of the tenth century left a lasting mark on the local life and folk ways. Overwhelmingly in the English Lake District the names of farms and hamlets and every minor topographical feature, through 'fell' and 'beck', 'dale' and 'tarn' and 'thwaite', proclaim the sound of the Scandinavian world. The dialect of Cumbria, virtually a living language until long after Wordsworth's day, was filled with words and structures descended from the Norsemen.

In northern England the Scandinavian raiders found an early base for their activities in the Isle of Man. One of the chief sources for the narrative history of the Vikings in the British seas, the *Orkneyinga Saga,* describes how the Isle of Man was occupied as a base through the winter months in preparation for the plunder raids of summer along the coasts of Wales and England. The security of its island site gave to Man the role that was played by Orkney and the Outer Hebrides in the Viking history of Scotland. In Cheshire, Lancashire and the

Lake District place names testify to an extensive Scandinavian settlement. For instance, in south-west Lancashire we find Ainsdale, Skelmersdale, Birkdale, Formby and Ormskirk and many like-sounding places that are now swallowed up in the suburbs of Liverpool. The character of this settlement of what must have been much empty land in north-west England is believed to have been largely of a peaceful kind. For one brief moment of history the darkness that surrounds the story of the Scandinavian settlements is broken by a reference for the year 910 in the *Anglo-Saxon Chronicle* to the colonization of parts of the Wirral, between the estuaries of the Dee and Mersey, by Norse-Irish settlers from the district around Dublin under their leader Ingimund. It is evident that this was not an enforced takeover of land in the wake of a conquering army but that Ingimund's farmer-colonists came to Cheshire by agreement.

The Scandinavian encroachment on a wide band of territory stretching from the Solway Firth to North Wales differed from the settlement of Caithness and the far north both in the source and the character of its colonists. By and large this was a secondary movement from Scandinavian centres already established in eastern Ireland and the Isle of Man. For instance, certain elements in the place names show the likely presence of Irishmen among the migrants as well as the intrusion of Irish elements among the topographical names.

The Norse-Irish role in the history of western Britain was intensified towards the end of the tenth century. The dominant wave in the Scandinavian settlement of the Lake District came across the Irish Sea in the early decades of the tenth century and by the year 1000 the Gallghaideal – the Norse-Irish sea raiders – were the greatest menace along much of the coastline of south-west Scotland. The complex history of the Scandinavians in highland Britain over a period of almost two centuries is most clearly illustrated in the parts of southern Scotland that border the Solway Firth. The first impact of the northern raiders seems to have reached the secluded lowlands of Dumfriesshire and Galloway from the east towards the end of the ninth century. In 880 the holy island of Lindisfarne, close to the Northumbrian coast, was threatened and devastated by North Sea raiders. The bishop of Lindisfarne, it is recorded, fled to the security of Whithorn, the remote monastery by the Solway where St Ninian had served as bishop in the fifth century. It is believed that the Scandinavian raid that caused the abandonment of Lindisfarne reached right across the Southern Uplands to the west, leaving in its trail a number of distinctive place names such as Eggerness, Almorness, Heston and Satterness by the Solway Firth. South-east Dumfriesshire has a scattering of places with Scandinavian elements in their names that have been attributed to a tenth-century movement of settlers from the English Danelaw – the separately governed territories in eastern England that stretched from Yorkshire to East Anglia in the years about AD 900. But the most persistent influence of the Scandinavian world upon south-west Scotland came in a secondary form from the Norse colonies in Ireland and the Isle of Man. For instance, as late as 1098 there is a record of a tribute of timber that was exacted from Galloway when Magnus Barelegs decided to establish his main base in the Isle of Man. It is said that 'he so exerted his power over the men of Galloway that he forced them to fell timber and transport it to the coast for the construction of these [Manx] fortresses'.

The cultural and archaeological legacy of these times seems remarkably sparse when compared with the extent and, in many parts, the abundance of place-name evidence. Until now archaeology has recovered little that can contribute to a detailed picture of the settlements and economy of the Scandinavians in Britain. One suspects that much colonization and land clearance of the inner valleys of the Lake District was pioneered by the Scandinavian settlers, but the ground has yielded little clear evidence to support such an idea. In Caithness the only detailed information has come from the archaeological investigation at Freswick Links, where a Norse settlement was buried beneath advancing sand dunes. Here three clear phases of occupation from the eleventh century to the later part of the thirteenth century were recognized. The main building was a large hall with slightly bow-shaped walls. The finds were composed of kitchen midden refuse, mainly limpet shells, cooking pots, implements for spinning, objects of bone and ships' rivets made of iron. For so much of the rest of Scandinavian western Britain the evidence of settlement sites is lacking, apart from burial-places such as the ship-burials at Gretna and Blackshaw close to the Solway Firth, and the influence of forms and motifs from the northern world in the shaping of stone crosses of the tenth and eleventh centuries. The Scandinavian years seem to be most clearly marked by the hoards of silver and precious objects that were lost or hurriedly buried in the uneasy decades of the pirate raids. The Cuerdale hoard, found in 1840 on the banks of the Ribble near Preston in Lancashire, comprised seven thousand coins and 1,000oz of silver in the form of ingots, armlets and rings. It is believed to have been a treasure chest belonging to a Viking army dating from about the year 903 when it was lost or hastily abandoned. Another such collection, the Talnotrie hoard, was deposited in south-west Scotland about the year 870. It contains much Saxon silver but one of the objects, an Arab coin, speaks of the far-flung trading and raiding of this sea-based people of northern Europe. One of the most telling items among the miscellany of objects that date back to the Scandinavian centuries in Britain is a macehead, made of bronze, found on a farm in Dumfriesshire. It was undoubtedly produced in Kiev, a Viking colony on the Dniepr in southern Russia, and the belief is that the mace was brought to Scotland by a Norseman who had served at some time in the tenth century as part of the guard of the royal household of Kiev.

### The effects of the Norman Conquest

The latter half of the eleventh century marks a crucial frontier in the evolution of upland Britain. The Norman Conquest of lowland England, swiftly accomplished in the years after the Battle of Hastings, brought an unceasing threat through the ensuing centuries to the societies and territories of Celtic

31　The Norman castle-mound at Rhuddlan, North Wales, situated on a bluff above the River Clwyd. Lately archaeologists have revealed some of the features of the small urban settlement that grew beside the Norman motte that was destroyed at the end of the thirteenth century with the founding of the Edwardian castle-town

Britain. As one writer, Lloyd Laing, has expressed it in his valuable survey of the archaeology of Celtic Britain in the centuries between the Romans and the Normans, 'the Anglo-Norman advance brought Celtic-speaking areas culturally into line with western Europe'.

By the twelfth century the Anglo-Norman culture was plainly marked on the landscape of upland Britain. Stone-built castles arose out of the primitive motte-and-bailey plan that the Normans had brought into the British Isles. In the quiet countrysides of those vulnerable territories on the borders of the Celtic west these earthworks of the uneasy decades of the Norman advance towards the uplands are found in abundance. From the plain of Glamorgan to the east bank of the River Clwyd at Rhuddlan, and even farther west at the approach to the Menai Strait in Anglesey, the overgrown earthworks of Norman castles mark out the Welsh marchland as a political 'shatter-belt', to borrow a geological term that has been used to describe zones of former stress in the earth's crust.

In Scotland the demise of the Celtic sphere of culture followed a different course. By the reign of David I, beginning in 1124, a state with the characteristics of feudal, Norman Europe had emerged in the eastern lowlands. This Scotto-Norman kingdom was based on Stirling, Fife and the Lothians. Its evolution through the twelfth century was marked by castle building, the introduction of the manners of Romanesque architecture and the founding of monasteries richly endowed with land. Several houses, such as Jedburgh, Selkirk and Kilwinning, were directly established from mother abbeys in France. None of the castle-mounds, the mottes, in Scotland predate the twelfth century. By the late Middle Ages this Norman style of military architecture reached far to the north, as far as Inverness and the Firth of Beauly.

The only part of Britain where a kingdom founded on the culture of the Celtic world effectively survived into the Middle Ages was the remote scatter of islands in Atlantic Scotland. There the Lordship of the Isles remained impervious, for some centuries longer, to the new ideas of social and economic organization that had taken root in much of the rest of Britain. There is evidence that occupation of the *duns* and *crannogs* – ramparted earthworks and artificial island dwellings in lakes that first appeared in Iron Age times – continued into the medieval centuries. A school of sculptors, producing ornate crosses and decorated grave slabs, carried on some of the art traditions of the Celtic world from its centre on Iona.

The material elements of the Celtic world in the communities of upland Britain were forgotten long before the customs, folk traditions and language. In Wales, for instance, the strongest links with the past – a past that reaches back into prehistory – were preserved in the mountain stronghold of Snowdonia, the princedom of Gwynedd. But even here the Anglo-Norman plainly exerted a powerful influence. The Cistercians planted their monasteries in Wales at the request of Welsh princes, motte-and-bailey techniques of castle building were adopted, and there is clear evidence that small communities engaged in trade at market centres – embryonic towns with the status of boroughs – had emerged in Wales before the great wave of urban plantations that followed the Edwardian Conquest at the close of the thirteenth century. Language and a sense of a common history whose roots lie in the distant centuries before the impact of the ideas of Anglo-Norman society form the basis of Welsh nationalism in our own times. But the material expressions of that culture were last in active creation many centuries ago. As E. Nash Williams wrote in his masterly study of the sculptured stones of Wales from the early Christian centuries, 'the dying flickers of Welsh Christian art were finally extinguished by the Norman Conquest'.

# 5

# Exploiting the Land

Man's demands on the resources of upland Britain have varied through his long occupation of the land since prehistoric times according to the needs of society and the technologies available for exploitation of those resources. For instance, the growing trade links between upland Wales and lowland England in the later Middle Ages saw the rise of the cattle traffic that took livestock on the hoof from the hill pastures of Cardiganshire and Snowdonia to the great fairs of the south-east. In turn, new farms were carved out of the mountain wilderness to supply the demands of this growing traffic. At a later time, in the early years of the nineteenth century, the profits to be drawn from sheep farming induced an economic revolution in Britain's uplands that has left, even to this day, the most painful scars on the landscapes of the far north. The sad green hummocks of the empty valleys of Sutherland that were the homes of active farming communities before the 'Highland clearances' of the early nineteenth century record this brief phase in Britain's economic history. After the sheep, large tracts of the Northern Highlands became the preserve of the deer as thousands of acres of wilderness were organized as sporting estates.

Within the changing patterns of man's exploitation of upland Britain over the past two thousand years the stable features of the personality of the uplands and their resources may be discerned. Ever since the Romans, and in some favoured parts of the west from much earlier prehistoric centuries, the presence of rich mineral ores has coloured regional development. The copper and tin lodes of western Cornwall and the rich deposits of lead in the Mendips and the Peak District have contributed much to the individuality of these parts of the uplands. The crumbling ruins of engine houses on the cliffs of Penwith or the long, thin lines of the lead rakes across the limestone upland of the High Peak – lines of gigantic molehills where men have burrowed deep into the earth along the veins of ore – represent only the final phase in the many centuries of exploitation of the richest resources of upland Britain.

## Man the farmer

In the realm of man's closer and more stable relationship with the land as a farmer the dominant feature of the environment of the Atlantic west has been the contrast between 'mountain country' and the lowlands and valley-plains, however restricted in extent, that surround and penetrate the upland tracts. The lowlands within highland Britain – the coastal plains of South Wales and Cardigan Bay, the Vale of Clwyd, the Solway lowland or the dissected hills of western Argyll from the Firth of Lorne to the head of the Kintyre peninsula, to take only a few examples – have formed cores of permanent settlement over many centuries. The higher lands, upwards above an indeterminate zone between the 600ft and 1,000ft contours, have played the role of an adjunct to the ancient cores of settlement. Already we have discussed the changing character of the upland environment in prehistory, whose dominant theme is a story of deforestation and degrading soils under the complex influences of climatic fluctuations and man's intrusion into the landscape. From the later centuries of the Bronze Age onwards the vast tracts of deforested upland – the moors of the South-West Peninsula, the rolling upland in Central Wales known most inappropriately as 'the Great Welsh Desert', or the bare spurs above the deep valley troughs in the Lake District – have provided many square miles of extra summer grazing for cattle, sheep and goats from settlements in the adjacent valleys and lowlands. In many regions of highland Britain evidence survives in place names and the footings of ruined primitive buildings of the one-time trek to the summer pastures and the crude huts that formed the temporary homes from June to September of the shepherds, cowherds and dairymaids who managed this transhumant economy. Transhumance as a way of life had disappeared from the greater part of Britain by the eighteenth century. Only in the north, in the Scottish highlands, was the trek to the summer pastures still a vital element in the rural economy, and even there it was to vanish in the years after Culloden with the severe economic and social changes that accompanied the 'clearances' of the first half of the nineteenth century.

On the use of the land in upland Britain over the past thousand years much research through documents and the direct exploration of the landscape, recording and interpreting features in the field, is still wanting. The great landmarks of history, such as the westward expansion of the Anglo-Norman frontier in the twelfth century, Henry VIII's Act of Union with Wales, and the later union with Scotland and ultimate extinction of its parliament, are well known. They mark important stages in the development of these different parts of highland Britain. The creation of Norman marcher lordships, for instance, in the valleys of eastern Wales in the twelfth and thirteenth centuries, saw the emergence of 'islands' of a lowland, English economy in a Welsh countryside. Nowhere is this revolution in the organization of society and the use of the land more clearly shown than in the upper valley of the Wye above Hereford and in the Vale of Usk, sheltered below the dark, ice-etched scarp of the Brecon

32 Tretower in the Vale of Usk is one of the many castle sites in the Welsh Marches that marked the advance of Norman power into the west. These were the cores of the *Englishries* – nodes of alien settlers – as opposed to the *Welshries* focused on the uplands between the major marchland valleys

Beacons. In the closing years of the eleventh century Bernard Neufmarché entered the territory of Brycheiniog that had been an independent Welsh princedom since late Roman times. Brecon was reached in 1091; in the following years castles were raised at Brecon, Bronllys, Talgarth, Tretower and Crickhowell. The castles became the centres of a new order; on the outskirts of Brecon, $1\frac{1}{2}$ miles to the north of the little castle town, the changes brought about by the Anglo-Norman intrusion into upland Wales have been recorded in a survey, made in 1326, of the manor of Llanddew, one of the properties of the bishop of St David's. Llanddew, a small nucleated settlement that even today reminds one of the villages of the English lowlands, was encircled by three open fields whose names are preserved in the 'extent' or valuation that David Francis, Chancellor of St David's, made there early in the fourteenth century. Hasfeld covered $34\frac{1}{2}$ acres, Lowefeld only 20, while Pengaer was another field of

133

open arable strips taking up some 30 acres. This medieval survey also made note of the crops that were planted there in the open fields: wheat was sown at $4\frac{1}{2}$ *truggs* to the acre, barley at 6 and oats at 8. The three-field village displays the primitive model of the manorial system in medieval England as it has been presented in history textbooks since the end of the last century. But nothing ever remains the same in this world. The open fields of Llanddew have long since vanished, the date of their demise going unrecorded. The tithe map of the parish, drawn in the 1830s, shows the final remnants of the land-use system that was brought to the Usk valley with the Norman conquest of Brycheiniog. Only a few unenclosed strips were left when the compilers of the Tithe Survey came to Llanddew.

The exploitation of the landscape of highland Britain has evolved under the pressure of economic and social forces that frequently emanated from sources to the east in the lowlands. Wales was profoundly influenced after the Edwardian Conquest at the close of the thirteenth century by the building up of landed estates, a process that was accelerated under the Tudors, after the Act of Union, when English laws governing the handing down of property upon the death of an owner replaced the ancient Welsh laws of inheritance that provided for the division of land among his descendants in equal shares. By the end of the seventeenth century the estate-building process, the making of individual farms, had done much in transforming the visual aspect of the landscape of Wales. The nuclear hamlets that formed one of the chief elements in the settlement pattern of earlier centuries had largely disintegrated. In fact, the dispersal of population over the past four hundred years has been so complete that the recovery of the outlines of the settlement geography of medieval Wales has become a matter of difficult research. The books of Welsh Laws, written down in the twelfth century before the transforming influences from the east had begun to affect this Celtic society, have been used, as have numerous extents and surveys of the thirteenth and fourteenth centuries, to discern the outlines of the ancient organization of the land, and shreds of evidence gathered from the present landscape suggest an ordering of the rural economy of a radically different kind. This work, pursued over almost a quarter of a century by an historical geographer, Professor Glanville Jones, has helped to destroy the view of medieval Wales and the working of its economy that prevailed in the histories of the country written in the early years of this century. Wales, along with the rest of upland Britain, was described as a largely pastoral realm where wealth was reckoned in flocks and herds, settlements were without any long and fixed location, and nomadism was part of the pattern of life. The heroic virtues of a remoter period, the late Celtic Iron Age, were thought to be expressed in the constant inter-tribal conflicts of this society. Above all the myth came to include the abhorrence of the nomadic, pastoral Celt for the steady, settled ways of the arable farmer engaged from year to year on the same acres of land in the seasonal, repetitive routines of sowing and harvest time.

Professor Glanville Jones's research, communicated in numerous articles

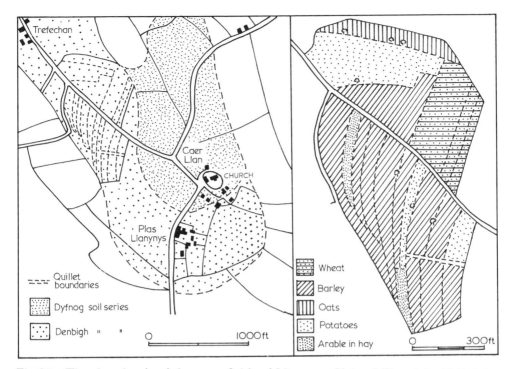

Fig 20   The sharelands of the open fields of Llanynys, Vale of Clwyd, in 1841 (*after Glanville Jones*). The Dyfnog and Denbigh soils are among the richest soils in North Wales

and lectures, has outlined a very different picture of the society and economy of Wales in the centuries before 1300. One of the most striking features of this early economy is the presence of arable crops growing on patches of open field within reach of nuclear settlements composed of up to a dozen farmsteads. As Jones has written, 'thus the general impression created by a study of the laws is of an old-established practice of *mixed farming* organized in the main on an open-field basis and with a degree of communal control'. At Llanynys in the Vale of Clwyd Professor Jones has demonstrated in a neat combination of fieldwork and documentary evidence the former presence of an open-field economy. The place is typical of the many lowland cores of settlement within upland Britain. It occupies a low ridge of well-drained sandy loams in the heart of the Vale of Clwyd, and the large parish of which the church on this ridge forms the focal point, stretches out westward to the bordering hills. The large circular enclosure that contains the parish church of Llanynys once held the buildings of a Dark Age monastic community. It has also been argued that the occupation of this site reaches back even further, to the Iron Age, when a circular fortification seems likely to have existed there. The evidence of settlement over the last two thousand years at Llanynys, tenuous as it may seem today, is enriched by documentary references from the fifteenth century: the phrase *seliones in campis de Llanenys* shows that the land was lying in open fields. Several

135

strips or quillets from these open fields were still surviving in intermixed ownership when the Tithe Survey was made and published in 1841. Along the lane that leads north-westward from Llanynys church towards Trefechan, the 1841 map shows fifteen unfenced strips on the site of Maes isa, the lower open field. These strips, making a ridge-and-furrow pattern, were faintly visible until 1971 when they disappeared as a result of ploughing.

Local studies, as research during the post-war years in North Wales has clearly shown, often undermine what seem to be established general theories. As Welsh historians and historical geographers have destroyed the romantic view of the Celtic peoples in the early Christian centuries as a race of nomadic pastoralists, so Wales is now seen to be part of a wider cultural sphere, the Atlantic façade of western Britain. Elsewhere, in the Peak District, Cumbria and Scotland, research has revealed a common pattern of land management that began to undergo substantial changes towards the close of the Middle Ages and whose demise was hastened in the seventeenth and eighteenth centuries by the enclosure and reorganization of open arable fields, by a widespread encroachment on the common upland grazings that contributed to the extinction of the summer trek to the high pastures, and by the building of estates, the making of individual farms and the 'improvements' in farming that were a factor in erasing the ancient communal settlements.

## The infield–outfield system

The systems of land use that once prevailed in upland Britain were first sketched out in an analysis of ancient fields and their organization that was made by an American economic historian, H.L. Gray, early in this century. Working from documentary evidence he published his *English Field Systems* in 1915. Here Gray argued that a distinctive pattern of farming belonged to the western parts of these islands and Scotland, one that was primarily pastoral but which included an arable element of some importance. Arable crops were grown, year in year out, from a field of modest size adjacent to the settlement – a string of buildings sheltering up to a dozen families arranged along the margin of the common field. This focus of arable farming is known as the 'infield' and an alternative Scottish name for it, the 'mukked land', shows that it was kept in good heart for its yield of oats and barley by the regular adding of manure from livestock. Away from the infield, its exact location depending upon local topography, slope, soils and exposure to sunlight, was a wide stretch of ground that was ploughed up by patches on a shifting system. This was the 'outfield'. In the Scottish Highlands, where the old systems of farming died out late, towards the end of the eighteenth century, records survive that tell of the working of the outfield. A patch of ploughed land in the outfield would be cropped for three or four years, usually with oats, and then rested for another five years. Beyond the outfield, its perimeter demarcated by a bank of turf or stone known as the head dyke, lay the common pastures – rough moorland

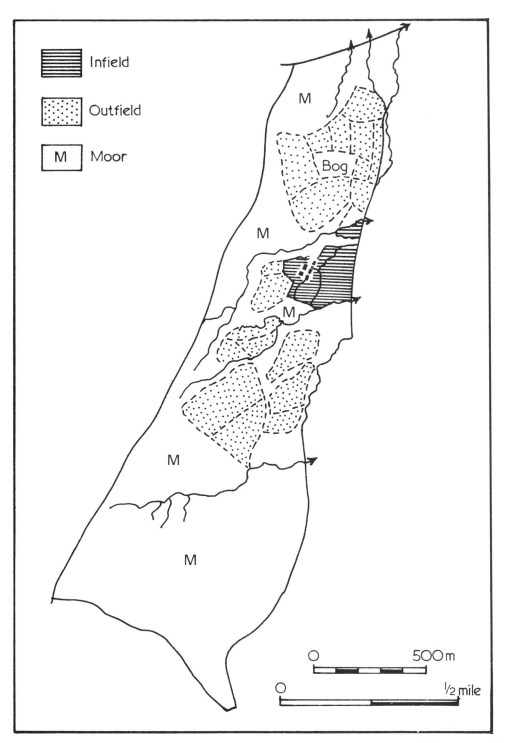

Fig 21   The infield–outfield system of the lands of Westertown, part of the estate of Pitkellony, Scotland, as it existed in 1753 (*after Whittington*)

where the cattle grazed through the summer months out of range of the growing crops around the main settlement.

Gray's model of the infield-outfield system, though best exemplified in Scotland where it survived for so long, can be discerned in many parts of highland Britain. In speculating upon the origins of the different field systems of the British Isles, Gray came to the conclusion that this method of land organization was something peculiar to the Celtic peoples – it was part of a 'race memory'. At the turn of the century, when Meitzen's great synthesis of settlement studies in Europe was in vogue, fashionable theories were put forward explaining settlement patterns and agricultural forms in ethnic terms. Dispersed patterns of settlement in which the hamlet and the lonely farmstead composed the chief units were associated with Celtic peoples, in this theory, wherever they were found, be it in Britain, Brittany or among the uplands of middle Europe. Gray's explanation of this system of land organization as peculiar to the Celtic peoples is now largely discredited. Instead, the infield– outfield arrangements are considered to be a reflection of the rainy, mountainous environments of Atlantic Britain in past centuries of greater isolation and self-sufficiency. As H.P.R. Finberg has written in a paper on 'The open field in Devonshire', 'all open-field types were a genus, of which the two-field system and its probable derivative, the three-field system, form one species, and the infield–outfield another. The two probably evolved side by side, moulded by the contrasting qualities of highland and lowland landscape'.

Research since World War II has revealed the widespread distribution of open fields in the past at many places in the hill country of northern England. Documentary evidence and the persistence of certain field names that point to the former presence of open-field farming show a circle of settlements in the wider valleys and lowlands around the Lake District where open fields formed an important element in the landscape before the eighteenth century. Practically every parish in the boulder-clay-covered Cumberland plain that reaches out to the dull, low coastline of the Solway Firth has abundant evidence of open-field agriculture, and the same kind of proof is forthcoming for the country around Penrith and the sheltered corridor of the Eden valley below the wall of the northern Pennines. Even the deep valleys in the heart of the Lake District's mountains are not without some evidence for a patch of cleared land, an infield, that was cultivated in common. At Wasdale Head, the highest hamlet in the wildest of the valleys, eighteen farmers held shares in a single common arable field, a field whose outlines we can still clearly trace, where two mountain streams converge to enter Wastwater from their sources on the stony lower slopes of Great Gable. The labour involved in the original clearance of this infield is evident in the present landscape, in the huge mounds of rubble that are scattered here and there within the tiny walled enclosures that have since taken the place of the common open field. But the open fields that existed in the mountain heart of the Lake District were insignificant patches of improvement when set against the thousands of acres of common grazing on the

138

33   The site of a former communal field at Wasdale Head, Cumbria. The huge stone heaps associated with the original land clearance in this rocky, unfruitful terrain can still be seen

fells that formed the chief resource of these sheep-rearing communities. In the sixteenth century the infield at Wasdale Head covered some 300 acres, while there were more than 6,000 acres of rough grazing on the surrounding fells. Most of the open fields among the mountains were tiny. The infield at Threlkeld, a string of farms below the southern slopes of Saddleback, covered only 14 acres. It was still unenclosed in 1849 at the time of the making of the tithe maps. Then there were eleven strips in the Town Field (a name that provides a reliable clue to former common ownership when practically all other evidence has vanished) that were farmed by five different owners.

Although H. L. Gray's ideas about the origins of the infield–outfield system of land management in upland Britain and its connection with the Celtic peoples have been dismissed, we are no closer to a satisfactory explanation and dating of the beginnings of this system of farming that was so widespread in the Middle Ages. Gray's hypothesis would fit in with the view that its origins go back to the migrations of the Celts into Britain during the final millennium of prehistory. And the visual evidence from the contemporary landscape in parts of Cornwall would support this idea. There, particularly on the coastal bench of the Penwith peninsula between St Ives and St Just, the tiny enclosures that surround such hamlets as Zennor date back to the Iron Age. The field pattern of the present landscape, in this instance, was in the making in prehistoric times. Further east in Cornwall, at Forrabury above the narrow twisting entrance to Boscastle harbour, the relics of an open field, the separate strips still divided from one another by low grassy balks, survive on the clifftop adjacent to the site of an Iron Age enclosure, Willapark. Here again we can see an open field that might have begun as the infield of an Iron Age community focused within the ramparted earthwork of Willapark's headland. But this is mere speculation, an inchoate suggestion from the disposition of features in a twentieth-century landscape. Professor Glanville Jones, from his study of the Welsh Law Codes written down in the twelfth century but harking back to the middle years of the tenth century, would date this mode of farming to the early Christian period 'that is at the latest in the seventh century and probably in the sixth century'.

A different line of thought has lately been pursued in Scotland through a documentary search for unequivocal references. G.W.S. Barrow has followed up I.F. Grant's statement that the earliest record of this system of land use in Scotland dates back only to the year 1606. A long search of the documents surviving from the twelfth to fourteenth centuries led Barrow to conclude that there is 'no indication in early documents of any system of infield and outfield cultivation, although the texts are not incompatible with the existence of such a system'. And this line of research led to the conclusion that the infield–outfield pattern of farming in upland Scotland emerged in the twelfth and thirteenth centuries under the pressures of growing population that caused 'a more extensive type of arable' to be changed into 'a mixture of intensive and extensive'. Expressing it in another way, G. S. Barlow believes that the Scottish agrarian system progressed in the Middle Ages from shifting arable farming associated with cattle keeping to a sedentary form in which cattle remained more important in the wetter west.

## Transhumance – farming the summer pastures

The special gift of upland Britain to its inhabitants in centuries past was the vast tracts of rich grazing that were available beyond the 1,000ft contour in the long, light days of summer. Today the details of this aspect of the farming year can only be gleaned from accounts written in the eighteenth century by travellers in Wales and the Scottish Highlands. Already by the time that

Pennant, a prolific recorder of the state of upland Britain in the years about 1800, was writing his detailed account of travels in Wales, the long-practised migration to the mountain pastures in summer was a thing of the past. Snowdonia was the last refuge of a way of life that had been rapidly forgotten, and Pennant's famous and much-quoted account of what he found at Llanberis is almost the only surviving description of what had formerly been a vital part of the rural economy in upland Wales:

> This mountainous tract scarcely yields any corn. Its produce is cattle and sheep, which, during the summer, keep very high in the mountains, followed by their owners, with their families, who reside in that season in *hafodtai*, as the farmers of the Swiss Alps do in their *sennes*. These houses consist of a long low room, with a hole at one end, to let out the smoke from the fire, which is made beneath. Their furniture is very simple: stones are the substitute of stools; and the beds are of hay, ranged along the sides . . . During the summer the men pass their time either in harvest work, or in tending their herds: the women in milking, or making butter and cheese . . . Towards winter they descend to the *hendref*, or old dwelling, where they lead, during that season, a vacant life.

Thomas Pennant's account of the *hafodtai* or *hafodau*, the clusters of temporarily occupied huts of the summer farms on the mountain slopes of Caernarvonshire, is matched in the same period by several accounts of the summer shielings in

34 Culkein, Assynt, North-West Highlands – a deserted settlement in Sutherland typical of the many places that suffered in the clearances of the last century

the Highlands of Scotland. For instance, one writer in the 1750s tells how 'in summer the people remove to the hills and dwell in much worse huts than they leave below; these are near spots of grazing and are called shielings, scattered from one another as occasion requires . . . Here they make their butter and cheese'. The contemporary discussions of the Highland shielings in the eighteenth century make clear the benefits of movement to the summer pastures. They note the preference of the cattle for the more fibrous hill grasses and weeds of the summer pastures with their richer content of minerals. The cattle were 'brought into good order' and the beef was 'extremely sweet and succulent'. The removal of livestock to the mountain pastures also gave a much-needed rest to the grassland within close range of the cluster of farms in the *clachan,* the all-the-year-round base at a lower level. These descriptions of the Scottish shielings convey something that is lacking in our knowledge of transhumance in the mountainous districts of England, a deficiency that is explained by the fact that this way of life was already a forgotten relic of the past in England and Wales. The Scottish accounts show clearly that the transfer of the community to the high pastures and the life that was lived there had a profound influence on the character of the Highlander and his outlook on the world. His 'superior degree of fancy and feeling' was put down to the leisure that accompanied the pastoral life. And 'when he was not fighting or hunting his time was taken up with music, poetry and lounging in the sun'. These were the characteristics of the Highlander's make-up that, after the severe puritanism of the Calvinist Church, were to be utterly banished by the break-up of the clans and ultimately by the 'clearances' that transformed large tracts of upland with their shielings into lonely sheep runs and sombre, empty deer forest.

Highland Scotland has preserved evidence of the ancient system of transhumance not only through the reports of travellers and estate surveys made in the eighteenth century, but also in the abundant proofs which still survive on the ground. In 1967 Professor Ronald Miller published the results of sample surveys from scattered parts of Scotland where transhumance had been an essential part of the pattern of rural life before the 'clearances'. In the district of Assynt, in south-west Sutherland, where the primeval shapes of the great mountains Suilven and Quinag brood over a grey lowland of Lewisian gneiss, ice-riven and splashed with countless lochs, Miller traced, through an eighteenth-century survey document and careful personal exploration in the field, the sites of almost 250 former shielings. The ruins of the bothies, now mere heaps of stone and turf deeply overgrown, could often be recognized against the dun, wet moorland as patches of bright green grass and bracken, places whose enhanced fertility, from the penning of livestock in the days when the shielings were occupied, has persisted down to the present time. Some of the Assynt shielings, Culkein for instance, had as many as a dozen bothies. Some were single-storeyed buildings, no bigger than 6ft by 4ft, with rounded corners and a door in the centre of one of the long walls; others were as much as 15ft in length.

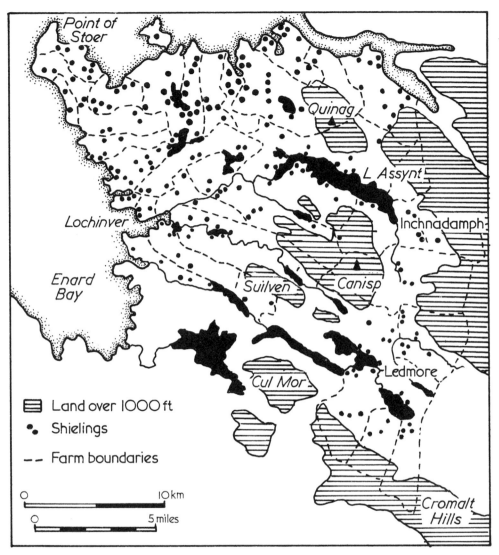

Fig 22   The summer shielings of the parish of Assynt, western Scotland, in 1774 (*after Miller*)

Frequently the walls were built of turf, though sometimes an inner stone wall would form a lining to an outer one of turf. Beside these huts that gave shelter to cowherds and dairymaids, the shielings of Assynt contained other buildings – small circular structures only a yard in diameter that probably acted as stores for cheese or butter. In addition the shieling grounds were often walled and there were stone-built pens for the livestock. At a few shielings, a dozen altogether, Professor Miller found evidence of former 'lazybeds', cultivation ridges where crops had been planted. The survey of Assynt that John Home made in the eighteenth century showed that arable cultivation had been widespread on the shielings. Between one-third and half of the sites had raised

143

35 An abandoned summer shieling near Culkein. In the distance the lonely mountains of Quinag, Suilven and Cul Mor rise up above the platform of Lewisian gneiss

corn crops and, as Miller comments, 'many of the Assynt shielings were virtually *outfield*'.

The shielings of the Assynt region diverge from the expected pattern of this kind of summer settlement in that many of them lay close to the permanently occupied sites. Along the intricately indented coastline and in the valley of the River Inver where it tumbles towards the sea from Loch Assynt, the sites of the shielings were no higher than the parent farms; a quarter of the 246 shielings surveyed by Professor Miller occupied sites at less than half a mile from the winter base, and another third lay not more than a mile away. The long trek to a cluster of bothies high in the mountains was not part of the way of life in Assynt; the highest shieling in the region occupied a hill pasture on the slopes of Quinag at about 1,000ft above sea level. Others, along the valley beneath the western slopes of Ben More Assynt where Cambrian limestones outcrop, were below 600ft and, as the notes of John Home's survey indicate, were prosperous summer farms in the eighteenth century, 'mostly arable, yielding fine grass'. If the economic catastrophe of large-scale sheep farming and the clearance of many settlements had not overtaken the North-West Highlands in the early years of the nineteenth century, it is evident that many of the shielings would have evolved into permanent farms, a process that was active in transforming the use of the summer pastures in Wales and south-west England before the close of the Middle Ages.

By the end of the eighteenth century the practices of transhumance were only part of the folk memory in Wales; when George Kay gathered information in Caernarvonshire, about 1790, for his *General View of Agriculture in North Wales,* he failed to find any evidence of transhumance. That the migration to the hills was part of the economy of medieval Wales, and a widespread practice, only becomes clear in George Owen's classic account of *Pembrokeshire* written early in the seventeenth century. He looked back across almost five hundred years to the time of Giraldus Cambrensis, the earliest of the Welsh travellers to leave an account of his native country. 'At the time of Giraldus', Owen wrote, 'the Welsh ploughed their oat fields in March and April, and then moved to the uplands for summer, returning to the *hendref* in time to harvest the corn, and to prepare the houses for winter.' Today the main evidence for the widespread pasturing of the uplands between May and September and the occupation of temporary settlements there rests in the silent witness of place names on the ordnance map. The term *hafod* usually locates a place that was once used as a temporary summer settlement. *Meifod,* another common Welsh place-name element, probably means 'the middle dwelling' – a halfway house between the *hendref* or *hendre,* the old homestead and parent settlement, and the *hafod* among the summer pastures. A varying interpretation of *meifod* is the 'May dwelling', a reference perhaps to the conventional date, 1 May, for the beginning of summer in medieval Wales and a time when the intermediate stopping place might be occupied for a few days on the way to the *hafod.* The term *lluest* too, meaning 'summer dairy cottage', is frequently combined with a personal name and serves to identify localities that were formerly concerned with transhumance. The largest number of *lluest* elements occurs in Cardiganshire, but they are also frequent further east in Montgomeryshire.

The sites of the *hafodau,* the clusters of rude huts that sheltered the families of cowherds and shepherds in the hills, are hard to locate today. Often they have been succeeded by a permanent, all-the-year-round farm. The place name alone frequently provides the clue to the early history of a solid stone farmstead of the seventeenth century as a medieval *hafod.* Elsewhere all traces of buildings have vanished completely and, as in the north, only an unusual richness of wild flowers and the brilliant green of the grass betrays the presence of a former summer settlement. However, careful fieldwork in the 1960s led to the recognition of the remains of summer settlements on the Brecon Beacons and Carmarthen Van, the highest and wildest tracts of mountain country in South Wales. Carmarthen Van rises to a height of more than 2,600ft above sea level and C.B. Crampton located at two sites the remains of huts from the days of the summer trek to these hill pastures. There were two single-roomed houses – one 24ft long and the other 13ft long – whose walls were still standing in the early sixties to a height of more than 3ft. The site of this long-abandoned summer

145

settlement occupies a bench on the north-east-facing slope of the mountain at a height of 1,550ft above sea level – a harsh, uninhabitable place through the long months of winter. Dr Crampton found no evidence, in the form of pottery or other objects, that could be used to date the period when the summer huts of Carmarthen Van were in use; its beginning and its end remain equally obscure. The *hafodau* on the northern spurs of the Brecon Beacons have likewise provided no clues to their history. An examination of the 1839 tithe map of the country below the summits of the Beacons shows no trace of the *hafodau,* an indication that they had been long abandoned by the early years of the nineteenth century. But the summer pastures above the Vale of Usk seem to have been grazed from clusters of crude huts during the sixteenth century. A native of Brecon, Sion Dafydd Rhys, who wrote a grammar in Elizabeth I's reign, makes passing reference to the occupation of a *hafod* in the upper reaches of Cwm Llwch at the time of his writing.

It seems strange that so little firm evidence has come down to us in the twentieth century about a way of life that formed such a vital part of the economy and society of upland Britain in the Middle Ages. It is mainly through the place names, fossils from a lost medieval world, that we can sketch the topographical outlines – the locations of the mother settlements and their out-lying *hafodau* – of this forgotten rural economy. For instance, at the head of the Tanat valley, where the road begins the steep climb westwards across the moors to Bala, the *hendref* of Llangynog is matched by the *hafod* of Craig Rhiwarth that looks down upon the permanent winter settlement from a bold rock spur scarred with slate quarries. But Craig Rhiwarth, if scarcely a mile from the *hendref,* opened the way to thousands of acres of moorland grazing in the Berwyns.

One of the threads that runs through accounts of peasant life among communities that divide the farming year and their lives between winters in the deep valleys and the weeks of high summer on the mountain pastures, be they from eighteenth-century Scotland or the fjords of Norway less than a hundred years ago, is the sense of joy and freedom that accompanied the movement to the uplands. Even today, if one takes the track to Craig Rhiwarth from Llangynog, one can regain, however faintly, some of the feelings that must have run through the hearts and minds of those medieval farmers. The gloomy head of the Tanat, a deep trough shaped by a glacier in Quaternary times, gives way to the bare, rolling moorland of the Berwyns – a simple landscape under a wide summer sky remote from the claustrophobic, sun-starved winter valley. But the uplands were a wider world in more than a topographic sense. There the common pastures formed a meeting place for communities from distant valleys on the other side of the mountain. The Berwyn Mountains provided a common ground for folk from the Tanat, the Ceiriog and the long, lowland corridor of the Dee that clasps the western and northern rim of this upland all the way from Lake Bala to Llangollen. There, in the long days of summer, marriages were made and the elements of a common culture were nourished through song and story and in the retelling of the heroic tales from an older Celtic world.

146

The widespread practice of transhumance in the former farming systems of upland Britain is not in question. From northern Scotland to Cornwall a legacy of names bears witness to innumerable places that must have originated as summer farms. How and when the grazing of the high pastures by communities based in the valleys and fringing lowlands began remains a problem to which no certain solution has yet been found. As with the parallel problem of the origins of the infield–outfield system of farming, there is hardly any evidence in documents through which the evolution of this aspect of the rural economy may be traced. As a local historian in Wales, researching into the history of the old summer pastures in Montgomeryshire, has written, 'the facts about transhumance in Wales are largely absent from the documentary record . . . it is another example of the curious silence of contemporary records about everyday things'. Even when the documents point to the grazing of the hill pastures and the establishment there of temporary settlements, they rarely go back beyond the later medieval centuries. For instance, the ownership of some of the shielings in Banffshire can be traced back through the records to the fifteenth century. C.B. Crampton, taking a very sober view of the scraps of evidence relating to the ruins of summer huts on the northern face of the Brecon Beacons, has suggested that their origin may date back only to the fourteenth or fifteenth century. In fact, given the lack of any firm evidence of dating, it seems reasonable to ascribe the widespread use of the summer pastures to a period between the twelfth and fourteenth centuries in response to a notable upsurge of population in western Europe. But there is also good reason to think that this mode of rural life has a much longer history. The Irish equivalent of the shieling and the *hafod* is the *buaile* – a cluster of two, three or four huts built of turf with a drystone foundation and a roof of rushes and heather. A reference to dairying at an Irish *buaile* survives in a document from the ninth century. This much earlier date for an economy and organization of settlements that may have involved transhumance could relate such a way of life to the Scandinavian colonization of western Britain. Norse elements in the place names of northern and western Scotland – in particular the term *shader* – indicate the location of former temporary summer settlements. It is highly likely that the exploitation of the pastures in the most mountainous parts of Britain was greatly extended in the tenth century at the time of the Scandinavian settlements. For instance, the overwhelming Scandinavian element in the place names of the Lake District suggests that this was the period when the upland grazings were brought into a much fuller use.

Nevertheless, there are further hints that the practices of transhumance and the accompanying settlement patterns in Britain may be even older. The

(*Overleaf*)
36 The Tanat valley, Powys. The limit of improved land, an economic frontier that had been fixed by the end of the Middle Ages, is clearly outlined by the fields and hedges of the valley floor. The upland pastures were in the past the scene of the great summer migrations to the *hafodau* (*Aerofilms*)

customs that governed life at the *hafod* and the shieling suggest roots in a pre-Christian world. For instance, Beltane, one of the major festivals of the Iron Age Celts, was observed at the settlements on the hill pastures even in the Middle Ages. In the Hebrides, Beltane cheeses were consumed on 1 May to protect the livestock from evil influences in the following season on the hills. Cattle were driven through the fire and smoke from burning branches of mountain ash – itself considered a powerful shield against the dark influences of a supernatural world. Christianity and paganism became mingled in the custom of tying crosses made out of rowan to the tails of cattle. The Welsh Laws, written down in the twelfth century but of much more ancient origin, laid down that the beginning of May, the festival of Beltane, was to be observed as the time for the migration to the *hafod*.

It seems possible that the migration to the high hills is an element in the life of upland Britain even older than the Celtic Iron Age. The Neolithic folk who searched the crags high above Great Langdale in the Lake District five thousand years ago for a rock outcrop that yielded material suitable for the making of stone axes were probably also there in the mountains with their cattle, goats and sheep. It is also likely that the quarrying of that fine-grained volcanic ash in the Borrowdale Volcanic Series on Pike of Stickle was a spasmodic summer activity – the first industry of Cumbria's mountains probably went hand-in-hand with the migration to the summer pastures from permanent bases on the rim of lowland beside the Irish Sea.

## The mineral wealth of upland Britain

Among the most important of the resources of Britain's highland west has been the mineral wealth locked in its mountains. Valuable metallic ores – copper, lead, zinc and tin – are profusely intruded into the fringes of the granite massifs of the South-West Peninsula, across the limestone plateau of the Peak District, and into the cold hills of the northern Pennines about Alston. The extraction and processing of metallic ores has coloured the lives and scarred the landscape of certain parts of the uplands over many centuries. The steep flanks of the valleys of inland Cornwall have been permanently disfigured by the primitive and ancient techniques for the extraction of tin ores – cassiterite – where they had been deposited by nature in terrace gravels. 'Hushing', a method of suddenly releasing large volumes of water from temporary ponds on hillsides above the tin-bearing gravels, contributed to the making of a deeply eroded landscape. The extraction of lead in the Peak District, an activity that certainly dates back to Roman times, has left indelible scars among the network of grey walls and green pastures on the limestone plateau. Here the lead rakes, narrow lincs of dishevelled, tortured ground – an unending succession of holes and hills – run for miles across this austere countryside where they coincide with the surface outcrops of the steeply dipping veins of ore.

The legacy of mining consists not only in deeply disturbed ground where the

37 The Langdale Pikes, Cumbria. The thin line of scree in the middle distance below the crags of Pike of Stickle was the site of the late Neolithic axe factory. On the bare upland in the distance the sites of other prehistoric axe factories have been located (*Aerofilms*)

relentless pursuit of the ore-bearing rock has gone on, but also in the place names, buildings, and the shapes of settlements in the districts that have been invaded by these extractive, 'robber' industries. In general, where rural ways of life have prevailed in upland Britain, the settlement pattern has evolved over the last four centuries into one of scattered, isolated farms and hamlets and only rarely larger places that may be described as villages. But wherever mining has entered a local economy on a substantial scale, a different type of settlement has emerged. This is nowhere more evident than in the interior of Cornwall, where the lonely 'churchtowns' – a farm, a rectory and a triple-aisled church in a raised circular churchyard – typify the places where mineral lodes are lacking and the rural economy has evolved slowly from the first prehistoric settlements into the twentieth century. By contrast, the mining communities that grew rapidly in the prosperous decades of the eighteenth and early nineteenth centuries straggle across a landscape littered with the cavernous openings and waste-hills of a defunct industry. Ruined engine houses, terraces of industrial cottages – many of which are now temporary summer homes for the great flood of holidaymakers that drowns the south-west every year – and huge, unfriendly Methodist chapels are the distinctive elements in a mining landscape.

151

Place names commemorate the techniques and processes of an economy that is practically extinct in upland Britain. In the South-West Peninsula the 'Wheals' – Wheal Busy, Wheal Cotes, Wheal Edward, Wheal Friendship, Wheal Kitty, Wheal Martyn, to mention only a few – mark the sites of the long-silent mines and their engine houses. A much older name in the Pennines records one of the early phases in the development of lead mining that came to a close before the end of the Middle Ages. The term 'bolehill' describes the place to which the lead ore was taken to extract the metal. The bole or bail hill was a shallow bowl-shaped furnace surrounded by a low retaining wall. The furnace was fuelled with a supply of brushwood on which the crushed ore was sprinkled. The heat of the fire caused the molten lead to drop into the bottom of the bowl, from which it was led away through a prepared channel into a collecting hollow. The essential feature of this furnace that was the chief means of smelting lead in the early Middle Ages was an exposed hilltop site where the natural force of the wind provided a draught to raise the heat of the brushwood fire. Today the evidence of these first smelting places is found in circular patches of black soil enriched with charcoal and remnants of lead slag. The bolehills of the Derbyshire lead industry are largely located on the rim of Millstone Grit moorland to the east of the Derwent valley. The ore was carried there, several miles from the lead mines on Longstone Edge and around Matlock, for the purposes of smelting. Today, except in the surviving place name, there is little left of this early phase of lead smelting – a process that was revolutionized in the sixteenth century when water power was harnessed to the driving of bellows to produce a more effective controlled draught. A relocation of ore hearths, housed in smelt mills, took place in the valleys of the Peak District where water power was available. Another place name that recalls a lost branch of the mining and processing of metallic minerals is Calamine House. In the northern Pennines the name denotes the places where zinc ores, usually a secondary product of the lead workings, were roasted and used particularly in the production of brass.

The beginnings of mining in upland Britain reach back into the centuries of prehistory, far back into the early Bronze Age in Cornwall, where there is indirect evidence of the working of tin deposits as early as 1700 BC. It lies in a bronze dagger of a type that was in circulation in the second millennium BC, found on an ancient tin-streaming site at St Ewe. Four centuries before the Romans reached Britain, tin extraction from the gravel deposits in the valleys of Cornwall and west Devon was firmly established. The Iron Age trade of the peninsula was in the hands of the Veneti, one of the tribes of western Gaul who controlled an overland trade route that led from southern Brittany by the northern flank of the Pyrenees to the Greek colony that had been founded on the site of Marseilles. Material proof of the exploitation of Cornish tin deposits in the later centuries of the Iron Age and of metallurgy comes from several sites. At Kenidjack Castle, a promontory fort on the north coast of the Penwith peninsula near St Just – the very capital of Cornish tin mining in the nineteenth century – thirty pieces of copper and smelted tin came from the foundations of a hut outside the rampart. An even more striking find and proof of the prehistoric export trade in tin was an H-shaped ingot dredged from the Falmouth estuary. It weighs 158lb, and the idea has been proposed that this massive ingot was brought by pack-horse to the coast to be loaded on to one of the merchant ships of the Veneti. Pewter, an alloy of tin and lead, was also produced in Cornwall, especially in late Roman times. Jugs and dishes were made of pewter, and it is believed that stone moulds for the shaping of dishes that have been found at St Just were used in their manufacture.

The taking of mineral ores from the limited number of sites in highland Britain where they have long been accessible – the gold-bearing hills of Central Wales, the lead veins of the Pennines and Mendips and the rich sources of tin and copper in the south-west – has been pursued over many centuries. Exploitation that in several places began before the Romans has only been extinguished in the twentieth century, though the long time-span of activity has seen many ups and downs, periods of prosperity and quiescence. The history of mining has been written into the landscape in an equally confusing way. Although there is abundant evidence that the Romans worked the mineral resources of upland Britain, scarcely anywhere is it possible to ascribe specific features of a mining landscape – shafts, adits, aqueducts or the foundations of buildings – to the period between the first and fourth centuries AD. The importance of lead mining under the Romans is indicated by the number of pigs of lead – ingots of smelted metal each weighing almost 200lb – that have been found over the past centuries in different parts of Britain. They represent losses in transit from the lead-mining districts on the way to the towns of the lowland south and east and to the coast for export. Over the years many lead pigs discovered by chance must have been lost to the archaeological record, several no doubt returning to the furnaces of medieval metalworkers. Some of the pigs carry inscriptions that tell of their place of origin. The letters LVTVD on one pig probably refer to the mineral-rich district of Derbyshire between Matlock and Wirksworth. It is believed that the centre of this district, a countryside scarred with centuries of lead mining, was known to the Romans as Lutudarum. The exact location is not known, but the holding of the Barmote Courts at Wirksworth since late Saxon times suggests that this place, the centre of jurisdiction for the lead industry in the Peak District in the Middle Ages, was the successor to the Roman Lutudarum. Apart from the evidence of half a dozen pigs found in the vicinity of Matlock over the past two hundred years, there is no means of showing that any particular patch of this mineral-rich ground of the southern Peak District was first opened up and worked by the Romans. The search for lead during the subsequent centuries has obliterated every distinct trace of Roman mining.

Though the visible evidence of Roman mining has largely vanished from the landscape of highland Britain, two places at least provide a closer link with the past. Charterhouse, on the lead-rich plateau of the Mendip Hills, at almost

38 The entrance to one of the levels at the gold mine of Dolaucothy, first exploited by
the Romans

1,000ft above sea level, has been shown to have been an important mining
centre in Roman times from the archaeological evidence concentrated in a
cluster of fields. At Dolaucothy, among the remote, wooded hills of south-west
Wales where gold occurs as a primary deposit in quartz veins, the link of the
present landscape with the Roman exploitation of Britain's mineral wealth is
even clearer. A Roman aqueduct can still be traced for 7 miles along the side of
the Cothi valley; it led the water that had been gathered from an almost
inaccessible gorge to tanks with sluice gates on the hill slopes above the mine.
The best-known parallels to this impressive and largely forgotten piece of
Roman industrial archaeology at Dolaucothy are the aqueducts at Roman
mines in Spain. Pliny the Elder described an aqueduct at a gold mine in Iberia,
saying that the Roman miners used sudden releases of stored water for
sweeping away the debris of mining and to uncover hidden outcrops of mineral-
bearing rock, as well as in the washing of the ore. Like most other mines in

Britain, Dolaucothy was a scene of considerable activity in the nineteenth century, largely as a result of a report by the Geological Survey in 1844 that gold was to be found there. By 1914 two shafts with engine houses and processing plants were in existence, and after some years of inactivity in the 1920s Dolaucothy was reopened with the digging of a fresh 500ft shaft and much unnecessary and expensive tunnelling in the search for gold. The enterprise collapsed in 1939. Today this complex array of adits, shafts, marshy storage basins and a half-forgotten aqueduct built by the Romans has the potential to become one of the most fascinating open-air museums in the British Isles – a site whose span of industrial archaeology from the Roman centuries to our own time cannot be matched anywhere else.

Altogether there are half a dozen different mines at Dolaucothy. The extension of mining with the reopening of the site in the last century resulted in a breakthrough into an area of former Roman workings where the parts of a wooden waterwheel that had been used for drainage purposes were discovered. Some of the tunnels, too, in this maze of mining operations from different centuries seem to date from the Roman epoch. Two long, gently sloping adits run into the hillside below the farm of Pen-lan-Wen; they are believed to be the work of miners almost two thousand years ago. In cross-section these tunnels are reminiscent of the Roman mines in the south of Spain, and there are characteristic tool marks on the walls and roof to suggest that they were cut by hand. The upper adit passes into a large cavern from which blocked tunnels lead in different directions. Other evidence of the presence of the Romans in the vicinity of Dolaucothy is provided by finds of pottery, jewellery and hoards of coins, as well as a Roman bath-house at Pumpsaint. Of the working of the mines in the Dark Ages or the medieval centuries there is no record. In fact, the extensive folklore about Dolaucothy and what must have seemed the mysterious entrances to a subterranean world makes no mention of gold. Here are two completely distinct archaeological periods inscribed on a fragment of the Welsh landscape – the Roman, when the exploitation of precious metals was a state monopoly, and the Victorian decades, when mining reached an all-time climax in the ore-bearing districts of upland Britain.

The Tudor period, and especially the reign of Elizabeth I, saw the making of new relationships between upland Britain and the lowlands of England. Henry VII's Act of Union with Wales hastened a transformation of Welsh society and economy that had started in the later Middle Ages after the Edwardian Conquest. The cattle trade with England flourished, a rising squirearchy engaged in estate building, sent its sons to Oxford and sought positions of power and influence in the running of the Tudor state and Church. The same themes of change may be observed in the evolution of the Lake District in the latter half of the sixteenth century. The dissolution of the monasteries by Henry VIII radically changed the ownership of land in the north-west where several monastic houses, the greatest of them all Furness, had possessed upland estates of thousands of acres. By the early decades of the seventeenth century a new and important element had appeared in the social structure of Cumbria: the 'statesmen'. This rural middle class enjoyed the right, at death, to hand on their estates to their next of kin, although they themselves were tenants of a lord. The rise to power of the statesmen was achieved not only through a firm foothold in their properties but also through the rising prices of wool through the Tudor decades.

In these changed conditions of society in the sixteenth century and the stronger links with distant markets that came through the traffic in cattle and wool, attention was turned towards the exploitation of the mineral wealth of the uplands in the interests of the lowlands. The state came to play a part in the development of mining and metallurgy in the north and west when two companies received royal charters in 1568. The company of the Mines Royal was concerned with the production of copper, while the Company of Mineral and Battery Works was engaged in the making of brass and the drawing of iron wire. The Company of Mines Royal opened up lead mines in Cardiganshire, but the chief region in which it entered into speculative developments was the Lake District. Late in the 1560s a smelter was built at Brigham, on the River Greta a mile outside Keswick, where ultimately half a dozen furnaces were in operation. The copper mines that fed the Brigham smelter with ore lay in Borrowdale, at the head of Derwentwater, and in the Newlands valley to the west of Keswick. The richest of the mines, Goldscope, was in the upper part of the Newlands valley. In addition to a highly productive vein of copper, 9ft thick, that had been exploited first of all in the early thirteenth century, there were two lead veins and the prospect of a yield of silver at Goldscope.

The sudden development of the copper resources of this remote part of the Lake District in the 1560s can be attributed to the interest and intervention of the state. Not only was capital for industrial equipment and the expansion of the mining of copper ores made available through the new chartered Company of the Mines Royal, but the technical skill of the most advanced mining communities in central Europe was called in to develop the resources of the region. Daniel Hochstetter, a German mining engineer from Thuringia – the most specialized of mining districts in the world in the sixteenth century – came to England and made an extensive survey of the country's mineral resources. His mandate took him to most parts of upland Britain. He toured extensively in the Lake District, visiting not only the valleys around Keswick but also the Coniston hills where the gloomy valley on the eastern face of the Old Man was cut through by rich lodes of copper. Hochstetter went on to Lancashire and Yorkshire and visited Wales and Cornwall in his assessment of the mineral potential of Tudor England.

Daniel Hochstetter's visit to Keswick was followed by the migration of German miners to develop the plans of the Company of the Mines Royal. They settled on Derwent Island, a colony set apart from the 'poor little market town called Keswike', as Leland, the first great writer on English topography, had described the place when he passed through in the 1530s. Keswick was part of the large primary parish of Crosthwaite that embraced the whole of Borrowdale and its tributary valleys. The parish registers of Crosthwaite recorded no fewer than 176 children of German fathers between 1565 and 1584. The intrusion of a large industry, the Brigham smelter and its outlying copper mines, must have brought a considerable economic stimulus as well as social disruption to the scattered sheep-farming community of Borrowdale at a time long before that later disruptive force in the traditional ways of life of the Lake District – tourism – was thought of. Between 1563 and 1590 the population of Crosthwaite parish rose from about 1,600 to well over 2,000. Keswick had been transformed into a busy little market town by the early years of the seventeenth century when it was the focus of life for the mining communities of the Newlands valley and Borrowdale. An act of politics in Elizabeth's reign, when Burghley encouraged the development of the mineral resources of Britain, added a new element to the economy of the Lake District. But the Company of the Mines Royal was an enterprise of state, of the Crown, and it fell into a time of troubles with the Civil War. Then the smelter at Brigham was destroyed, as much a target for the anti-royalist as any proud Midland castle. The copper mines in the Newlands valley closed down after Goldscope had been working continuously for almost a century. The mines around Keswick came back into production towards the end of the seventeenth century. Goldscope, for instance, was reopened by a company of Dutch capitalists in 1690 – a minor regional reflection of William of Orange's accession to the English throne. For the next century and a half, until the final closing of the mine in 1866, the history of Goldscope is typical of mining in upland Britain. Brief phases of prosperity were succeeded by years of slump; the changing pattern of the local economy was woven against a background of the ups and downs of metal prices and the occasional discovery of fresh sources of ore in local mines. Goldscope's main history was as a producer of copper, but its last brief phase of activity in the 1850s was in the output of lead.

The second half of the seventeenth century and the decades up to the Napoleonic War saw a succession of technical developments that encouraged mineral extraction on an ever greater scale. The mining districts of upland Britain found that their communal life and the very landscapes were deeply influenced by the new economies – ways of life that were almost completely divorced from the land. One of the most revolutionary among the technological changes, equal in importance to the introduction of steam power in the eighteenth century, was the driving of horizontal tunnels or adits into the depths of established mines that were threatened with flooding. The lowering of the water table that was achieved by this new technique of drainage meant that lead and copper veins at previously inaccessible depths could be reached. The drainage of flooded mine workings by the cutting of adits started in the Peak District in the seventeenth century. There the science of a Dutchman, Cornelius Vermuyden, whose name is connected with the management of the Fenland rivers in Charles I's reign, was brought to bear on the problems of the flooded Dovegang mine, at Cromford, in 1629. By the eighteenth century the driving of ever more expensive adits, 'soughs' as they are known in the Derbyshire dialect, became one of the chief technological means for expanding the outputs of the Peak District's ore fields. After a century of increasing exploitation the Derbyshire limestone plateau was riddled with 150 soughs. The construction of many of them demanded immense amounts of capital, and often they were many years in the making. Hillcarr Sough, for example, was started in 1766 and took twenty-one years to complete. It was driven for $4\frac{1}{2}$ miles into the limestone plateau beneath Youlgreave, into a countryside whose fields are now pockmarked with the evidence of long-forgotten surface workings for lead. £32,000 had to be invested in the making of Hillcarr Sough, money that was raised by the London Lead Company, a name familiar in the history of all the major lead-ore districts by the later decades of the eighteenth century. The first 2 miles of the sough ran through soft shales beneath Stanton Moor, but the last section through another 2 miles of hard Carboniferous limestone did much to retard its completion. Nevertheless, it has been calculated that the profits from extended mining in the two years after the opening of Hillcarr Sough provided for the recovery of the capital outlay.

The drainage of mines by adits and the later addition of steam engines for pumping out water increased the output of all the ore-bearing regions of highland Britain up to the early years of the nineteenth century. For instance, the mining of copper in the South-West Peninsula was remarkably revived by the new technology. There, as in the Peak District, the cutting of adits up to 300ft below the surface of the ground at old and flooded workings also revealed rich new lodes of metallic ores. One of the earliest of the Cornish 'unwaterings' was achieved with the construction of the Pool Adit in 1740. It emptied into the Red River at Tolvaddon, below Camborne, a valley that is littered with the evidence of Cornwall's eighteenth-century industrial revolution. In its making, the Pool Adit struck an abundantly productive copper vein that became the basis of the fabulously rich Trevenson mine. The success of the Pool Adit began a mania for drainage in the district of Camborne, Redruth and Chacewater. Several famous mines came into existence as a result of the drainage of old and flooded working; the Cherry Garden Adit gave rise to Cook's Kitchen, Tincroft and Carn Brea mines. But the greatest venture of all, outshining the ventures of the lead-mining companies of the Peak District, was the cutting of the Great County Adit that was started in 1748 near Bissoe in the Carnon valley. The adit led westward towards St Day under rolling hills that are still thick with the silent evidence of the prosperous decades that followed the drainage. The Great County Adit was built to unwater the Poldice mine; by the end of the eighteenth century the length of its many ramifications reached out to 20 miles and forty-six mines were drained by this underground system of miniature canals that in places went as deep as 300ft below the surface.

For the greater part of the nineteenth century, roughly from 1820 to the 1870s, the ore-bearing districts of upland Britain reached the highest peak of their activity. The time was ripe in every sense. The industrial revolution made ever new demands upon the resources of lead and copper, the generation of capital in those days meant that finance was available for fresh ventures, and it was a time of a rapidly changing technology that constantly found new means to overcome the problems of ever deeper mines, of ore extraction and processing and the menaces of flooding. It was the working of the ore fields in the nineteenth century that produced the distinctive landscapes of those districts that remain to us today – the silted ponds, the cuttings and embankments of abandoned tramways, the stone emplacements and leats where busy waterwheels once worked, the ruined chimneys, the footings and the crumbling walls of buildings whose purposes are now so hard to recognize without the help of old plans – and, dominating all, the sense of desolation and the acres of waste land, miniature mountain ranges and grey canyons whose poisoned soils are slowly and sparsely being colonized once more by vegetation.

Copper mining in Cornwall reached its climax between 1820 and 1870. It is perhaps here that the exploitation of the metallic ores has left its deepest impression on the landscape of upland Britain. Camborne and Redruth emerged in the middle years of the nineteenth century as a miniature 'conurbation' serving the extraction of copper and its associated engineering industries. This untidy, sprawling landscape of industrial cottages, huge gaunt chapels and the forgotten wastelands of a century's activity in exploiting the subterranean wealth is held together by Cornwall's two chief lines of communication – the A30 trunk road and the Western Region's main-line railway to Penzance. Today the silent engine houses and spoil heaps of Camborne–Redruth and its ring of mining villages form one of the richest museums of industrial archaeology in the British Isles. The Holman Museum in Camborne sums up in its displays the history of a district of the south-west that has been determined by the presence of rich mineral resources, now practically exhausted, over the past two thousand years.

Elsewhere in upland Britain the mines of the Victorian decades failed to generate urban communities with the vitality of the little towns of western Cornwall. The site of Devon Great Consols, above the Tamar gorge on the western fringe of Dartmoor, is now a desolation with just a lonely standing chimney or a ruined row of cottages where Wheal Maria, Wheal Fanny, Wheal Anna Maria, Wheal Josiah and Wheal Emma raised three-quarters of a million tons of copper ore in half a century from what was, in the years about 1850, the greatest copper mine in the world. Today the acres of waste ground at Devon Great Consols are softened by an ever-extending cover of dark green planted conifers.

The evolution of mining landscapes in the Pennines and Wales took somewhat different forms in the nineteenth century. North Wales contains two of the most ravaged landscapes of Britain, from the copper mining of Parys Mountain in Anglesey and the long history of lead working on Halkyn Mountain above the estuary of the Dee. Both places have a tradition of mining,

39   Amlwch, the port whose brief period of high prosperity belonged to the working of the copper ores of Parys Mountain in the late eighteenth century

supported by firm evidence, that goes back to the Romans, but the scenes of desolation that greet the traveller today are the result of the last hundred years of this robber economy that mines to the point of exhaustion a natural resource that cannot be replenished.

Large-scale mining began on Parys Mountain in the 1770s; by the 1820s it had attracted a population of six thousand to Amlwch, a nearby harbour where copper smelters were erected and where most of the miners lived. The last mine on Parys Mountain closed in 1883. Today at this site, where mining and opencast methods were used in pursuit of the copper ores, the dereliction of the landscape seems to lie beyond any hope of recovery or reclamation. Halkyn Mountain is a lead-rich upland of Carboniferous limestone, the last of the hills of North Wales before the land falls away to the narrow coastal plain and salt marshes of the Dee estuary. The intensive exploitation of the ores of Halkyn was foreshadowed when the Company of the Mines Royal extended its interests from the Peak District into the ore-bearing regions of Wales. The London Lead Company succeeded the Company of the Mines Royal in the eighteenth century. They introduced the new technology that was to lead in the nineteenth century to a vast expansion of output. In 1731 steam power was introduced with the first Newcomen engine at Trelogan, and in 1774 the problem of drainage and access to the deep, rich lodes of ore was tackled with the cutting of the

160

Holywell Tunnel – an adit wide enough to take barges. The climax in the mining history of Halkyn Mountain extends from 1838 to the first decade of the twentieth century. In 1838, after the introduction of mining engineers from Cornwall, the 9ft lode, a vein of pure lead ore, was discovered in the extension of an adit. The hundreds of acres of derelict land on Halkyn Mountain – a grey wilderness when the winter mists envelop the uplands of North Wales and a garish desert under a bright summer sun – form a landscape that came into being only in the last half of the nineteenth century.

The Peak District presents a different mining landscape again from those of the intensively worked places in North Wales. Nowhere, either at Sheldon or Chelmorton, in the anciently exploited ore field around Winster, or in the copper mines of Ecton in the Manifold valley, does one feel the desolation of Parys Mountain. Around the gathered settlements of cold grey farms on the limestone plateau – Chelmorton, Monyash and Sheldon, to mention only a few of the places that are already recorded in Domesday Book – the activities of the lead miners have not savaged the landscape. The lead rakes are often marked by long lines of spindly ash trees; green lanes bounded by limestone walls mark old rights of way to forgotten lead workings. And here and there, scattered among the fields of the once open commons, grassy hillocks and overgrown hollows show where someone tried his luck for lead in a forgotten century. The landscape of mining in the Peak District reflects an economy and society in which farming and the extraction of lead played equal roles. Even the parts of

40   At Halkyn Mountain in Clwyd, North Wales, a famous source of lead ore which was highly productive until the middle years of the nineteenth century, dereliction has come with the closing of this latest mine

the Peak District where the London Lead Company gained important interests in the eighteenth century have not much to show for their activities today. The Bowers lead-smelting mill, near Ashover, in a countryside of tangled woodland and enfolding gritstone edges, has all but vanished, even though the London Lead Company installed the latest technical development in smelting, the reverberatory furnace or cupola, when they took over the site in 1734. One of the most attractive relics of lead processing in the Peak District is found at Alport in the shallow gorge of the Lathkill just below its junction with the River Bradford. Here two cupolas were built on the valley floor and two condensing flues ran up the steep, overshadowing valley side to a chimney on the windy plateau above. Supplies to the Alport smelter from lead mines in the neighbourhood began to fail after 1850. Alport finally closed in the 1870s, after its smelter had fallen back on supplies of waste material, rich in lead, from older mining.

A final explanation of the contrasts in the mining landscapes of Wales and the Peak District is hard to come by. The disposition of the lead ores in nearly vertical dipping veins in the Carboniferous limestone, marked now by the rakes that run for miles on end across the Derbyshire landscape, may be a factor preventing the total destruction of large tracts of ground at the surface. The exhaustion of resources at several sites before the middle of the nineteenth century and the age of exploitation on an ever larger scale may help to complete the explanation, though one must not forget that Mill Close mine on the edge of the Winster ore field has a recorded output of half a million tons of lead ore and was active until the late 1930s. It ranks among the most prolific mines in Britain. Even so, the small scale and lesser visual impact of mining in the Peak District probably has much to do with the early start and long history that enabled a society of farmer–miners to exploit the resources of the region and to surround themselves with rights that were already embodied in a code of law before the end of the Middle Ages.

The last quarter of the nineteenth century witnessed a sudden collapse of most mining in the hills of Britain, a decline that was brought about by the entry into the world's markets of new sources of cheap copper, lead and tin from mines in Peru and Chile, Australia, south-east Asia and the Rocky Mountains of North America; besides, the search for ore-bearing rock in Britain was becoming ever more difficult and costly. But more recently, in a time of soaring metal prices since World War II, it has been found profitable to rework some of the ancient lead-rich spoil heaps. Modern earth-moving equipment has been used to open up the lead rakes on Longstone Edge in the Peak District to depths of almost 100ft to extract the valuable gangue minerals – fluorspar, barytes and calcite – leaving deep wounds in an historic landscape. On Grassington Moor, in the West Riding, the recent quarrying of the waste heaps has obliterated most of the evidence of earlier mining – the bell pits that marked the prospecting of individual miners along the outcropping lead veins over the 6 square miles of Grassington Moor in the eighteenth century, the dressing floors, watercourses, silted reservoirs and sites of early smelt mills. Only a chimney stack and flue and the ruin of a smelt mill remain as a record in the landscape of the lead industry of Grassington. Mining had ceased in the 1860s; the smelt mill closed in 1880, and now only the names of half-forgotten shafts – Peru, New Peru and West Peru – recall the hopes of the boom years of the last century, when the mines of Craven were expected to rival the legendary wealth of the Andes.

And if the Peak District escaped the desolation that could be created by industry in the last century, it now faces many worse threats to its familiar landscape. The need for limestone for cement and fertilizers, as a raw material of the chemical industry, and, hungriest demand of all, for road-stone after it has been crushed, has imposed tremendous stress upon the very foundations of this landscape. An ever-moving quarry face, a naked wall of rock, has pushed back the valley sides of Great Rocks Dale. The pale spring green of the woods in the Via Gellia valley is soon coated with a film of grey powder from the quarries and crushing plants in the adjacent limestone plateau. The skies of the Peak District become a luminescent grey on brilliant summer days from the ring of limeworks and their smoking kilns that lies just beyond the northern perimeter of the National Park. The mineral wealth of upland Britain in the latter half of the twentieth century finds new uses and economic values beyond anything previously imagined. The search for gold took the Roman mining engineers to Central Wales, where they opened up mines that drew a water supply from a 7-mile-long aqueduct. The hunger of the closing years of the twentieth century is for uranium, a mineral and source of energy that threatens the remote landscapes of Orkney with the kind of destruction that twentieth-century technology has already brought to the southern Pennines.

# 6

# The Taming of the Uplands

---

The fifty-year period between 1770 and 1820 is remarkable in that it saw an almost spontaneous attempt in many parts of Britain to tackle the reclamation of the upland wastelands, which had long been abandoned to rough grazing or grouse and deer shoots. For the first time since the monasteries had used the upland pastures as great sheep runs, there was a feeling that these wastes could make a valuable contribution to the wealth of the country if reclaimed and properly managed. The end of the eighteenth century was an age of Romanticism and, to a lesser extent, philanthropism. To wrestle with nature and in the end see two blades of grass grow where none had grown before appealed to an enlightened few amongst the new class of landowning gentry. In the untouched acres of heather moorland or the vast expanse of tough, tussocky and unpalatable grasslands there was a tremendous potential for improvement. Provided adequate capital was available there appeared no reason why nature and man could not combine to produce a landscape that was both appealing to the eye and yet yielding of her goodness. The judicious planting of woodland, especially the hardwood trees like the oak and beech, could ultimately bring worthwhile economic returns and yet, at the same time, vastly improve the appearance of the bare mountain slopes and provide shelter belts to aid cultivation.

Seen through the eyes of the eighteenth century Romantics, the harsh realities of the hostile upland environment tended to be overlooked once the fervour of the improvement drive got under way and an upland Utopia seemed an attainable goal. With little scientific knowledge available, especially as regards climate, it was difficult for improvers to assess the true potential of a particular site, and often a decision for improvement was based on no more than a single visit undertaken in summer when conditions were at their best. Drainage problems following the winter snowmelt or troublesome gales were often not considered in this casual preliminary assessment. Rather, the decision might rest solely on an aesthetic approach and a desire to improve on nature. The influence of Claude Lorraine (1600–82) was still very much in evidence, and in the 'Age of the Picturesque' it is not surprising that adherents

164

like Richard Payne Knight (1750–1824) of Downton Castle in Shropshire and Ulvedale Price should seek to model their ideas on landscape improvement on his teachings. Although improvement began in the laid-out garden and the informal swards of the country estate like that of Downton Castle, the same influence was later to find expression in the attempted taming of the upland wilds. It is significant that a relative of Knight who came under his influence, Thomas Johnes, was one of the earliest practitioners of improvement. Before he began his great experiment of taming a remote Welsh valley in Cardiganshire, Johnes often discussed architectural theory and the aesthetics of landscape improvement with Knight. Another member of the Knight family, John (1765–1850), was later to embark on a great plan for reclaiming thousands of acres on the plateau top of Exmoor. Although of a more practical bent than his cousin Thomas Johnes, John Knight was fired with the same enthusiasm to create an ordered, productive landscape out of desolation. Measured in purely economic terms, Knight was no more successful than Johnes in making the upland desert bloom, at least in his own lifetime, although a present-day judgement might come to a different conclusion: there is now no doubt that the hopes that Knight nurtured through the difficult years of the early nineteenth century have been largely fulfilled.

That the time was ripe for attack on the upland wastes is shown by the atmosphere of agricultural improvement that spread through the country in the second half of the eighteenth century. The Board of Agriculture came into being in 1766 and soon Arthur Young was busy educating through his writings. In Scotland, John Sinclair of Ulbster (1754–1835) was anxious to make the wastes of his native Caithness productive and thereby improve the lot of the small tenant farmer. The creation of better strains of seed and the improvement of animal husbandry through cross-breeding were being realized for the first time. Improvement often meant a considerable change of farming practice and life style and in Scotland, in particular, there was resentment and considerable opposition to a changeover to more profitable sheep farming. It was one of Sinclair's main tasks to try to resolve the conflict which arose between landlord and tenant farmer as the former sought to turn the Highland estates into huge sheep runs. In theory the changeover could be beneficial to all, for the wool produced could form the basis of a local cottage industry to give regular employment to displaced tenant farmers. Sinclair was responsible for initiating and editing the First Statistical Account of Scotland in twenty-one volumes between 1790 and 1799. He had already been President of the Board of Agriculture and it was at this time that he started county surveys with Arthur Young, the Secretary.

Sinclair attempted to put over his views on agricultural development and improvement, and perhaps more than any other Scotsman he succeeded in transforming the landscape, especially in his native Caithness. The peculiar problems facing the Highlands after the unsuccessful insurrection of 1745 are highlighted in the attempt to found new settlements and through them exploit the resources of a country which had long been torn in strife. As one contemporary writer put it, 'Highlanders had to be won from their idle and wicked practices to commerce and trade'. Many of the new settlements like Newtonmore, Fochabers or Grantown were set in coastal or valley situations and therefore took advantage of the most favourable physical conditions. Others, however, were established in what can only be described as unpromising situations, where the inhabitants could only survive if imbued with an almost missionary zeal. Tomintoul, on the eastern borders of the Cairngorms and set at a height of over 1,100ft, comes into this category. The settlement was founded in 1775 by the Duke of Gordon as a planned upland village to rival Grantown, recently built down in the Spey valley by Sir James Grant. Because of its site and the fact that it has survived, somewhat astonishingly, as a viable entity, Tomintoul can claim to be the most interesting of the Scottish planned villages. The name means 'barn on the knoll' and must refer to the appearance of the area prior to the laying out of the village. Thomas Milne the surveyor was given the task of preparing a map of the proposed layout with the various buildings, cottages and land holdings shown in detail. The survey was carried out in 1775, but it was a further five years before the first of the plots was taken up. The oblong plots, fifty-six in all, were arranged on either side of the main road across the Banffshire uplands between Braemar and Inverness. In the centre, eight of the plot frontages were set back to form an open square, the hub of the village. An alehouse for travellers passing through the area, a schoolhouse and itinerant meeting house were also envisaged. Each of the plots of about 2 acres was designed to give the owner a degree of self-sufficiency.

Transfers for the dispersed cottagers from the area around into the new village went on slowly in the closing years of the eighteenth century, and by 1794 there were thirty-seven families living in the village. This number was to increase steadily throughout the nineteenth century even though the projected lint mill and spinning school, associated with a locally based linen industry, did not materialize. In consequence the villagers were forced to rely almost entirely on subsistence agriculture, with crops of oats, potatoes and hay from their plots and cattle grazed on the common ground of the village at Tomnabat. The village did provide a useful stopping place on the journey across the uplands and by 1820 there were three inns located around the square, a useful asset to the village during the grouse-shooting season. Fortunately there was no difficulty in obtaining local building materials with freestone available at Achriachan, limestone at Craighalkie and slate from the Knockfergan quarry. The limestone was also a valuable asset in that it could be used for improving the newly ploughed lands, and near Faindouran there were no fewer than nine kilns for burning the lime. What looked at first sight an unpromising settlement scheme did manage to survive, and by 1842, in spite of a lack of industry, the population had increased to over five hundred. Its survival into the last quarter of the twentieth century is equally remarkable. In a car-conscious age

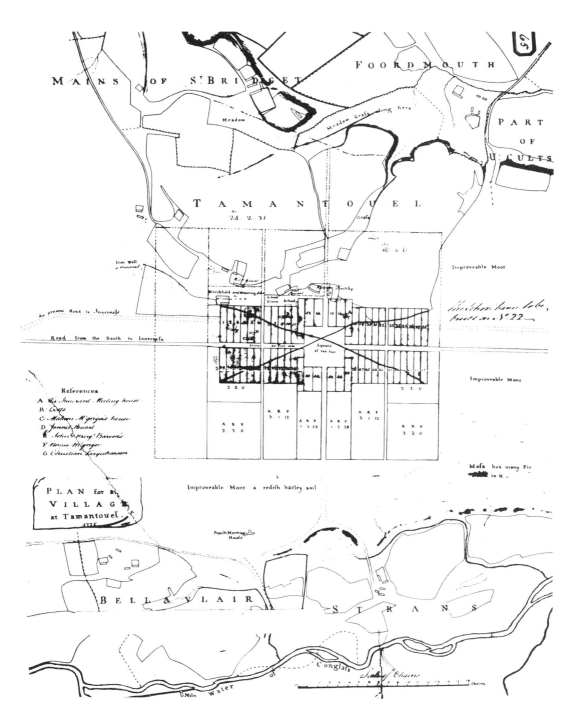

Fig 23　The map which Thomas Milne prepared in 1775 to show the proposed layout for the new settlement of Tomintoul

Tomintoul, at 1,160ft 'the highest village in Scotland', as the guide book proclaims, is much visited, forming a convenient stopping place on the road between the Spey and Dee valleys. Coach operators, too, find its hotel useful for overnight accommodation on their wide-ranging Highland tours. There was a brief period when Tomintoul almost became a spa, for, as Thomas Stuart remarked, 'I find that here there is one, perhaps, of the most excellent medicinal or mineral wells in the North of Scotland which, was it properly laid out, managed and cared for, would add not a little to the improvement of the village'. In the event Tomintoul did not become another upland spa like Buxton, so that today, with many of its plots uncultivated and returning to the waste, it remains a curious anomaly, hardly justifying the faith placed in it by its founder, the fourth Duke of Gordon, who thought it would lead to a marked improvement in the lot of the Highlander.

Similar schemes to that of Tomintoul were fashionable in other parts of the Highlands in the closing years of the eighteenth century. The landed nobility, including in particular the Duke of Argyll, the Duke and Duchess of Sutherland and Sir John Grant, were very much to the fore. Many projects were tried for the improvement of both farming and the fishing industry, and foremost amongst the beneficent landowners was the previously mentioned Sir John Sinclair of Ulbster in Caithness. The family had a long association with this remote north-east corner of Scotland and lived in Thurso Castle. When he was only sixteen, John Sinclair inherited the family estate on the death of his father in 1770. For a while he went away to study in Edinburgh, and it was probably at this time that he became interested in agricultural reform and met people who would help him to carry out his ideas in later years. He soon realized that the problem of the Highlands could only be solved by providing better roads, and that it was essential to have Wade's military network extended into remote areas like Caithness. He himself showed the way by employing local labour to build access roads in his own area. The appointment of Thomas Telford as engineer to the newly created Commission for Roads and Bridges in 1803 quickly led to the building of the coastal road southwards from Wick to Helmsdale to a 15ft width specification. Even the formidable obstacle of the promontory of the Ord of Caithness was overcome by skilful engineering practice. With this link to the south firmly forged, Sinclair rightly believed that the isolation which had contributed to the neglect of farming in Caithness was now at an end and that he could now press ahead with his improvement schemes.

While at Edinburgh and later at Oxford, Sinclair laid plans which would help forward his vision of turning the wastelands of Caithness into productive farmland. In the 1780s emigration to America was beginning to build up, and as it involved the most able families, the outlook for those who remained was bleak. The despair that Sinclair felt was compounded by the harvest failure of 1782 and the resulting food shortage. Only the potato saved many from starvation. Scottish agriculture was still almost feudal in character, with several

41  Abandoned cottages at Broubster in Caithness. Here, and at the neighbouring settlements of Shurrery and Shebster, a total of 192 families lost their homes during land clearance

tenants on a farm each cultivating strips in a big field. With scattered holdings and land they did not own there was little incentive for improvement, and without capital the necessary reorganization was virtually impossible. The whole question came to a head in the 1780s in an unexpected way. In 1784, the chiefs who had been deprived after the Jacobite rebellion were allowed to return to their original estates. During their years of exile, often in southern Britain, they had learned much about current farming practice in the lowlands, especially the financial rewards that were available from sheep farming. Although in lowland England sheep were part of a mixed farming economy of arable and animal husbandry, the Scottish exiles were not slow to realize that the vast upland pastures of their native country could sustain great flocks of sheep with the minimum of effort. The returned lairds therefore resolved to do away with the existing system of tenant farming and replace it with sheep rearing. This would give a much quicker return on capital, but it would mean the tenant farmer losing his security and often the only means of supporting his family. The imposition of this change undoubtedly caused great hardship in parts of Scotland and aroused considerable ill-feeling. Even Thomas Telford felt he had to comment on the sad state of his kinsmen when he wrote in 1802 that 'the lairds have transferred their affection from the people to flocks of sheep'.

It was against this background that John Sinclair began his quest for improvement. He himself was enthusiastic about promoting sheep farming as he felt that in the long run, if carefully and humanely handled, it provided the best chance of improving the lot of the Highlander. On a visit to London in 1788 he discussed the whole problem with Sir Joseph Banks, and as a result he purchased the Langwell estate for £9,000. It was here that he began experimenting with large-scale sheep farming for the production of both meat and wool. From the Border Country he brought in five hundred Cheviot ewes which quickly established themselves and flourished on the green pastures of coastal Caithness. To make way for them Sinclair had to displace eighty of his tenant farmers, but, aware of his responsibilities, he gave them land on the clifftops of Badbea. His plan was to give each tenant farmer a cottage and 2 acres of land where basic necessities could be grown. As they could not be self-sufficient Sinclair guaranteed them a certain number of days of work a year in order to supplement their income. The resettlement scheme included a proposal to promote a cottage industry using the wool from his own sheep ranch. It was while the Langwell experiment was getting under way that Sinclair founded the British Wool Authority, doubtless using contacts he made in London while Member of Parliament for Caithness. Unfortunately for Sinclair the resettlement at Badbea was not a success, and after two generations of struggle in its new environment the whole community emigrated. Nothing therefore remains of the Sinclair project, save that the site of the former village is marked by an obelisk set within the stone-walled fields which are rapidly returning to waste.

If Sinclair's attempt at resettlement at Badbea was an undoubted failure, some of his other improvement ventures were more successful and have left their mark on the present landscape. In 1794 he was appointed the first President of the Board of Agriculture and immediately began putting into practice some of his ideas on agricultural improvement. The old open fields would have to give way to walled enclosures, and new farmhouses would be built along newly driven roads that would give access to the farms from the main highways. In less than a generation he aimed to transform the whole appearance of the landscape around his ancestral home at Thurso Castle. The new scheme began at Thurso East in 1798 and during the next fourteen years went on steadily in the lands around the town of Thurso. About fifty 25-acre cottage farms were established in the vicinity of Skinnet, Lieurary and Scrabster Common. It has been estimated that the resettlement scheme cost Sinclair about £6,000 over a twenty-five-year period. On the credit side, he could point to a profitable, regular crop rotation of turnips, clover and rye grass in place of the former wasteful open-field system. Sheep rearing, following the methods recommended by Townshend, also became established on many of his Thurso farms.

Agricultural Sir John, as Sinclair became known, was willing to try various approaches in his quest for improved farming. The planned village of Halkirk, lying on flat land to the south of the River Thurso, was laid out on a gridiron plan with individual cottages lining a wide grass-fronted street. Each cottage had an acre of land attached to it to provide the occupier with basic necessities

42    The main street of Lybster, one of several planned villages on the Caithness coast
aimed at improving the standard of living of the Highlander by combining farming with
fishing

by way of vegetables. As at Tomintoul, many of the plots are now uncultivated
as the function of the village has changed since its inception. Being close to
Thurso, the cottages have been sought after by those coming to the area
following the building of the Dounreay atomic power station. Only the basic
layout of the village and its siting in the wilds now give a hint that Halkirk must
have a history of artificial plantation. Sinclair's other attempt at village
foundation was at Sarclett on the coast, 5 miles south of Wick. Here, on an
exposed clifftop, a single street of cottages runs down to the head of a small
harbour. Access to the harbour is not easy, and in any case it is too small to
house more than a few fishing boats on which the Sarclett pioneers were
expected to depend for part of their livelihood. Today Sarclett looks desolate
and not as attractive as the other planned village along this coast, Lybster. The
brain-child of Temple Sinclair, who, like his namesake, was concerned with the
fate of evicted tenants of the Highland clearances, Lybster was better endowed
by nature and its harbour, even today, can still attract vessels of the Caithness
fishery.

It is in the present towns of Thurso and Wick, rather than in the agricultural
resettlement villages, that Sir John Sinclair has left his mark as an innovator.

Both towns are of ancient foundation, but Sinclair succeeded in redeveloping them to the extent that the present plan is very much of his creation. At Thurso, new wide streets were laid out on a grid pattern and the blocks filled in with terraces of well-built stone houses. Wick attracted Sinclair because of its great potential as a fishing port, provided an adequate and safe harbour could be built. To this end, as early as 1787 he had urged the British Fisheries Society to build harbour works that would give safe anchorage to a large fishing fleet. It was, however, many years before Thomas Telford was called in and the construction work begun under his overall guidance. On the south side of the new harbour, which came into use in 1809, an additional quarter of the town – known as Pultneytown after the President of the British Fisheries Society – was laid out, and here again we see the influence of Sir John. The early-nineteenth-century developments at Wick and Thurso allowed both towns to enter a period of prosperity, so that when the Highland Railway was pushed to the north in the second half of the century, both became termini.

The Caithness experiments had their counterparts in other areas of Britain, especially after Arthur Young had produced a whole series of county agricultural reports which stressed the under-utilization of good land in upland areas. This was not the only approach, however, and in North Wales Richard Pennant used his industrial interests to further upland colonization and settlement. As early as 1782, when he bought out the interests of a number of small slate-quarry owners and began to rationalize the industry, he saw himself as a benefactor to those who lived on his extensive estates bordering the Ogwen valley in Snowdonia. He was soon to become Lord Penrhyn, and his interest in settlement is shown in the laying-out of a model village, Llandygai, at the gates of Penrhyn Castle. It was designed for workers on the estate, and became the focal point, with a dairy and sawmill. The slate-quarrying industry at the end of the eighteenth century underwent many changes of fortune. By rationalization and improved methods of extraction, Penrhyn outstripped his rivals and soon developed a flourishing export trade. The best slates were not near the coast at Llandygai but 5 miles inland on the edge of the mountains by the Ogwen valley. The only difficulty with the inland quarry was the transport of the slates to the coast for shipment. Lord Penrhyn solved this problem by building a horse tramway from the Ogwen quarries to a new port built at Bangor. More and more men were taken on at the ever-growing Penrhyn quarry, and many travelled long distances to work each day. The model village of Llandygai – without a corrupting alehouse – was now too small to house the workers, so Lord Penrhyn allowed his men to build their own cottages on his land close to the quarry. Each had a plot attached to it so that when work slackened in the quarry it was possible to be gainfully employed as a smallholder.

The idea of part-time quarrymen–farmers so attracted Lord Penrhyn that he ultimately decided to lay out a small settlement of sixty cottages near the quarry, each with an acre of land to graze a cow or keep a few pigs and poultry. The site chosen was on open moorland at a height of over 1,000ft just under the

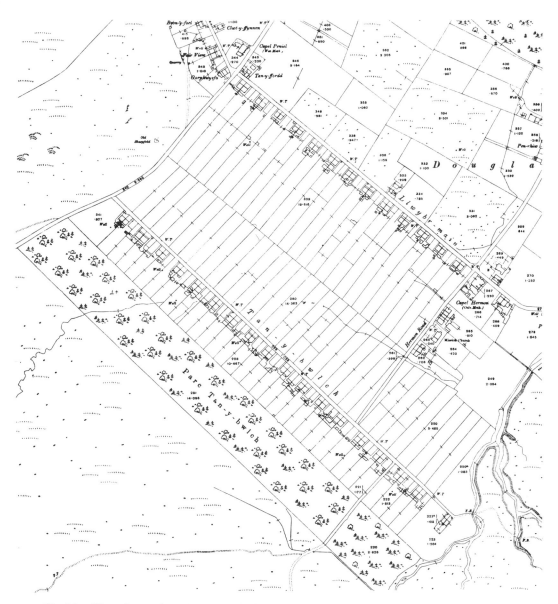

Fig 24    The planned settlement of Mynydd Llandygai close to the Penrhyn quarry,
Snowdonia

shadow of Elidir Fawr. The planned settlement, usually called Mynydd
Llandygai, consisted of two parallel rows of cottages with land at both the front
and rear. A shelter belt of mixed deciduous and coniferous woodland was
planted on the exposed south-west side. During the period of the Methodist
revival, Capel Hermon was built (1847), and later Capel Peniol. It was not until
1873 that a daughter chapel of the established Church was built. It was no
part of Lord Penrhyn's plan for an alehouse to be built, and this has remained

173

43  Mynydd Llandygai, a planned upland settlement close to the Penrhyn slate quarry

the case right through to the present day. Many quarrymen, however, preferred to live in the rapidly growing Bethesda, a village which had begun to grow up alongside Telford's Holyhead road from about 1820 onwards. Mynydd Llandygai, in consequence, has preserved its original design and identity, though its chapels and church now have a care-worn look. Many of the cottages are no longer occupied by Penrhyn quarrymen, and in recent years many have been bought by people working in Bangor, only 6 miles away.

It was in Cardiganshire rather than in the slate belt of Snowdonia that the greatest experiment in taming the wild upland landscape took place. The bare headwater reaches of the Ystwyth valley had long been exploited for the lead ores they contained in numerous veins. The result was that the original forest cover had long since vanished as the timber was used as a fuel to smelt the ores. It was the vision of Thomas Johnes to transform this despoiled landscape into his idea of Arcadia that led to perhaps the greatest experiment in landscape design in Wales, an experiment that was ultimately to consume his vast fortune. He first came to this quiet backwater of the Welsh hills in the summer of 1780 and was immediately struck by the possibilities of this once verdant valley now raped of its woodland cover. Johnes was a friend of Sir Walter Scott and shared the latter's Romantic feelings. At Hafod, an estate which he had acquired through the marriage of his father into the Herbert family, he decided to put ideas which seemed right when expressed in prose, poetry and on canvas into practice by creating a 'natural' landscape setting.

The first requirement was to build a modern country house which would serve as a focal point for this earthly Utopia. Here he could call on the expertise of his cousin Richard Payne Knight, who had recently built the modern Gothic castle at Downton-on-the-Rock in Shropshire. His friend Ulvedale Price was busy at this time designing a formal garden and rides on his estate at Foxley and it is likely that Johnes discussed his own project with Price too. The Bath architect Thomas Baldwin was brought in and asked to supervise the building of a light and spacious mansion with Gothic pointed windows. The house was started in June 1786 on a low, flat terrace above the pebbly bed of the youthful Ystwyth, but almost immediately Johnes found it inadequate for the plans he had in mind. A library to satisfy his interests as a bibliophile became urgent, and for this he called in a relatively unknown architect, John Nash of Carmarthen, long before the latter had established his reputation in fashionable quarters. A whole army of workers was employed in building the

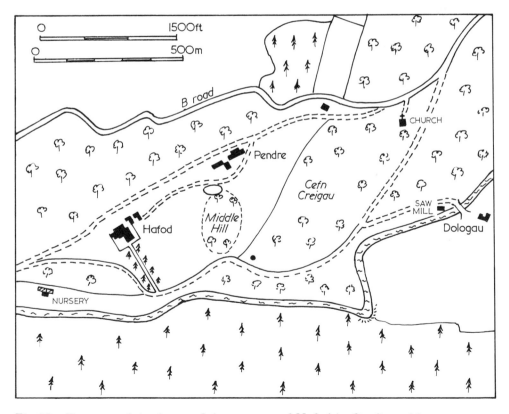

Fig 25   Features of the former Johnes estate of Hafod in Cardiganshire

175

44 Hafod in its prime, before the house was allowed to become derelict and finally demolished

house and laying out the formal gardens around. The rest of the estate was transformed by the establishment of walks and rides, as far as possible conforming to the natural contours of the valley. The waterfalls of the Ystwyth were suitably incorporated into the grand design and, in keeping with the spirit of the Romantic Age, secretive grottoes were opened up into the bare rock faces. No wonder Hafod was being spoken of as 'one of the wonders of Wales', with Johnes lavish in his entertainment of the constant stream of eminent visitors who came to view. Coleridge stayed here for a while and probably had Hafod in mind when he wrote of Kubla Khan's Xanadu. There were oddities which the visitor was expected to view, not least the peacocks wandering freely in the woods or the flock of merino sheep grazing on the valley-side slopes. Turner came to Hafod in 1798 and has left us a painting of the house as it was then, with the two long wings which John Nash had added to the original Baldwin design. Another frequent visitor was Sir John Smith, first President of the Linnean Society, who gave Johnes advice on botanical matters.

Some measure of the impact which Johnes made on the landscape within a generation can be seen from his tree-planting schemes. He realized that many slopes were too steep to be farmed but were sufficiently sheltered to grow valuable timber. The best farmland was on the plateau top, but this was so exposed that shelter belts were a first priority. Both aspects of arboriculture were in the mind of Johnes when he took over the Hafod estate in 1783 and he soon embarked on a massive programme of tree planting. Records show that between 1796 and 1813 close on four million trees were planted. Over half were of species of the European larch but there were also stands of beech, elm, oak, alder and ash. Larch was usually favoured for the plateau tops up to a height of 1,200ft because of the relative thinness of the soil and the known ability of the tree to survive the exposed windy sites. Hardwood trees like the oak and beech were restricted to the better-drained lands of the valley sides, and in spite of doubts expressed by local farmers about the advisability of planting these so-called 'exotic' species, they did grow surprisingly well. Most of Johnes's woodland has long since disappeared, as the fully grown trees were cut down and sold once they reached maturity, but a few stands of beech and oak remain, a welcome relief from the ubiquitous conifers planted by the Forestry Commission who now own the estate.

Johnes went to great lengths to ensure the success of his upland afforestation. As a pioneer in the field he had to experiment and also learn from his mistakes. He made his own nursery to raise the vast number of tree seedlings, and we are told that between 1798 and 1802 almost a million oak seedlings were raised from acorn seed. When the saplings were two years old they were planted out at the rate of four thousand to the acre, the normal work-load of two men for a week. The failure rate was surprisingly low, and with a subsequent growth of about 2ft a year, the experiment could be judged a success. A water-powered sawmill was erected by the side of the Ystwyth and when the timber was mature – long after Johnes's death – Hafod sawn oak became well-known both in the neighbourhood and further afield.

The Thomas Johnes improvement experiment has been admirably told in Elizabeth Inglis Jones's *Peacocks in Paradise,* with its reference in the title to the many peacocks which roamed at will over the Hafod estate. The story, for all its pioneering theme, is one of personal family tragedy. The original house was soon burnt to the ground, and though Johnes had it rebuilt in 1807, it took much of the family fortune. A further blow came with the death of his only daughter Marianne in 1811. Chantrey was commissioned to sculpture a memorial, but even this was severely damaged by fire at Hafod church in 1932. The death of Marianne drained Johnes of much of his early enthusiasm, and the estate gradually became too much to manage, until finally he found the cost of upkeep altogether too great. On his death in 1816 the estate passed into the hands of the Duke of Newcastle, and with this came the end of the Hafod improvement experiment. The new owner was never interested in the estate, concentrating his efforts instead in building a new hotel at nearby Devil's Bridge in the style of a Swiss chalet. The house at Hafod gradually fell into disrepair, and after being stripped of its valuables it was finally demolished in 1958. The area, now under the control of the Forestry Commission, is leased today as a caravan park. Although a mere shadow of its former glory, the Hafod estate still retains the barest imprint of its illustrious past. The driveways, terrace walks, parkland setting and exotic trees are still there, as much out of character with the Welsh countryside as they were in Johnes's day. The church of Eglwys Newydd, an early creation of the Romantic Age by Wyatt, has been recently restored and is now perhaps the most obvious surviving feature of Johnes's excursion into Arcadia. As with another great pioneer who aimed at re-shaping the Welsh landscape, William Madocks, with his scheme for

reclaiming the Glaslyn estuary, Johnes might have looked upon his efforts as being a dismal failure. His real monument lies not perhaps in the tangible remains but rather in the lead he gave to the improvers by tackling a most unpromising upland situation and encouraging others to do likewise.

The spirited attack on the upland wastes by a relatively small group of individuals at the turn of the eighteenth century was undertaken with a burning idealism that was their main hope of success. What is remarkable is that one family, the Knights of Shropshire, should have provided two of the leading figures. Thomas Johnes's father had married the daughter of Richard Knight of Croft Castle, and she had brought him a dowry of £70,000 as well as an inheritance of estates near Ludlow and in west Wales. We have already seen how Thomas maintained a close contact with his cousin Richard Payne Knight of Downton Castle prior to the building of Hafod. The latter's cousin, John Knight (1740–95), lived at Lea Castle, and it was his son, John Knight, Junior (1765–1850), who undertook perhaps the greatest of the upland reclamation schemes, that of Exmoor Forest. Through the masterly and authoritative study by the agricultural economist C.S. Orwin, the Knight imprint on the Exmoor landscape has been fully documented. The sandstone plateau, rising to almost 1,600ft at the Chains, is one of a series of uplands that make up the backbone of the South-West Peninsula. It differs from other uplands like Dartmoor and Bodmin Moor not only in its basic rock type but more significantly in that it has a thick superficial cover of a stony clay called 'head' which gives it relatively deep soils. Although the potential for farming has always existed on Exmoor, historical circumstance dictated otherwise. For almost a thousand years the area was a royal hunting preserve, but in 1815 this protected status came to an end and the land was sold to the highest bidder, John Knight, for £50,000. Most of the 10,000 acres were treeless sheep pasture, with only a house and homestead at Simonsbath.

It did not take Knight long to begin the scheme for upland reclamation which he had clearly had in mind when he bought the Exmoor holding. The first task was to surround his land with a wall 29 miles in length and then open up the area with a network of tracks. The main link between Simonsbath and Exford was made into a fine metalled road and this became the main access route to the Knight estate. All was ready to attack the wilderness of purple moor grass and the ill-drained land. After trying unsuccessfully to get rid of the surface water by normal drainage techniques, Knight was forced to adopt a deep ploughing method to break up the crusty impervious iron pan just below the surface. Once this had been achieved it was possible to use the full depth of good soil. After heavy dressings of lime had been applied, the ploughed land was sown with grass. This quickly developed into fine pasture, its bright green colour standing

45   The church which Thomas Johnes built on the edge of his Hafod estate, the only substantial building to remain from his attempt to create an earthly paradise in the Cardiganshire countryside

179

46 Warren Farm, one of several which Knight built for his tenant farmers on the Exmoor plateau top. A south-facing site was chosen and a screen of trees planted to lessen the effects of exposure

out in contrast to the duller tones of the unimproved purple moor grass. In thirty years of effort up to 1845 Knight had ploughed, limed and sown about 2,500 acres. The import of lime from South Wales through the tiny port of Combe Martin proved his biggest expense, and from time to time Knight sought a more local source of supply, but without success.

With sown grassland now occupying about a quarter of the total area of the estate, there was a sound basis for pastoral farming. High hedge-banks of loose stone and clay were built around the newly created fields and then planted with hazel saplings. The hazel hedges still figure prominently in the appearance of the landscape. Knight travelled widely throughout Britain looking for suitable stock, and in one single purchase he obtained seven hundred head of cattle, mainly Hereford and Highland breeds. Sheep, particularly the Cheviots, a breed favoured by Sinclair in Caithness, were introduced in 1840. Much of his work was on a trial-and-error basis, and although he had his successes, like the introduction of the Cheviot breed, Knight also had his failures. The local Devon cattle, for example, have in time proved much more suitable than some of the exotic breeds which Knight introduced. His knowledge of Midland farming led him to adopt a four-course rotation system, but at heights of over 1,200ft it was never successful, and it was later abandoned. These apparent failures were only minor hiccups in what must be judged overall as a successful experiment in upland management. The present landscape around Simonsbath contains all the elements of the original Knight plan, with his great enclosing wall, the road network and above all the farms which he established like Cornham, Honeymead, Wintershead and Emmett's Grange. Knight originally intended to run the whole enterprise himself, perhaps with cottages to house workers on the estate. As he grew older he found the pressures too great and was therefore forced to adopt a different method of farming. Eleven new holdings were made in the 1840s and staffed by tenant farmers who were rewarded for any improvements they made. This different approach undoubtedly helped to save the original Knight scheme, which was at that time threatened with total disaster. Not only did it produce an annual rental income of £3,500 but it led to a wider range of expertise being made available. The growing of wheat and barley was abandoned in favour of oats, which formed an important winter feed for horses and cattle. Greater emphasis was now placed on a pastoral economy, and this led to the sowing of more root crops. Turnips were especially favoured,

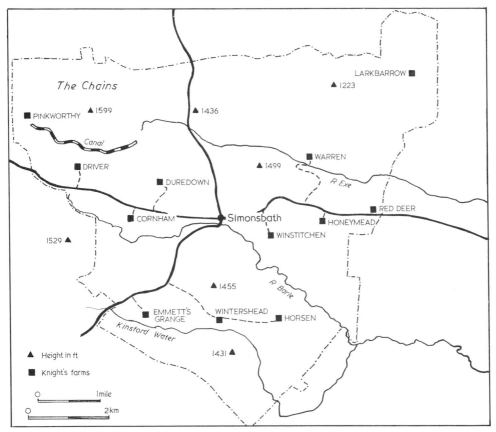

Fig 26   The Knight estate centred on Simonsbath, Exmoor

181

particularly after sheep rearing became more popular in the latter half of the nineteenth century. From 1868 onwards the sowing of rape also became widespread after its value for fattening sheep was discovered.

The recent concern felt about ploughing large areas of the Exmoor plateau provides an interesting contemporary comment on the Knight scheme. With modern methods available, and much more known about the management of upland grasslands following the work of Sir George Stapledon at Aberystwyth, the full potential of the area is at last being realized. The basic physical attributes of a deep soil derived from the head deposits and the provision of good drainage through deep ploughing techniques undoubtedly give Exmoor a great advantage in terms of upland improvement, as does its more favourable climate due to its position in the South-West Peninsula. Although above the 1,000ft contour, it is in the unique position of having to resist further attempts at improvement, while land at a similar altitude in areas like Snowdonia and the Highlands has now tended to go out of cultivation.

# 7

# The High Ways

## Prehistoric and Bronze Age roads

Early man, perhaps surprisingly, found the uplands attractive as a means of moving from one part of the country to another. As most journeys were on foot, severe gradients did not pose the problems which wheeled transport had to face in later centuries. Once the steep ascent had been made to the top the route could then be relatively flat, especially when advantage could be taken of high-level plateau surfaces. Even ridgeways, following a watershed between two adjacent drainage basins, could mean only the occasional ascent and descent and they, too, often gave a relatively easy passage. Compared with lowland routes, the high ways were more open and seldom had to contend with impenetrable forests or areas of poor drainage. Many of the early tracks used by prehistoric man have long since disappeared, but some have left tangible remains in the present landscape, though the routes themselves are much less important than in the past.

Prehistoric routes, perhaps going back for five thousand years, form a tantalizing subject of study and speculation. Neolithic man, because of his more settled mode of life based on cultivation and the pasturing of animals, has left us the clearest picture of the earliest upland routes. Though the exposed uplands with their lack of shelter and unfavourable climate precluded permanent settlement, necessity often dictated that the highest parts had to be crossed in the interests of trade and other forms of economic activity. The plateau lands of Central Wales or the summit plain of Exmoor come immediately to mind as areas where the topography could be used to advantage in fashioning long through ways linking areas of settlement. Many of the prehistoric tracks have been lost, as the conditions which brought them into being disappeared over the centuries. As with present-day footpaths which are not continually walked over, vegetation soon obliterates all trace, sometimes in less than a decade. In our upland areas a climatic deterioration such as occurred at the end of the Bronze Age encouraged the growth of peat which quickly smothered the early tracks. Even in later centuries, paved ways which had once felt the tramp of Roman legions were to be covered up by a spreading mat of peat. Often it is only the chance stripping away of the vegetation cover, perhaps by gullying following a particularly heavy rainstorm, that brings to light a former road or track. Some roads have been in continuous use for over four thousand years, perhaps as prehistoric ridgeway tracks, then as Roman roads, medieval pack-horse trails and eighteenth-century droveways, right down to the present-day country lane. Many early upland routes have survived not as metalled roads but as delightful 'green lanes' which made ideal cross-country walks in parts of the Pennines. Paradoxically, ancient lowland routes have often been obliterated through later rebuilding and widening to take the ever-increasing flow of traffic. The best section of Roman road to survive is not the Foss Way or Watling Street, but the now neglected route across the Pennines climbing Blackstone Edge between Rochdale and Halifax.

The tracing of early upland routes calls for a detective approach both on the ground and, more especially, in the use of maps to pinpoint concentrations of prehistoric features. Even where a former road has virtually disappeared from the present-day landscape, archaeological finds like artefacts and pottery, or the more obvious monuments to the past – burial chambers or standing stones – can often indicate a once important upland route.

Contrary to popular belief, early man was extremely mobile and some of his trade routes, especially for valuable commodities like stone axeheads or flint scrapers, extended for hundreds of miles across the length and breadth of the country. Good implements were of such value to Neolithic man in his forest clearance that once a suitable stone had been found, the quarry site was quickly developed and its products distributed far and wide. Remarkably few rock outcrops, as opposed to the ubiquitous flints of the chalklands, satisfied the requirements for making stone tools, so there are only a handful of known prehistoric quarry sites. Graig Llwyd, on the flanks of Penmaenmawr Mountain in North Wales, and the Langdale Pikes in the Lake District were notable centres of production. Both were found to have rock outcrops that gave stone which could be cleft into fine cutting edges. That of Langdale is a volcanic tuff which can be easily recognized in hand specimens, so that a distribution map of finds can give a good indication of trade routes in existence about 3000 BC. The same is true of the igneous rocks of Graig Llwyd, which have been found in excavations as far away as Land's End and along the shores of the Solent. Because the quarry was so close to the coast it is possible that many of the axes from Graig Llwyd were carried by sea and not overland. The inland site of Great Langdale, by contrast, would mean that for at least part of the journey the distributive routes would be across upland areas. Most of the axeheads were only roughly hewn at the quarry site, for the altitude precluded permanent settlement. The slopes around the 'factory' are littered with chippings from the initial rough-hewing. It was the chance find of some forty axeheads by an archaeologist about fifty years ago that first drew attention to the Graig Llwyd site, and it was much the same story at Great Langdale, where a factory was found that must have been worked between about 3000 and 2600

BC. It must have been a similar chance find by some Neolithic wanderer that led to that initial discovery of a rock type that could be split to give fine cutting edges which was to play such an important role in the economy of prehistoric Britain. Although so much has been learned in recent years about the working sites, we are still very uncertain about the exact routes followed by the traders of the axeheads.

When we come to the succeeding Bronze Age, we have more tangible proofs of the use of upland routes as trade and communication links. Three areas in particular – Exmoor, the Kerry Hills of Central Wales and Rombalds Moor in the Pennines – have yielded evidence of a carefully planned and much used ridgeway route. In each case a plateau top is used to minimize changes of gradient, and it is clear that these early travellers had a fine sense for the form of the country. The Exmoor trackway begins in the west, close to the north Devon coast at Morte Point where it quickly makes for the flat-topped ridge at a height of just over 600ft. Beyond Mullacott Cross (the crossing point of the present main road linking Barnstaple and Ilfracombe) the prehistoric route strikes due east and rises to over 800ft on Berry Down. Further on, at Blackmoor Gate, present-day roads are left behind with the ridgeway now firmly along the line of the Exmoor watershed past Chapman's Barrow and Wood Barrow. From this point the route continues southwards as a grassy track, still along the ridge crest to Mole's Chamber: a most exhilarating walk with wide panoramic views for much of its length. Money raised from the appeal following the Lynmouth flood disaster of 1952 has been used to metal the next section of the original track as far as Sandyway Cross, so that although the motorist has benefited, the rambler lacks a soft cushion underfoot and cannot gaze unconcerned at distant

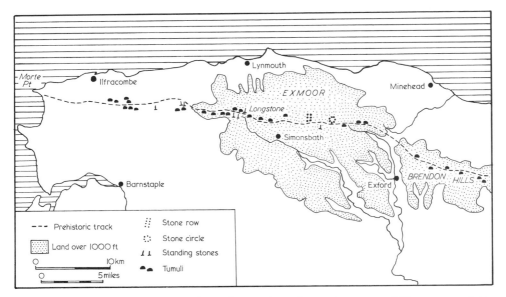

Fig 27 The prehistoric upland track running along the crest of Exmoor and the Brendon Hills

185

views. The height of the ridgeway now drops gradually as the eastern end of Exmoor is reached, and at Sandyway Cross it is below the 1,300ft contour. From here to Dulverton in the Barle valley the prehistoric track keeps to the ridge crest and is still followed by a minor road.

Wood Barrow must have been a major junction of this Bronze Age trackway, for here another prehistoric track led off to the east to Chains Barrow and, by keeping to the main watershed north of the Exe headwaters, ultimately reached Wheedon Cross. The ridgeway itself continues along the crest line of the Brendon Hills without ever dropping below the 1,000ft contour. C.B.Grundy, who forty years ago made a detailed study of the ancient highways of Devon and Somerset, referred to this route as the Brendon Hills Ridgeway and suggested that after dropping into the lowland at Lydeard St Lawrence it made for the Quantock Hills where it linked up with the equally fine ridgeway route on this sandstone massif.

How can we be certain that these ridgeway routes represent ancient features of the landscape going back for at least four thousand years? The dating of the early part of the Bronze Age rests largely on the tangible remains of this period which are strung out along its entire length. Apart from the ubiquitous burial chambers (tumuli), now often only low mounds or piles of disturbed stones, there are a number of standing stones (menhirs), stone circles and stone rows. Although the exact purpose of these monuments has long been the subject of speculation, there seems no doubt that they had a religious significance. The stone circles, like the one on Almsworthy Common, lie close to the ridgeway and seem to be a Bronze Age development of the earlier Neolithic henge monument. Many of the stones of Almsworthy have gone so that there are a number of possible interpretations of those that remain. Whatever the original form of the monument, it seems clear that it was carefully set out by Bronze Age man close to what was one of his major routes of the South-West Peninsula. Could the arrangement of the stones have an astronomical signficance, as first suggested by Sir Norman Lockyer? This theory has recently been revived by Professor Thom and others who imagine that these structures formed a gigantic visible seasonal calendar. Other stone circles are known to have existed, like the one on Mattock Down, mentioned by the seventeenth-century antiquary Tristram Risdon, who recalled a circle of stones, many bigger than the height of a man. All have now completely vanished, but they serve as a reminder of the fragmentary nature of the present archaeological evidence. Most seem to have been purposely removed by local farmers requiring gate posts or lintels. Isolated standing stones have fared better, and there are many lying on or close to the Exmoor trackway. The best is probably Longstone, standing on a saddle between Chapman's Barrow and Longstone Barrow. It is over 9ft high and consists of a wide slab of slaty stone, ideal as a track marker, though some believe that it might represent a memorial to a Bronze Age chieftain. Whatever the true explanation, it is clear that the Exmoor top was well known and used throughout the Bronze Age, certainly to a much greater extent than in the succeeding Iron Age when climatic conditions seem to have deteriorated.

The Welsh Borderlands also had their Bronze Age ridgeway routes, the most notable being that which ran along the crest of the Kerry Hills from the Severn valley near Newtown in the west towards Bishop's Castle in the east. It seems likely that the Kerry Hills section was only part of a much longer trade route which ran from the English Midlands across the full width of Central Wales to the shores of Cardigan Bay where there was contact with Ireland. The Kerry Hills track is remarkable for the way in which it keeps to the plateau top, seldom dropping below the 1,500ft contour in its western section. Known in Welsh as Yr Hen Fford (the old road), this remarkable track has survived the passage of centuries and today it is still possible to follow it by car for much of its length. Prior to the Enclosure Acts of the early nineteenth century, it must have been a broad green track used by drovers and others wishing to avoid the toll roads of the adjacent Clun valley.

Though Bronze Age monuments are less in evidence along the Kerry Hills track than on Exmoor, there is no doubt as to its age, for an astonishing number of flint implements, as well as large quantities of chippings, have been recovered from the fields alongside the road. With no natural flint deposits closer than the Marlborough Downs, over 80 miles away, the Kerry Hills must have been an important long-distance trade route, perhaps linking Wessex with Ireland. Alternatively the ridgeway could have been part of an east–west route running from the Grimes Graves flint mines in north Norfolk right across to the shores of Cardigan Bay. The finding of thousands of flint chippings in certain definite localities on the Kerry Hills implies working areas where the flint head could be finally shaped and trimmed. In turn this must have meant permanent settlement at times, using the more favoured south-facing slopes. After their initial use in the early Bronze Age, the Kerry Hills and adjacent Clee–Clun ridgeway routes took on other functions. The discovery of an igneous rock called picrite on the slopes of Corndon Hill not far away to the north added to the importance of the routes, for it was found that the picrite could be split and shaped like the Langdale Pikes material. Miss Lily Chitty, in a detailed study of the Clun ridgeway, has carefully plotted the distribution of the Bronze Age finds, and her map leaves no doubt as to the importance of the route over the centuries. The more southerly route left the Kerry Hills trackway at Croes y Sarnau and followed the main watershed separating the Clun and Teme valleys. The gradients on top were fairly easy, though at times the road had to climb to cross higher sections like Spoad Hill, Rock Hill and Black Hill before dropping down into the basin country around Clungunford. A journey along this ancient track can still be made by car through a countryside that is pleasant rather than dramatic.

Not all the early routes were of the ridgetop type, for in crossing dissected mountain country the way often led early man along valley floors to their head and then across low cols into the opposing valley. One such prehistoric route led from a small port at the mouth of the Afon Artro on the shores of Cardigan

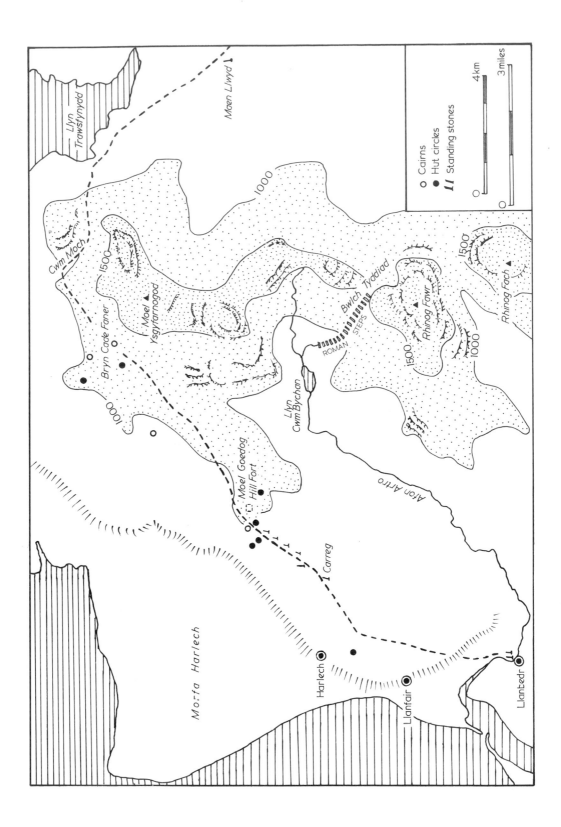

Llyn Trawsfynydd

Maen Llwyd

Cwm Moch

1000

1500

Moel Ysgyfarnogod

Bryn Cader Faner

1000

1500

Bwlch Tyddiad

STEPS

ROMAN

Rhinog Fawr

1500

1500

1000

Rhinog Fach

Llyn Cwm Bychan

Moel Goedog

Hill Fort

Carreg

Afon Artro

Morfa Harlech

Harlech

Llanfair

Llanbedr

4km

3miles

○ Cairns
● Hut circles
▲ Standing stones
11

Bay and then penetrated the rugged country of the Harlech Dome. This mountainous area, rising to almost 3,000ft in its twin peaks of Rhinog Fawr and Rhinog Fach, is still a wilderness of bare rock crags and boulder trains, and once off one of the few tracks, walking is extremely difficult, if not impossible. Physical conditions must have imposed severe limitations on routes available to travellers in such country, and any track forged is likely to have been the result of trial and error, taking care to avoid steep ascents, boggy hollows or unstable scree slopes. Once a route had been finally settled, it is likely to have remained in use over a long period of time because of the lack of a suitable alternative.

In the case of the Artro–Rhinog route, a whole series of standing stones have survived to mark the way. Although standing stones belong to several periods of history – many stone pillars were set up in the fifth to seventh centuries – there seems little doubt that those of the Harlech Dome date from prehistoric times. One of the most impressive lies at the seaward end of the route, close to the present village of Llanbedr and within a short distance of the sheltered waters of the Artro estuary. This magnificent Maen Hir is 11ft high with a broad base and a column of stone which gradually tapers towards the top. Its size and marshland situation, well away from any quarry, meant that considerable pains must have been taken with its transport and erection, and this points to a specific purpose such as the marking of the beginning of an important land route. From Llambedr the trackway made for the north-east by climbing on to the rolling plateau country behind Harlech in the general direction of Moel Goedog. A succession of standing stones mark the way, the survivors of a whole string which lined the route across the desolate countryside of rocky crags, small lakes and marshy hollows. Beyond Moel Goedog there are no further standing stones, but a number of small cairns and circles are now in evidence. After entering Cwm Moch the route passed over a high-level col and on towards the stores of Llyn Trawsfynydd. It was in Cwm Moch, in the early years of the nineteenth century, that a remarkable hoard of bronze spearheads was found under a stone. The isolated situation of the Cwm Moch hoard points to a trackway that was in use in the middle Bronze Age as a major trade route with Ireland. Although its ultimate destination in England is unknown, it is possible to trace the route further east into the Bala trough and thence across the Berwyns to reach the lowlands of Shropshire.

Another important trade link with Ireland used a route further south. Again a small harbour at the mouth of the Dysynni marked the starting point. The mountain trackway, known as the Fford Ddu, ran along the root of the Cader Idris escarpment and, as with the Rhinog route, there were marker stones at intervals along its length. Their exact age has never been determined, but there

Fig 28    The prehistoric route from the coast at Llanbedr around the northern edge of the Harlech Dome, together with a later route through the Bwlch Tyddiad, popularly known as the Roman Steps

47 A standing stone marking the route of the prehistoric track which winds its way around the northern end of the Rhinogs

is no doubt of their prehistoric origin. In 1832 a gold torque was found close to the trackway in the vicinity of Gilfachwydd farmhouse. A local farmer came across the torque half buried in the heather when out walking on the hillside below the Cadair ridge. It was subsequently sold for £50 once its significance was realized. As with similar torques found near Harlech in the late seventeenth century, the object is of a type associated with Tara in Ireland and dates from the period after 1000 BC. One can only speculate as to how it came to arrive in this situation, but it seems that it was either lost or hidden for safety while in transit. In either case it indicates that this sub-scarp track was in use as a major trade troute between Ireland and England in the middle Bronze Age. It is still possible to follow the way first navigated by prehistoric man, for a metalled road now runs from Dolgelly up to Llyn Gwernan and then on past lonely farmhouses, former *hafods* and ruined cottages. Ultimately the road has to drop back to the Mawddach, but the old trackway continues as a green way across country to reach the coast near Llwyngwril.

## The Romans

Although the Romans are rightly given credit for establishing the first comprehensive road network of the country, it is clear that in upland Britain at least they were often content to use and develop existing prehistoric tracks, especially if they had a strategic value. There were obvious advantages in the takeover of existing routes, for they provided a rudimentary communication system in the first century in advance of the Romans' own road-building programme. In upland areas the prehistoric trail was often the only practicable route and therefore had to become part of the Roman road network. A good example of a Roman takeover is in the Lake District where the prehistoric ridgeway known as High Street became a through route of the Romans linking the fort at Brougham in the Vale of Eden with the Cumberland coast at Ravenglass. In its High Street section it climbs to well over 2,000ft along the top of the fells for several miles before making the gradual descent down the western side of the Vale of Troutbeck to reach the fort at Ambleside. Before it acquired its present name of High Street the road was named Brethestrete (the road of the Britons), and it first appears in this form in a thirteenth-century document. Here we have a slight clue to its pre-Roman antiquity, when perhaps it formed part of the trade route used by the carriers of the Langdale axeheads. From Ambleside fort the Roman road continued through Little Langdale, but before it could reach the coast two formidable obstacles had to be crossed – the Wrynose and Hardknott passes. Both taxed the ingenuity of the Roman engineer, and in the case of the Hardknott it meant a steep, zigzag climb with gradients approaching 1 in 3. Even the modern road builder has to follow the example of his Roman predecessor in taking the road over the col at a height of 1,200ft. Dropping down the other side to a long spur, the road reaches Hardknott Fort, perhaps one of the most exciting of those built by the Romans, with its far-reaching views down the length of Eskdale. Although Hardknott could not have been a popular posting, the garrison had to be maintained even in winter because of the strategic importance of the fort on the through route to the coast. As with the High Street section, it seems likely that the Roman engineer followed the line of a much older track, possibly one used in carrying the roughly hewn axeheads from the working sites located on Langdale Pikes and around Scafell.

Some of the finest remaining sections of the Roman road system are found in upland areas, particularly where later centuries found only a limited use for them. Although it was customary for the Roman engineer to build his road on a slightly raised embankment or *agger*, local conditions often determined the method of construction. In the steep climb up the western face of the Pennines, for example the road was set in a deep hollow, and as this could often become an artificial stream channel it was found essential to provide a paved surface of slabs. Two of the Pennine roads are built on these lines. One, with the curious name of Doctor's Gate, linked the two Roman forts of Brough and Dinting

48    The Roman road over the Hardknott Pass *en route* to the coast at Ravenglass. The
Roman fort lies close to the road and on a relatively flat site near the end of the spur
looking down Eskdale (*Aerofilms*)

Vale. In this bleak, gritstone upland of heather and peat hags, the building and maintenance of a road to carry wheeled traffic was a major undertaking. From the east it climbs up a tributary valley of the Derwent close to the present Snake Pass and ultimately reaches the plateau top at a height of over 1,600ft. Even today the Snake Pass is often blocked by snow in winter and needs constant attention through the slipping of the unstable valley sides. It is therefore surprising that such an apparently difficult route should have been chosen across the northern part of the Peak District. Perhaps military needs dictated the forging of a link, however difficult the country to be crossed. Great slabs of gritstone had to be laid to form a reasonably stable foundation, with kerbs formed of stones set on end. The road was not entirely satisfactory and probably was abandoned when the Roman legions withdrew from these islands. This is perhaps the reason why such a good paved section has survived to the present day.

The other trans-Pennine road has even more impressive remains. Forged as a link between the fort at Manchester in the west and the Roman town of Aldborough in Yorkshire, the road ran for almost 50 miles. The steep western edge of the Pennines posed problems, but the road was made to cut a broad gash running directly up the hillside at Blackstone Edge. A pavement of stone blocks or setts about 15ft wide was used as a surface and bordering kerbs were added. In the centre there is a broad groove which until recently has been looked upon as the result of wearing by a brake attached to carts using the steep incline. An alternative view, which is now gaining support, is that the groove was purpose-built to carry turves which would allow horses to obtain a better footing both on ascent and descent. Once on the moorland top the centre groove disappears, which would be consistent with either explanation. Further east the paved surface gives way to a raised embankment of stones. Few roads of this age are better preserved than this Blackstone Edge section, and today it stands as a testimony to the skill of the Roman engineers working under adverse conditions which must have tested their ingenuity to the full.

Upland topography seldom acted as a deterrent to the Roman road builder, and routes which even today are considered impracticable were laid out as the need arose. A good example is provided by the road built to link the fort at Caerhun in the Conwy valley of Snowdonia with the town of Segontium, near the present-day Caernarfon. Advantage was taken of a high-level col at a height of 1,404ft in the northern hill ranges of the Carneddau. The ascent from the Conwy valley was gradual and used the relatively easy gradients of the Afon Tafolog. After crossing the col of Bwlch y Ddeufen the road is edged with large stones as it follows a twisting course down to the coastal plain at Aber. This direct route is obviously more difficult than the present coastal road (A55), but it must be remembered that the latter is only made possible by the tunnels under the headlands. Certainly in Roman times the inland route, with all its inherent difficulties, was the only possible link through the northern part of Snowdonia. With plenty of conscript labour available and a ready supply of stone, perhaps the task what not as formidable as it might appear. Nevertheless it is a route that the twentieth-century road engineer continues to shun, in spite of the pressing need to provide a good trunk road which would avoid bottlenecks like Conwy and Colwyn Bay. The Caerhun to Segontium road was built relatively early in the period of Roman occupation, for it was certainly in being by AD 121, as is clear from a milestone found near Rhiwiau which records the eighth mile out from the fort at Caerhun. Another milestone found nearby dates from AD 208, the time of a military reorganization in Wales when roads were being brought up to standard. Three other milestones have been found at various places en route to Segontium, a remarkable concentration for a single road considering that only 110 milestones are known for the whole of Roman Britain. Most of the milestones have been fashioned out of local rock, but those at Rhiwiau are unusual in that they are made from millstone grit, even though the nearest outcrop of this rock is over 40 miles away near Llangollen.

49  The largely overgrown paved way of the Roman road across the Pennines now known as Doctor's Gate

## Post-Roman Britain

The official ending of Roman government in Britian in the year AD 410 must have gone virtually unnoticed in many parts of the highlands. Life would have gone on much as before and established routes would have continued in use throughout the succeeding centuries. Maintenance would have been minimal, but it is evident that the Roman network survived in a recognizable form right down to perhaps the late ninth century when the parish boundaries were established. The well-defined roads made good estate boundaries too for the Saxon nobles, and also determined the siting of many Saxon villages, which today retain the *strat* element in their place name. Another Anglo-Saxon element in common use is *stan*, meaning stone, as in Stanford – a reference to the metalled road in existence when the settlement came into being. Anglo-Saxon charters which demarcate the boundaries of estates also make use of existing roads for reference. Indirect evidence of this nature leads to the conclusion that many of the Roman roads continued in use throughout the Saxon centuries, especially in upland areas where there was virtually no extension of the frontier of settlement. Saxon colonization occurred mainly in the lowlands, and it is only here that any additional roads would have been built in the period leading up to the Norman Conquest.

The brief interlude of Norse penetration into the uplands of the north and west probably led to new trackways coming into being as part of a general attack on woodland clearance and the creation of upland pastures. Without supporting documents it is impossible to be sure of the details, but the abundance of Old Norse place-name elements leaves no doubt as to its effectiveness. In the Lake District names like Tirril, meaning 'the shieling built of fir wood', or High Winder, 'the windswept shielding', tell us of this colonization of the uplands and hint at the creation of tracks. Even the mountainous interior was settled at this time as new farms were established in some of the most lonely and inaccessible valleys. The *thwaite* element which occurs repeatedly in the place names of Borrowdale – Rosthwaite, Stonethwaite and Thornythwaite, to mention only three – speaks of the clearing of woodland to make way for pastoral farming. Features on the surrounding uplands and peaks were also given Norse names, so it is clear that these formerly neglected areas were being colonized. Most of the well-used fell tracks in the Lake District probably date from the brief period of Norse penetration. No clearly defined Norse settlement has been excavated, but collections of long houses found above the 1,000ft contour are possible sites. One on the limestone slopes above Kingdale in the western Pennines is known as Braida Garth and includes a hut 50ft long with walls 2ft thick built of the local limestone. Until a proper archaeological examination has been made we cannot be sure whether Braida Garth is a Norse hut or a later medieval long-house farm complex. Either is possible, because between about AD 1000 and 1250 there was a distinct amelioration of the upland climate which might

195

encourage settlement at heights well above the 1,000ft contour.

This utilization of upland fell pastures for sheep grazing was to reach full maturity in later centuries under the influence of the monasteries, especially in the Lake District and Pennines. In the central Pennines, Fountains Abbey acquired thousands of acres of upland pasture and even had land holdings as far away as Borrowdale in the Lake District. Sheep grazing areas were eagerly sought in the Middle Ages as wool became a highly valued commodity both for use in the home cloth industry and for export to Europe. Some idea of the vast scale of the monastic enterprise can be gathered from the fact that, in the Craven Uplands alone, Fountains Abbey held over a million acres by grant or lease. So vast was the area under their control that the monks established outlying granges which functioned as local centres for sheep rearing and the clipping of the wool. The gathering together of the huge bales of wool at the parent abbey or occasionally for direct shipment abroad meant that a transport system and network of routes had to be established. Pack-horse trains were the

50 Capon Hall, nestling at the foot of Fountains Fell, was one of several farms in this part of the Pennines which formerly served as shepherds' lodges to Fountains Abbey

most favoured and indeed the only practical method of carrying goods across the vast upland areas. It was usual to organize the train to consist of twenty to forty animals each carrying about 2½cwt in panniers. Many of the ponies were of the hunter (*jaeger*) type imported from Germany, and it is not surprising that the name is remembered in designations like Jagger Lane and Jagger Hill. In carrying the wool and other products of the monastic farm, the trains usually took the most direct route that was practicable and soon the pack-horse trails became very much a feature of the upland landscape. Apart from exceptionally steep slopes, gradients were not a problem, so the route made few detours to avoid obstacles. One former pack-horse route, now part of the Pennine Way, climbed over the summit of Pen y Ghent at a height of 2,271ft.

On the flat plateau surfaces of the limestone Pennines, the monastic trails ran across country for long distances almost on the level. One of the best-known of the surviving trails is Mastiles Lane, which led from the monastic pastures on Fountains Fell near Malham Tarn due east in the direction of the parent abbey. It crosses the bare plateau top at about the 1,250ft contour and for part of its length on Malham Moor it is still a wide 'green road' set between walls. Further west the road has been metalled as it makes its way down to the crossing of the upper Ribble valley. En route it passes the farm known as Capon Hall, first mentioned as early as 1206 when the Countess of Warwick gave the land round about to Fountains Abbey. In its early form the name was Copmanhowe, possibly derived from the Scandinavian form of *ceapman* or trader, so that in the present farm we could have the site of the original Norse settlement. When Fountains Abbey took over the area, the farm became one of their shepherds' lodges. Another former lodge, West Side House, lies a mile further along the track, now known as Henside Road. At this point a monastic pack-horse trail ran northward along the top of Ravenscar Edge. This part still remains as a green road to Dale Head Farm. Just before the farm is reached the road junction shows the base of a cross, mentioned as Ulfkil Cross in the early charters. Dale Head Farm was an important staging post for the pack-horse trains and once had a range of stables to accommodate the ponies who made repeated crossings of Fountains Fell and Malham Moor.

Apart from the green roads which came into being during the full blossoming of the monastic wool trade there were other tracks in the uplands which developed as connecting links between the growing market towns. In this same part of the Pennines, centres like Skipton, Settle and Sedbergh held frequent markets by the fourteenth century, and numerous primitive roads converged on them. The present attractive road through Kingsdale connecting Dent and Ingleton first came into being as a tenuous link between these once important market towns. Dent with its attractive curved streets, still with a cobbled surface, and surely the most unspoiled of the Craven market centres, was formerly much more important than its sleepy state today would indicate. From the town there was an important route around the northern shoulder of Whernside where it is still clearly seen as a distinct terrace at a height of 1,700ft.

197

The grassy track, once known as the Old Craven Way, forms an excellent walk, wending its way between a succession of shake or swallow holes where streams from the upper slope disappear underground once the limestone beds are reached. There are old coal pits with their bell-shaped openings where coal was once won from a succession of rather thin seams. Small-scale mining for coal took place from medieval times onwards and continued well into the nineteenth century. Tracks like the Old Craven Way provided a ready-made transport network, allowing the miner to carry off the coal by pack-horse to nearby towns and lime-burning kilns. Until the railways brought in cheaper and better coal from afar, the bell pits of Whernside and Fountains Fell played a very important role in the economy of the area and undoubtedly helped to preserve many upland tracks that would otherwise have been abandoned and lost. With the nineteenth-century enclosures leading to the building of hundreds of miles of loose stone walling, the former pack-horse trails became fossilized in the landscape and have survived in this form for the pleasure of the present-day walker.

Much of the Craven Uplands and the vast moorland tracts further north have survived as a relict landscape of the past untouched by the industrial explosion which occurred in the adjacent lowlands. South of the Stainmore Gap there is a great expanse of untenanted country developed largely on a thick cover of glacial drift. Occasionally harder beds of the underlying Millstone Grit break through to the surface and sometimes, as around Tan Hill, they contain thin coal seams. Although only a few feet thick the coal has been worked since the thirteenth century and from this isolated spot pack-horse trains radiated in all directions. One running off to the south-west is still known as the Jagger Road and at Ravenser the original pack-horse bridge can still be seen alongside the farm. On difficult sections the trail is paved with local slabs from the Millstone Grit formation. There were also routes leading to Brough and Kirkby Stephen, while another followed the Sleightholme valley to Bowes. With so many routes radiating out from Tan Hill it is perhaps inevitable that an inn should have been built at the crossroads. At a height of 1,758ft it lays claim to be one of the highest inn sites in the country. Over the centuries Tan Hill has played host to a wide variety of visitors, including the pack-horse driver and his assistant, the local collier, the merchant traveller, huntsman, cattle drover and others. It was a favoured resting place for the Scottish drover making the long journey from the 'tryst', as the cattle fair at Falkirk was known, down the backbone of the Pennines to Malham Moor in time for the great October fair.

### The drovers' ways

When the monastic influence on upland farming began to peter out following the dissolution of the monasteries in 1536, many upland routes were threatened with abandonment, as the need for a transport network was severely curtailed. Many survived, however, either as stony mountain tracks or delightful green

51 The inn sign at Farmers in mid-Wales, once a favourite stopping place of the drovers

ways with lush turf underfoot, because other uses were found for them. As the demand for fresh meat grew in the developing towns of the country, so cattle became as prized a commodity as sheep. The upland pastures were sought out as breeding and grazing grounds even though they suffered from relative isolation and distance from their main markets. To overcome this handicap, great cattle herds were assembled and then driven across country, often for hundreds of miles. Even areas as remote as the Highlands of Scotland became suppliers of beef cattle and towns like Falkirk had their great sales gatherings prior to the long overland journey, perhaps to the fattening pastures of the Midlands and southern England and ultimately the Smithfield Market in London. All the uplands of Britain participated in the cattle-droving traffic, but it is in areas like Central Wales, Scotland and the central Pennines that it has made its greatest impact on the present landscape. Malham Moor, for example, was a great gathering ground for the drovers, and each autumn a vast fair was held in the huge field known as Great Close, east of the tarn. At its height, Malham Fair could attract perhaps twenty thousand head of cattle, all assembled in the 700-acre field. The cattle came from Scotland, the Lake District and the northern Pennines, with drovers in charge of herds of up to two

199

hundred animals using the old monastic sheep and wool trails. The cattle fair on Malham Moor was a great annual event for both the participants and local people and, not surprisingly, there was an alehouse at the foot of Great Close Scar. On their way to fairs like that on Malham Moor the drovers could only hope to cover about 10 miles a day and would be content to sleep rough in the open. Occasionally a night's lodging would be sought at an inn like Gearstones near Ribble Head with its patchwork of small enclosures to prevent the cattle straying overnight.

It is to Wales that we must turn for the most recent, authoritative account of the cattle drovers and the routes used by them. Forty years ago a schoolteacher, P.G.Hughes, produced a slim, readable book on Wales and its drovers, and until recently this has remained the most useful account. In 1976 Richard Colyer assembled a vast amount of material relating to the Welsh cattle trade, and two years later the same subject attracted two enthusiasts, Fay Godwin and Shirley Toulson, who followed and wrote about the former roads of the drovers across the uplands of Wales. The life led by the drovers and the hardships they encountered as they made their way towards the English fattening pastures and markets make fascinating reading. Only when the railways entered the scene in the latter part of the nineteenth century was there a real threat to their livelihood, and even then the droving trade carried on into the present century. The cross-country routes forged over the years can still be recognized, and occasionally, in an inn name like the Drover's Arms, we have a more tangible reminder of this once flourishing trade. Figures for the number of cattle moved are difficult to obtain, though Dr Colyer mentions that three thousand cattle were made to swim the Menai Strait from Anglesey each year in the seventeenth century. A hundred years later some thirty thousand cattle were passing through mid-Wales to the Hereford market each year. The drover was well rewarded for his effort and even in 1830 could earn 2s a day.

The routes he chose to follow had been mapped out across the uplands over the centuries. Many were original prehistoric tracks which had managed to remain in use. It was essential to deliver the cattle as quickly as possible and therefore the most direct rather than the easiest route was deliberately chosen. This often meant climbing to well over 2,000ft but, provided a reasonable track was available and grazing grounds at hand, mere height did not prove too great an obstacle. The cattle were assembled from the farms at specific collecting points, usually small market towns. Tregaron in west Wales became a famous centre and when the droving traffic was at its height there were no fewer than twenty inns to cater for those about to embark on the long journey across the tops to England. There were inns or cider houses en route, and local farmers advertised accommodation by the curious practice of planting three Scots pines near the house. These not only told the drover that he was welcome, but in murky weather were often useful as a marker. Pastures were provided in the fields around – often known as halfpenny fields, for this was the standard charge per beast for grazing rights. There were also smithies for shoeing the

200

52 The former inn of Gearstones near Ribble Head, a resting place for the drovers as they crossed the Pennines *en route* for the great autumn fair on Malham Moor

cattle, the shoes consisting of twin arcs of iron designed to fit the cloven hoofs.

Many of the former drovers' ways have left a permanent mark on the contemporary landscape, either as rough upland tracks, wide green roads or even metalled country lanes. One such route that can be followed by car provides both an exciting journey into the past and a scenic drive across an unpopulated area of Central Wales long known as the 'Welsh Desert'. The starting point is the Talbot Inn in Tregaron, where formerly the great herds of cattle were assembled in the fields behind. The road leaves the town near the church and follows the valley slopes of the Afon Berwyn to make height. Once the valley head is reached near Diffwys Farm the route now crosses the rolling landscape of the Central Wales plateau with its vast new plantations of conifers. After dropping down into the valley which feeds the Brianne reservoir there is a further steep climb over a col at 1,400ft into the Cloddiad valley, which then leads down to Abergwesyn. At the Grouse Inn the present road follows the twisting valley floor, but the original drovers' route took a more direct course by making straight up the hillside to the summit cairn. From this viewpoint there is a steady descent down a long spur to Beulah. Many drovers had to deliver the animals in their charge to Hereford market, and this amounted to a week's work. Tregaron was left at midnight on Sunday – no droving was allowed on the Sabbath – and by taking only limited rests they could deliver the herd by Wednesday and then be back home by Friday evening.

In Scotland the pattern was rather different because of the much greater distances to be covered. Nevertheless the trade began early and in the seventeenth century cattle were being brought from the island of Lewis in the Outer Hebrides across the Minch to the mainland. They were then driven along valleys and through passes until they finally arrived at the cattle sales at places like Falkirk or Crieff. Falkirk in particular became a great trading fair and routes converged on it from all parts of the compass. Long overland routes were possible because the animals could obtain free grazing on the way and therefore transport costs were kept to a minimum. It was Adam Smith in his *Wealth of Nations* who wrote that 'live cattle are, perhaps, the only commodities of which transport is more expensive by sea than by land. By land they carry themselves to market'.

Although valley routes, especially from the west coast, were favoured, high-level passes were occasionally pressed into service if they shortened the journey. The outstanding example is the Lairig Ghru, the great north–south trench cut deep into the 4,000ft Cairngorm plateau. Even today it is still the only practicable route through the mountains and is favoured by walkers as a testing 25-mile hike to Braemar. Anyone picking his way carefully across the Rothiemurchus Forest in the north and then on through the narrow defile towards the summit col must wonder how drovers managed animals in their charge on such a difficult route. In spite of the problems involved and the sheer physical hardships to be endured, the Lairig Ghru continued to be used until 1873 as a main drovers' trail. Each spring men from the Rothiemurchus district were sent up into the Cairngorms to clear the tracks of fallen boulders brought down by the snow and frost of the winter months. It was only with the coming of the Highland Railway northwards to Inverness that the droving trade began to decline and finally petered out altogether.

Away to the west lay another of Scotland's great trackless deserts, the Monadhliath Mountains, which even by Highland standards are still a wilderness of nature, with no road crossing them and few penetrating the periphery for more than a few miles. The mountain mass, however, lay across the direct route from Skye to Crieff and therefore could not be avoided by the drovers. Fortunately, General Wade in 1731 had planned and built a road to connect Fort Augustus and Dalwhinnie. Because of the difficult terrain Wade was forced to make use of the Corrieyairack Pass, but even this entailed a difficult climb up to a summit height of 2,507ft. Although planned for military needs, the road proved ideal for the drovers, and they continued to use the route right up to the end of the nineteenth century, long after it had been left in a state of disrepair. Like the Lairig Ghru, this former drovers' track still makes an excellent long-distance walk through one of the loneliest parts of Britain. A sense of isolation is everywhere apparent, and it is difficult now to appreciate the past military circumstances which dictated the building of the original road.

## The modernization of communications

The Wade roads of Scotland, amounting to about 250 miles in total and dating from the period between 1724 and 1740, emphasized the value of a good communication network, not only to serve military needs but also as a means of quicker travel and promotion of trade. In England and Wales the creation of turnpike trusts by Act of Parliament had been taking place since the beginning of the eighteenth century, and by 1750 had reached the proportions of a 'road

53 Telford's Holyhead road (the present A5) as it climbs the side of the Nant Ffrancon valley near Ogwen Cottage. The old road which it replaced lies below the great retaining wall built by Telford

mania'. Most of the progress was in lowland areas and aimed at improving coach travel and the carrying of goods between the main urban centres. It was only in the latter half of the century that the upland areas came under scrutiny. In Snowdonia, for example, the route between Corwen and Llanwrwst in the Conwy valley was turnpiked in 1777, but it was 1802 before a through route via Capel Curig to Bangor came into being. It was Thomas Telford, more than any other engineer, who improved roads through mountainous areas and made them suitable for rapid coach travel. His achievements span the length of Britain but it is perhaps in North Wales, in his Holyhead road with its fine bridge across the Menai Strait, that we see the culmination of his efforts. He was first called in by Henry Parnell after the Irish Members of Parliament had pressed for the improvement of road links with their country. Telford suggested that the number of existing turnpike trusts should be drastically reduced and money spent on improving gradients, drainage and the actual surface. After being given £15,000 in 1815 he immediately set to work and for the first time an adequate foundation of large stone capped with smaller rubble was constructed. A pronounced camber and drainage lessened damage by heavy rain or winter snowmelt. Large sections of the original turnpike through the mountain areas were reconstructed, often leading to a reduction in the gradient to less than 1 in 20, a figure Telford thought necessary in the interests of speedy coach traffic. In order to climb the 300ft step at the head of the Nant Ffrancon he started the ascent 2 miles lower down and cut his road into the hillside as a gradual incline. Similarly the twisting climb out of the Conwy valley at Bettws y Coed with a more evenly graded road. Even after 150 years of continuous use Telford's Holyhead road remains as a living memorial to his skill as an engineer. His iron milestones, the walled lay-bys that housed the stone to repair the road, the embankments across marshy ground and the buttressed sections cut into steep valley slopes have all survived. Even though the road climbs to over 1,000ft in places, it is still a fast route because of the finely engineered gradients on which Telford was so insistent.

Telford's contribution to the building of an adequate road network for the country, coming as it did at the beginning of the nineteenth century, followed his period of great activity as a canal engineer. The main phase of canal building had passed its peak by 1800 after a decade in which artificial waterways had sprung up in every part of Britain. Upland areas were, for the most part, excluded because of the unsuitable terrain and the cost of building tunnels or great flights of locks to surmount major topographic obstacles. There were instances of canal building even in upland regions and in this connection the unique High Peak Railway provides an interesting commentary on the way in which engineers tackled the problem. The railway link was designed to connect two canal sections lying on opposite sides of the Peak District, one at Cromford in the east and the other at Whaley Bridge in the west. Between the two canal termini the land rose to over 1,200ft in the core of the Peak District, so a canal route across the top was clearly impracticable. Railways in the 1820s were still in their infancy and largely untried in hilly districts. The High Peak Railway, as it became known, was therefore built to principles which had been developed in the canal age. Inclines were used to climb on to the plateau top, and once there the railway kept to a constant level save for one intermediate incline. On reaching the western side there were further inclines for the descent. The whole concept was very much in the thinking of the canal era; the only thing that was absent was an actual high-level waterway. On the level stretches horses pulled waggons along a metalled track following the contours of the countryside. The inclines, corresponding to the lock systems, were served by a stationary engine which hauled the trucks up by a wire rope. One of these engines has recently been restored at the top of the Middleton incline just west of Wirksworth and is now maintained in working order as a tourist attraction.

The engineer responsible for the High Peak Railway was Josiah Jessop, the son of the builder of the Cromford Canal. Close to the highest point on the route there is a fine memorial plaque to Jessop on the bridge where the Ashbourne to Buxton road crosses the former track. Work on the railway was begun shortly after the necessary Act of Parliament had been passed, and after its completion many lime and stone quarries were opened up along its length to take advantage of the transport facilities offered. By 1841 the original horse-drawn trucks had been replaced by steam traction and in 1855 the operating company was given permission to carry passengers. Any journey on the High Peak Railway must have been either a tiresome or an exhilarating experience, depending on the attitude of and the time available to the passenger. Because the line functioned primarily to carry goods traffic and only one passenger carriage was included on each train, the journey was extremely slow: it took a day to travel the length of the line, a mere 30 miles. On a fine day the leisurely amble through the Peak District provided excellent views of the plateau landscape. With frequent stops, especially at the inclines, passengers could disembark, along with the driver, and retreat to the local inn. There were frequent breakdowns, and this could mean hours of waiting while a relief engine was found. For over seventy years the line provided the only cross-country link in the Peak District, but after 1892, when the western section was abandoned, it was mainly used to carry stone from the numerous limestone quarries around Wirksworth and Middleton. In this attenuated form the High Peak Railway continued to function right up to the 1950s. Fortunately its closure came at a time when the Peak National Park Authority was creating walks and the former track was soon turned into a long-distance trail.

In the early years of the nineteenth century, a mere decade could see radical changes in railway engineering concepts. Whereas the High Peak Railway of 1820 was cast very much in the mould of the canal era, the Stephenson rail projects in upland areas were to a very different design. The first real challenge came with the building of the main west-coast route into Scotland. Robert Stephenson favoured a coastal route through Cumberland, thus avoiding the long haul through the high ground of the eastern part of the Lake District.

Another suggestion was a route up Long Sleddale and then a long tunnel to reach the Haweswater valley and ultimately the Vale of Eden. Both these suggestions met with opposition, and the final choice of route favoured a line across Shap Fell. This involved a climb to almost 1,000ft at Shap summit, and could only be achieved by building the line with a steady gradient from Tebay. Even then it was necessary to use banking engines to haul both passenger and goods trains over this section of the route. Diesel and electric locomotion has ended all this, so that today the railway cottages at Tebay, where the banking engine drivers were stationed, have a forlorn appearance.

Of all the lines that have had to meet the challenge of an upland route, it is the Settle to Carlisle Railway which can claim the most exciting history of construction and operation. It was the last of the main-line railways to be built, and during the six years it took to construct there was a succession of disasters and costly failures. Dandy Mire, a desolate spot on the western side of the Pennines, proved difficult to cross, and various solutions were tried. Initially an embankment was proposed, but after a quarter of a million tons of stone had virtually sunk into the bog the idea was abandoned in favour of a long viaduct of twelve arches. This ultimately proved successful, though not before considerable efforts had been made to find satisfactory foundations for the brick piers. The railway was the last to use gangs of navvies who lived in shanty towns on the moor as the work went forward. Even the normally resilient navvies found the winter conditions difficult to endure, and over half the labour force left each year in December even though they could earn up to 10s a day. While the wages were good there was plenty of money to be spent on drink in the nearby towns, the only antidote they knew to the bleak conditions under which they had to work. The most formidable difficulty lay in driving a long tunnel under Blea Moor. Its total length was almost $1\frac{1}{2}$ miles and it took four years to build. Working in the damp and dark, with only candles to light the way, the navvies removed thousands of tons of rock by hand. Inevitably, many did not survive the experience, so that perhaps the most telling memorial to their efforts is not the tunnel nor the great brick viaducts which grace the line, but rather the scores of gravestones in Chapel-le-Dale churchyard of those who died at work.

The Settle to Carlisle route was finally opened in 1876, giving the Midland Railway its much-needed line into Scotland. Compared with the east- and west-coast routes of rival companies it could hardly be considered as a serious rival for in climbing the 'long drag' up to the summit of Ais Gill (1,169ft) – the highest point reached by a main line in England, though not in Scotland – there was an inevitable loss of time. Perhaps the most surprising thing is that the line has survived to the present day, and although the Thames–Clyde express is no longer on the timetable, there are still through trains from Nottingham to

(*Opposite*)

54   A tunnel on the High Peak Railway as it passes under the main Buxton to Ashbourne road. The plaque on the stone facing records the efforts of its engineer, Josiah Jessop

55   The long viaduct on the Settle to Carlisle Railway near Ribble Head, with Great Whernside in the background

Glasgow. In spite of the slow journey times compared with the electrified route over Shap, it provides one of the most scenically attractive upland routes in the country. On a clear winter's day the bare expanses of moor under a blanket of snow, with great tabular hills like Pen y Ghent or Whernside rising above it, provide unforgettable views. Further along the line there is a brief enticing glimpse down Dentdale after the train has emerged from Blea Moor tunnel. Although the Victorian shareholders who raised the capital to build the 72 miles of line at a cost of £3½ million never saw an adequate return on their money, they undoubtedly created the most exciting stretch of main-line railway in England.

The Victorian interest in rail travel, which offered a very quick though not cheap method of moving around the country, was a major reason for an astonishing growth in tourism in the latter half of the nineteenth century. Tours of the Highlands of Scotland or the mountains of North Wales became almost commonplace as the search went on to discover the most remote parts of the kingdom. It was not long before there was a clamour for railways to scale the mountain peaks as they had already done in the Alps and Rockies. Following the success of the railway up the Rigi in 1871, attention was focused on a similar mountain line to the summit of Snowdon. In 1872 a Bill was promoted in Parliament for a railway from Llanberis to the top of Snowdon, but the owner of the Vaynol estate – Assheton-Smith – on whose land the railway would be built was implacably opposed and so that matter was dropped. It took a generation of persuasion to make him change his views, but he finally relented in 1894, and it was not long before work was begun on the railway. The initial opposition meant that Snowdon could not claim priority in the opening of a mountain railway, an honour that went to a similar line up Snaefell in the Isle of Man. This was one of three mountain lines considered in the 1870s; the others were on Skiddaw in the Lake District and Ben Lomond in Scotland. Schemes for the latter never materialized and so it was left for Snaefell to boast the first mountain railway, opening in August 1895, just a few months before that on Snowdon. With a height of only 2,100ft and a rather unspectacular climb to the summit of what is a dull mountain, the Snaefell project cannot claim to be a serious scenic rival to that up Snowdon, where the line hugs the Clogwyn edge with its fine views on either side. Both railways operate in the summer months only, but in spite of this limited season they have shown a steady increase in traffic over the years. The type of summer obviously plays a great part in determining the total number willing to pay for a ride to the summit. On a fine summer's day something like 2,500 visitors will arrive on the top by train, with perhaps 100,000 passengers in a year. As there are something like 300,000 other people who each year walk to the summit, there are now immense problems of conservation and management to be faced by the National Park Authority.

Privately owned mountain railways were very much the product of the Victorian period and, as far as Britain is concerned, are unlikely to be repeated. The growth of winter sports now offers another way for the ordinary visitor to reach the mountain tops – by chair lifts such as those now found on the Cairngorms. The building of new roads to open up remote areas is a much more likely development in the future and already in recent years some high-level roads have been built. The continued decline of the rural population in Scotland, especially in remote areas, prompted the building of the Applecross road, and because of the delightful scenery it passes through it has also become a valuable tourist asset. With a circular route from Loch Kishorn to Shieldaig completed, the problem now is one of controlling the traffic using the road in the summer. In its most impressive section it climbs up from Loch Kishorn to over 2,000ft in a few miles, past former shielings long since abandoned as the people left the area. It is by no means clear whether the new road will arrest the population decline, but it certainly will attract holidaymakers to what was once a remote west-coast peninsula.

The policy of the Forestry Commission to open up areas by dirt tracks for

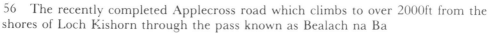

56    The recently completed Applecross road which climbs to over 2000ft from the
shores of Loch Kishorn through the pass known as Bealach na Ba

access to its plantations could also have sinister repercussions, for it is but a
short step from there to allowing public access by car, and thence to the
clamour for metalled highways. While the motorist undoubtedly gains by such
changes, it is inevitably at the expense of those seeking absolute solitude, a
commodity that is becoming ever more scarce in upland Britain.

# Epilogue:
## Past, Present and Future

It is a curious, yet perfectly explicable, anomaly that in a country which feels the full effect of population pressure, most of our upland areas are suffering from under-population. Whether it stems from the events of the distant past, as is the case in the Scottish Highlands, or from a slow but continuous drift towards the lowlands which is still going on today, the end result is the same. Many parts of the country above the 800ft contour now no longer have enough people to maintain an acceptable social structure. The first thing to suffer is rural transport, with bus services gradually becoming more fragmentary until they reach the point of extinction. Long before this ultimate state is reached, the younger and more active members of the community have found their own transport to give them the necessary flexibility for travel to work. Older people are left stranded, and in an ageing population structure even the problem of obtaining basic necessities can become acute. The days of the travelling grocer, butcher or baker have long since passed, and it is only council-maintained services like mobile libraries that go the rounds of the isolated upland communities.

Little-used bus services are clearly uneconomic, and even where subsidized by local authorities they are fighting a losing battle against the tide of events. It was an attempt to grapple with this problem and provide a more viable alternative that led in 1967 to the experiment of using post buses to carry passengers to and from isolated hamlets. There are, inevitably, advantages and disadvantages to post-bus operation. Although a circuitous route has often to be adopted to deliver the mail, some degree of regularity is assured. The provision of small units, perhaps carrying twelve passengers in a minibus or only four in an estate car, driven by the regular postman, is clearly more cost-effective than using a large bus with its own driver, though the loss of the latter inevitably means greater unemployment. The minibus or estate car means that upland tracks can be used, and as most of these have been metalled during the past twenty-five years they provide more than adequate arteries of communication. The initial experiment of 1967 covered four services, one in the

211

57 The post bus at Scourie – a method of rural transport which has become increasingly popular in the Highlands of Scotland in recent years

Lake District, one in Devon, one in Central Wales and one in Scotland. The choice of the Lake District route is interesting, for it lay between Penrith and the remote eastern valley of Martindale, where no transport had previously been available and farms were being abandoned. After the Post Office became an independent organization in 1972, the post-bus service was expanded, especially in the Highlands and islands of Scotland where it has proved its worth. Scotland now handles three-quarters of the total number of services; dying communities are being revitalized, and there is some hope of arresting the steady decline which has been going on for decades.

The provision of a rudimentary rural service has gone hand in hand with road improvement; this in turn has helped local employment prospects, while at the same time allowing young people with their own transport to travel further afield in search of employment. Whether in the long term it will have the desired effect of keeping young people in the remoter upland areas remains to be seen. At present, where population decline has been halted it often results from lowland emigrés seeking solitude and an escape from the pressures of an over-organized society. For them there is a willingness and indeed a desire to accept the challenge of 'primitive living', without a piped water supply or even electricity in extreme cases. Subsistence farming, based on a limited number of crops and an occasional animal, is looked upon as being a fulfilling way of life, though the deep-freeze is there as back-up should things go wrong.

The penetration of electricity supply into remote upland areas has been one of the great advances seen in recent decades, so that the most isolated hamlet is now within its compass. Even lonely farms which cannot justify the expense of a public supply have installed small oil-engine generators, while the ubiquitous calor gas has proved invaluable for heating and cooking once there is adequate road access. Contact with the outside world has been improved by television, especially since small booster relay stations allow reception in well over 95 per cent of the country.

What the future holds, in view of diminishing energy supplies and the increased cost of remoteness, is problematical. Wind power might provide an answer in view of the high average wind speeds experienced in upland areas (see Chapter 2). A well-designed wind-powered generator – one that can withstand severe gales as well as functioning at moderate wind speeds – has still to be developed, and seems a long way off. And yet, as more than one eminent scientist has pointed out, wind provides a much more realistic natural source of power than either solar or tidal energy for the country as a whole. For the uplands it would seem the only possible solution to an ever-deepening problem.

The resources of our uplands, though seemingly limited at present and making only a small contribution to the total wealth of the country, are likely to assume a much greater importance in the future, especially in less quantifiable aspects like recreation. There was a short period in the eighteenth and nineteenth centuries when the mineral wealth – principally copper, lead and exotic products like wolfram, manganese and tungsten – brought a short-lived period of prosperity to certain parts. Once the more accessible deposits had been worked out, the sites were abandoned and left to decay so that it is only now, perhaps a hundred years later, that the scars are being healed. Fortunately future investment is not likely to be in similar robber industries but rather in more lasting assets like forestry, water resources, tourism and a more specialized upland farming. The problem here lies not in the nature of these activities, all of which have a valuable role to play in an upland economy, but rather in their competing interests. In a leisure-conscious age, tourism offers the greatest prospects while at the same time presenting the greatest challenge. Private and government-aided investment has led to hotel improvements and the provision of more accommodation in areas like the Lake District, Snowdonia and the North-West Highlands. Motels have proved most popular of new buildings as they provide the ideal solution for the car tourist. Unfortunately, along with ordinary hotels, they have an intense seasonal peak-booking period in July and August, while the demand can slump to zero during the winter months save in favoured winter resort areas like Aviemore and Glenshee in Scotland. Marked seasonality means correspondingly high charges for accommodation during peak periods. More serious is the fact that tourism provides only limited employment opportunities for local people, often at a time when they would prefer to be working on their own smallholdings.

Seasonality is a problem which also affects the road investment programme. Narrow roads, perfectly adequate for local traffic for nine-tenths of the year, can become a nightmare when crowded with visitors during July and August. The impact of thousands of cars pouring into the Lake District on a summer's day or speeding along the single-track roads of the Highlands can be disturbing for the local community. In some areas the extreme solution of total banning has had to be introduced, but this has only been done where an alternative method of transport can be provided. Far-sighted National Park Authorities have in recent years encouraged the provision of minibus routes along some of the more popular and crowded stretches. Routes pioneered in recent years for climbers and walkers include one to the head of the Llanberis valley in Snowdonia, the 'Mountain Goat' service over the Kirkstone Pass and the 'Wasdale Flyer' to Wasdale Head, both in the Lake District, and the Goyt valley scheme in the Peak District. Although in their infancy, minibus routes seem destined to become part of the upland scene in that they give access to the less popular and less crowded parts for the ordinary walker, while helping to lessen pressure on the narrow roads. To ensure success, restriction on private car use seems essential, for if the motorist is given the choice he will naturally prefer his own independent means of transport. Some careful thought and planning by the National Park Authorities, who largely determine the way we now use most of our upland areas, seem necessary to evolve a sensible and rational approach to a problem which will grow during the next decade.

The minibus transport revolution in the form of a post bus or privately sponsored service has lessened, though not solved, the difficulties of the non-car-owner in rural areas. One scheme aimed at benefiting both the local community and the tourist has been attempted in the western Pennines. The fine scenic route of the Settle to Carlisle Railway – the last major railway line to be built in this country – had long been losing money in operating a passenger service and had only survived with the aid of subsidies from the taxpayer. Small stations, once the only link with the outside world, were allowed to close so that the line became only a through route to Scotland and did little for the areas through which it passed. In May 1975 five stations on the line were reopened as part of an integrated road–rail amenity scheme connecting the small market towns of Hawes and Sedbergh. Chartered trains were organized to allow shoppers from the countryside around to visit towns on a Saturday, with buses arranged to connect with the train services. Walkers and climbers in the towns were encouraged to use the same service, though in the opposite direction. The Dales Rail attracted enough support to make the service viable for its initial season, and gave the hope that it could become a permanent part of the life of the isolated communities in this corner of the Pennines.

A potential source of conflict between the varying needs of the community

214

has arisen with the great expansion of forestry in upland areas of Britain. Compared with Europe as a whole, Britain is at the bottom of the forestry league with only 9 per cent of its total area under trees. The vast untenanted acres of huge sheep runs and more particularly deer 'forests' in Scotland provide an outstanding example of the under-utilization of upland resources. The Forestry Commission, since its birth in 1921, has pursued a vigorous policy of planting as much land as purchase would allow, but increasingly in recent years it has found opposition to its proposals and an inability to obtain suitable land. In 1978 forestry plantings were down to only 7,000 hectares (17,000 acres), only about a third of the average of recent decades. Opposition from local farmers, absentee landowners, amenity bodies and countryside users in general has been considerable and well orchestrated, partly because of past sins of the Commission. The regimented plantings of conifers in pre-war years and the lack of accessibility to planted areas because of fire risks did not endear the Commission to the general public, while the sheep farmer was increasingly hesitant to see his former runs steadily cut back through the ceaseless march of the woodlands across the valleys and hilltops of a once pastoral countryside. Since the war a more enlightened approach, using arboricultural consultants like Dame Sylvia Crowe, has improved the public image, though sheep farmers still tend to resist overtures from the Commission. The mass planting of hill slopes and plateau tops in Wales and Scotland has undoubtedly led to a loss of panoramic views, but on the credit side the provision of forest parks like Grizedale in the Lake District is an indication of what is possible in establishing a better working relationship with other countryside users.

Water authorities, too, particularly in Wales and the Lake District, have had to face their critics in the past because of their exclusionist policies. The development of the natural lake of Thirlmere to provide Manchester with water as long ago as 1909 sparked off a controversey which still continues today, surfacing again at every opportunity. The exclusion of the public from the lake shores and surrounding hill slopes in the very heartland of the Lake District was deeply resented and later led to considerable opposition to similar developments not only in the Lake District but further afield as well. Even a recent proposal by the North West Water Authority, with the support of Cumbria County Council, to raise the level of Ennerdale by 4ft provoked a storm of protests from respectable bodies like the Countryside Commission, the National Park Authority and amenity societies, as well as from farmers and walkers. On the face of it the scheme seems modest enough, especially as the lake has been supplying water to Whitehaven since the beginning of the century. Feelings aroused seventy years ago at Thirlmere still colour present-day views and attitudes, even though the two schemes have little in common. The opposition to the Ennerdale proposals arose from the fact that no other Lake District valley has survived in such a state of dramatic and pristine beauty, and that an alternative, though more costly, scheme for abstracting water from the River Derwent is available. Opposition to an earlier scheme for

58   The branching arms of the Clwyedog reservoir near Llanidloes in Central Wales

Ullswater led to water being pumped across to the existing reservoir at Haweswater and the pumping house being buried so that the effect on the environment was minimal.

The drowning of valleys for water storage basins has also led to heated arguments, for where good land is at a premium, the loss of valuable waterside meadows can mean the abandonment of a hill farm. In purely aesthetic terms, however, the creation of an artificial lake can represent an improvement, for it adds diversity to the landscape. The most outstanding example in recent years is the Clwyedog scheme near Llanidloes in Central Wales, where a deep valley has been dammed and a branching lake formed. From the specially created platform by the road joining Llanidloes to Machynlleth, the view is one of unrivalled splendour, giving a new dimension to the whole setting. The appearance, once due allowance has been made for scale, recalls not the rock-girt basins of Snowdonia nor the Lake District's wooded slopes running gently down to the water's edge, but rather the fjord coastline of western Norway.

In spite of the importance of tourism, forestry and water-storage functions, the future of the uplands cannot be divorced from the efforts of the local farming community. Because of the climatic conditions associated with the higher altitudes, cereal cropping must remain uncertain even with the introduction of new faster-ripening varieties. Livestock provides the best means of livelihood, with sheep rather than cattle the most worthwhile investment. Sheep farming inevitably relies more on hay than silage, and this can prove difficult after a wet summer. Grass growth can be seriously curtailed by a late spring or a dry May followed by a damp June. A wet summer can mean that hay is not gathered in until September and may have to be abandoned altogether to rot in the fields. In an exceptionally hot summer like that of 1976 the hay is stacked away in the barns by the middle of July, even in some of the highest areas. Subsidies paid to hill farmers have undoubtedly helped to maintain marginal land for sheep farming, even after bad summers, but they are not the real solution. The future of upland farming would seem to rest on rationalization rather than cash handouts. The amalgamation of the smaller units, as has taken place in the Welsh upland counties like Powys, has led to the building up of a single, high productivity unit. Land up to 1,500ft has been improved with heavy dressings of lime, while at slightly lower levels drainage and ploughing have allowed crops of rape and rye grass to be grown successfully. In a number of upland farms a certain diversity of crops, including seed potatoes – the altitude limits the effects of damaging aphids – has proved practicable and provides a valuable additional source of revenue. Road improvement to give access to the higher pastures for harvesting the hay and distributing winter feed is of vital importance in any future plans. In Central Wales the presence of the thick layer of stony clay or head resting on a shale substratum has meant that it is relatively easy to construct firm access roads by bulldozer and scraper without the need for a costly foundation. In other parts of the country, particularly Scotland, natural conditions are not quite so favourable, and this has inhibited road improvement. In some parts little progress has been recorded since Sir John Sinclair showed the necessity and the way almost two hundred years ago.

The fact that so many of our upland plateaux and mountains have been designated as National Parks or Areas of Outstanding Natural Beauty is recognition that there is much here worth preserving – and much to preserve it from. The creation of the first area in the Peak District in 1949 came not a moment too late, for already there were threats of much greater development in many parts of upland Britain. Even so, mineral workings had already made deep inroads into the Peak District as well as Snowdonia, leading the National Park Authorities to create boundaries with a very irregular course to exclude the worst-affected areas. Strict planning control over building development – save for local farmers – has prevented many of the excesses which undoubtedly follow an unrestricted play of market forces. Mineral working still poses the greatest problem, especially in the Peak District, where the size of limestone quarries has grown enormously in the last decade. Purchase of small quarries and adjacent land by the big roadstone companies has led to an already quite

59   Sheep shearing by hand is still a family occupation in the more isolated parts of the Pennines

unacceptable scale of working, mainly to provide stone for concrete aggregate. This development is relatively recent and partly reflects the substitution of limestone for gravel in the making of concrete. Large-scale barytes extraction presents another problem, for it has led to the tearing up of the landscape and the creation of unsightly settling basins. As with limestone quarrying, the amount of traffic is far too heavy for the narrow roads and has brought about the wholesale destruction of roadside verges as the heavy vehicles plough deep ruts across them. The white dust from the limestone quarries blankets the countryside for a considerable area around, and must make conditions intolerable for those unfortunate enough to live on the lee side.

Fortunately the problem is at present mainly restricted to the Peak District, but there is a lesson to be learned by other Park Authorities if faced with a similar conflict of interests in the future. If highland Britain is to retain its beauty and its essential character, conservationist policies must be pursued with vigour and determination. The lessons learned by experience over the past thirty years have to be assimilated, and if necessary further protective legislation will have to be introduced as an additional safeguard.

# Short Glossary of Technical Terms used in the Text

*accordant level*: flat surface due to past erosion at a uniform height

*breccia*: rock composed of angular fragments cemented together in a fine matrix

*cleavage*: the facility which certain rocks possess for splitting along distinct planes which do not coincide with the deposition layers of sediment

*conglomerate*: rock composed of rounded pebbles cemented together in a fine matrix

*doline*: large depression on the surface resulting from the underground collapse of limestone caverns

*dyke*: narrow vertical emplacement of igneous rock often harder and more resistant than the surrounding rocks so that it stands up as a wall

*epiphyte*: plant growing on another which acts as host and from which it derives some sustenance

*false bedding plane*: horizontal break in a compact rock like granite due mainly to cooling and not the mode of deposition

*gangue*: matrix in which mineral ores are found

*gneiss*: rock composed of quartz, felspar and mica in the form of laminated crystals resulting from pressure and heat which have altered their original structure

*inversion of temperature*: rise of temperature with height instead of the usual decrease

*isopleth*: any line which joins points of equal magnitude

*karst*: area of limestone scenery with distinctive landform features

*loess*: fine-grained deposit which has accumulated as a result of wind transport

*magma*: molten rock material at depth which can reach the surface through vents or fissures where it rapidly cools

*natural climax forest*: mature woodland that has evolved under stable environmental conditions and without interference by man

*pedunculate*: stalked; also refers to a variety of oak with acorns carried on short stalks *pluton*: the feature formed by the emplacement at depth of a slowly cooling rock magma which produces a coarse crystalline rock like granite, only revealed by the later removal of the capping beds

*quartzite*: rock formed almost entirely of pure quartz recemented by silica and commonly occurring in veins

*tuff*: fine ash particles resulting from volcanic eruption; also a fine-grained rock, suitable for making slates, formed by the compaction of such ashes.

# Sources and References

## 1   Landscape of Rock and Stone

Clayton, K., 'The origin of the landforms of the Malham area', *Field Studies*, 2, p 359
Condry, W., *The Snowdonia National Park* (Collins, 1966)
Craig, G. Y. (ed), *The Geology of Scotland* (Oliver and Boyd, 1965)
Davies, M. (ed), *The Brecon Beacons National Park* (HMSO, 1967)
Ford, T. D. (ed), *Limestone and Caves of the Peak District* (Geo, 1977)
Greig, D. G., *The South of Scotland*, British Regional Geology Series (HMSO, 1971)
Johnstone, G. S., *The Grampian Highlands*, British Regional Geology Series (HMSO, 1966)
King, C. A. M., *Northern England* (Longman, 1977)
Millward, R., and Robinson, A., *The Lake District* (Eyre and Spottiswoode, 1970)
—— *The South-West Peninsula* (Macmillan, 1971)
—— *The Welsh Marches* (Macmillan, 1971)
—— *Cumbria* (Macmillan, 1972)
—— *The Peak District* (Eyre Methuen, 1976)
—— *Landscapes of North Wales* (David and Charles, 1978)
—— *The Welsh Borders* (Eyre Methuen, 1978)
Parry, J. T., 'The limestone pavements of north-east England', *Canadian Geographer*, 16 (1960), pp 14–21
Pearsall, W. H., *Mountains and Moorlands* (Collins, 1950)
Pitty, E., 'The scale and significance of solutional loss from the limestone tracts of the South Pennines', *Proceedings Geologists Association*, 79 (1968), pp 153–8
Raistrick, A., *The Pennine Dales* (Eyre and Spottiswoode, 1968)
Richey, J. E., *The Tertiary Volcanic Districts*, British Regional Geology Series (HMSO, 1961)
Simmons, I. G. (ed), *The Yorkshire Dales National Park* (HMSO, 1971)
Sissons, J. B., *The Evolution of Scotland's Scenery* (Oliver and Boyd, 1967)
Tarn, J. N., *The Peak District National Park Architecture* (Peak Park Planning Board, 1971)
Whittow, J. B., *The Geology and Scenery of Scotland* (Penguin, 1977)
Worth, R. H., *Dartmoor* (David and Charles, 1970)

## 2   A Hostile Environment

Baldwin, H., and Smithson, P. A., 'Wind chill in upland Britain', *Weather*, 34 (1979), pp 294–306
Chandler, T., and Gregory, S., *The Climate of the British Isles* (Longman, 1976)

Curran, J. C., *et al*, 'Cairngorm summit automatic weather station', *Weather*, 32 (1977), pp 61–3

Finch, C. R., 'Some heavy rainfalls in Great Britain', *Weather*, 27 (1972), pp 364–77

Garnett, A., 'Diffused light and sunlight in relation to relief and settlement in high latitudes', *Scottish Geographical Magazine*, 55 (1939), pp 271–82

George, D. J., 'Temperature variations in a Welsh valley', *Weather*, 18 (1963), pp 270–4

Glanville Jones, R. J., 'The distribution of bond settlements in north-west Wales', *Welsh History Review*, 1 (1961), pp 111–32

Green, F. H. W., 'The transient snow line in the Scottish highlands', *Weather*, 30 (1975), pp 226–31

—— 'Climate and weather', in Nethersole-Watson, D. (ed), *The Cairngorms* (Collins, 1974), pp 228–36

Harding, R. J., 'Upland radiation', in *Summary of papers presented at a meeting of the Association of British Climatologists* (1978)

—— 'Altitudinal gradients of temperature in the northern Pennines', *Weather*, 34 (1979), pp 190–201

Harrison, S. J., 'Problems in the measurement and evaluations of the climatic resources of upland Britain', Ch 2 of Taylor, J. A. (ed), *Climatic Resources and Economic Activity* (David and Charles, 1974)

Hunter, N. F., 'The effect of altitude on grass growth in eastern Scotland', *Journal of Applied Ecology*, 8 (1971), pp 1–19

Kidson, C., 'The Exmoor storms and Lynmouth floods', *Geography*, 38 (1953), pp 1–9

Lamb, H. H., 'The history of our climate: Wales', in *Climatic change with special reference to Wales and its agriculture*, Memoir 8, Symposium in Agricultural Meteorology (1965)

Manley, G., 'Topographic features and climate of Britain', *Geographical Journal*, 103 (1944), pp 241–58

—— 'The helm wind at Crossfell', *Quarterly Journal Royal Meteorological Society*, 71 (1945), pp 197–219

—— *Climate and the British Scene* (Collins, 1952)

—— 'The climate of Malham Tarn', *Field Studies Annual Report*, 1955, pp 43–5

—— 'The mountain snows of Britain', *Weather*, 26 (1971), pp 192–200

—— 'Scotland's semi-permanent snow', *Weather*, 26 (1971), pp 458–71

Parry, M. L., 'Secular climatic change and marginal agriculture', *Institute of British Geographers*, 64 (1975), pp 1–14

Paton, J., 'Ben Nevis Observatory observations 1883–1904', *Weather*, 9 (1954), pp 291–305

Pedgley, D. E., 'Why so much rain?', *Weather*, 22 (1967), pp 478–82

—— 'Heavy rainfall over Snowdonia', *Weather*, 25 (1970), pp 340–50

—— 'Field studies of mountain weather in Snowdonia;, *Weather*, 29 (1974), pp 284–97

Rodda, J. C., 'Rainfall excesses in Great Britain', *Transactions Institute of British Geographers*, 49 (1970), pp 149–60

Rorison, I. H., 'The influence of climate and topography on plant growth in a Derbyshire dale', in *Summary of papers presented at a meeting of the Association of British Climatologists* (1978)

Spink, P. C., 'Scottish snow beds in the summer of 1978', *Weather*, 34 (1979), pp 135–7

Steadman, R. G., 'Indices of windchill of clothed persons', *Journal of Applied Meteorology*, 10 (1971), pp 674–83

Taylor, J. (ed), 'Hill climates and land use with special reference to Highland Britain', *Geography Department, University College of Wales Memoir 3* (1960)

—— (ed), *Climatic change with special reference to Wales and its agriculture*, Memoir 8, Symposium in Agricultural Meteorology (1965)

—— 'Upland climates', Ch 12 of Chandler and Gregory, op cit

——'The role of climatic factors in environmental and cultural changes in prehistoric times', in *The Effect of Man on the Landscape in the Highland Zone*, Council for British Archaeology Research Report, 11 (1975), pp 6–19

Taylor, P. J., and Heasman, A. J., 'A local wind in Snowdonia', *Weather*, 34 (1979), pp 135–7

Thomas, T. M., 'Tree deformation by wind in Wales', *Weather*, 28 (1973), pp 46–8

Thom, A. S., 'Mountain summit weather', in *Summary of papers presented at a meeting of the Association of British Climatologists* (1978)

## 3   The Ancient Landscapes of Upland Britain

Collingwood, R. G., 'The hill-fort on Carrock Fell', *Transactions of the Cumberland and Westmorland Antiquarian and Archaeological Society*, (NS) (1938), pp 32–41

Cunliffe, B., *Iron Age Communities in Britain* (Routledge and Kegan Paul, 2nd ed, 1978)

Evans, J. G., Limbrey, S., and Cleere, H., *The Effect of Man on the Landscape in the Highland Zone*, Council for British Archaeology Research Report, 11 (1975)

Feacham, R. W., *A Guide to Prehistoric Scotland* (Batsford, 1963)

—— 'Ancient agriculture in the highlands of Britain', *Proceedings Prehistoric Society*, 39 (1973), pp 332–53

Forde-Johnston, J., 'Fieldwork on the hill-forts of North Wales', *Flintshire Historical Publications*, 21 (1964), pp 1–20

—— 'The hill-forts of the Clwyds', *Archaeologia Cambrensis*, 114 (1965), pp 146–78

Hicks, S. P., 'Pollen-analytical evidence for the effect of prehistoric agriculture on the vegetation of north Derbyshire', *New Phytologist*, 70 (1971), pp 647–67

—— 'The impact of man on the East Moor of Derbyshire from Mesolithic times', *The Archaeological Journal*, 129 (1972), pp 1–21

Hogg, A. H. A., 'The size-distribution of hill-forts in Wales and the Marches', in Lynch, I., and Burgess, C., *Prehistoric Man in Wales and the West* (Adams and Dart, 1972)

Jones, G. D. B., and Thompson, F. H., 'Excavations at Mam Tor and Brough-on-Noe', *Derbyshire Archaeological Journal*, 75 (1965), pp 123–6

King, A., *Early Pennine Settlement* (Dalesman Publishing Co, 1970)

Laing, L., *Ancient Scotland* (David and Charles, 1976)

Mercer, R., 'The excavation of a Bronze Age hut-circle settlement, Stannon Down, St Breward, Cornwall, 1968', *Cornish Archaeology*, 9 (1970), pp 17–46

—— 'The Neolithic settlement on Carn Brea: preliminary report, 1970', *Cornish Archaeology*, 9 (1970), pp 53–67

Mitchell, G. F., 'Post-Boreal pollen diagrams from Irish raised bogs', *Proceedings of the Royal Irish Academy*, B57 (1956), pp 185–251

Pearsall, W. H., *Mountains and Moorlands* (revised W. Pennington, Collins, 1968)

Pennington, W., 'Pollen analyses from the deposits of six upland tarns in the Lake District', *Philosophical Transactions of the Royal Society of London*, Series B 248 (Biological Sciences) (1964–5), pp 205–44

Preston, F. L., 'The hill-forts of the Peak', *Transactions of the Derbyshire Archaeological and Natural History Society*, 74 (1954), pp 1–30

Radley, J., 'A Bronze Age ring-work on Totley Moor and other Bronze Age ring-works in the Pennines', *Derbyshire Archaeological Journal*, 123 (1966), pp 1–26

Raistrick, A., and Holmes, P. F., 'Archaeology on Malham Moor', *Field Studies*, 1 (1962)

Savory, H. N., 'The excavations at Dinorben hill-fort, Abergele, 1961–9', *Transactions of the Denbighshire Historical Society*, 20 (1971), pp 9–30

Simmons, I. G., 'Environment and early man on Dartmoor', *Proceedings of the Prehistoric Society*, 35 (1969), pp 203–19

Smith, A. G. and Willis, E. H., 'Radiocarbon dating and the Fallahogy landnam phase', *Ulster Journal of Archaeology*, 24–5 (1962), pp 16–24

Smith, A. G., 'The influence of Mesolithic and Neolithic man on British vegetation', in Smith, A. G., Pilcher, J. R., and Pearson, G. W., 'New radiocarbon dates from Ireland', *Antiquity*, 45 (1971), pp 97–102

Smith, A. G., 'Neolithic and Bronze Age landscape changes in Northern Ireland', in Evans, Limbrey and Cleere, op cit

Thom, A., *Megalithic Sites in Britain* (Oxford University Press, 1967)

Turner, J., 'A contribution to the history of forest clearance', *Proceedings of the Royal Society*, Series B, 161 (1965), pp 343–53

Walker, D., and West, R. G. (eds), *Studies in the Vegetation History of the British Isles* (Cambridge University Press, 1970)

## 4 The Cultural Remoteness of Highland Britain

Alcock, L., 'Wales in the 5th–7th centuries AD: archaeological evidence', in Foster, I. Ll., and Daniel, G., *Prehistoric and Early Wales* (Routledge and Kegan Paul, 1965)

—— 'Wales in the Arthurian Age', in Ashe, G., Alcock, L., Raleigh Radford, C. A., Rahtz, P., and Pacy, S., *The Quest for Arthur's Britain* (Pall Mall Press, 1968)

Bowen, E. G., 'The travels of the Celtic saints', *Antiquity*, 18 (1944), pp 16–28

—— 'The saints of Gwynedd', *Transactions of the Caernarvonshire Historical Society*, 9 (1948), pp 1–15

—— *Britain and the Western Seaways* (Thames and Hudson, 1972)

Breeze, D. J., *The Antonine Wall*, (HMSO, 1973)

Chadwick, N. K., *Studies in Early British History* (Cambridge University Press, 1959)

—— *Celtic Britain* (Thames and Hudson, 1963)

Davies, E., *Celtic Studies in Wales* (University of Wales Press, 1963)

Foster, I. Ll., 'The emergence of Wales', in Foster and Daniel, op cit

Henderson, I., *The Picts* (Thames and Hudson, 1967)

Hogg, A. H. A., 'Garn Boduan and Tre'r Ceiri – excavations at two Caernarvonshire hill-forts', *The Archaeological Journal*, 117 (1960), pp 1–39

Jackson, K. H., *Language and History in Early Britain* (Edinburgh University Press, 1953)

Johns, C. N., 'The Celtic monasteries of North Wales', *Transactions of the Caernarvonshire Historical Society*, 21 (1960), pp 14–41

Jones, G. R. J., 'Early settlement in Arfon: the setting of Tre'r Ceiri', *Transactions of the Caernarvonshire Historical Society*, 24 (1963), pp 1–20

—— 'Post-Roman Wales', in Finberg, H. P. R. (ed), *The Agrarian History of England and Wales, AD 43–1042* (Cambridge University Press, 1972), pp 281–382

Laing, L., *The Archaeology of Late Celtic Britain and Ireland, AD 400–1200* (Methuen, 1975)

Nash-Williams, V. E., *The Early Christian Monuments of Wales* (University of Wales Press, 1950)

Nicolaisen, W. F., 'Norse settlements in the Northern and Western Isles', *Scottish Historical Review*, 48 (1969), pp 6–17

Reece, R., *Iona* (Iona Community Publishing Dept, no date)

Richmond, I. A. (ed), *Roman and Native in North Britain* (Nelson, 1958)

Ritchie, R. L. G., *The Normans in Scotland* (Edinburgh University Press, 1964)

Robertson, A. S., *The Antonine Wall* (Glasgow Archaeological Society, 1972)

Scott, J. G., *South-West Scotland* (Heinemann, 1966)

Simpson, W. D., *The Historical St Columba* (Oliver and Boyd, 1965)

Thomas, C., *Britain and Ireland in Early Christian Times: AD 400–800* (Thames and Hudson, 1971)

—— *The Early Christian Archaeology of North Britain* (Oxford University Press, 1971)

Wainwright, F. T. (ed), *The Problem of the Picts* (Nelson, 1955)
—— (ed), *The Northern Isles* (Nelson, 1962)


## 5 Exploiting the Land

Barrow, G. W. S., in Baker, A. R. H., and Butlin, R. A., *Studies of Field Systems in the British Isles* (Cambridge University Press, 1972)

Barton, D. B., *Copper Mining in Cornwall and Devon* (Barton, 1961)

—— *An Introduction to the Geology of Cornwall* (Barton, 1961)

Booker, F., *The Industrial Archaeology of the Tamar Valley* (David and Charles, 1967)

Bouch, C. M. L., and Jones, G. P., *A Short Economic and Social History of the Lake Counties 1500–1830* (Manchester University Press, 1961)

Crampton, C. B., 'Hafotai platforms on the north front of the Brecon Beacons', *Archaeologia Cambrensis*, 115 (1966)

Dodd, A. H., *The Industrial Revolution in North Wales* (University of Wales Press, 1951)

Elliott, G. G., 'The enclosure of Aspatria', *Transactions of the Cumberland and Westmorland Antiquarian and Archaeological Society*, 44(NS) (1945), pp 55–67

Evans, M. B., 'Gadlys and Flintshire lead mining in the 18th century', *Journal of the Flintshire Historical Society*, 18 (1960), 19 (1961), 20 (1962)

Fell, C., 'The Great Langdale stone-axe factory', *Transactions of the Cumberland and Westmorland Antiquarian and Archaeological Society*, 50(NS) (1951)

Finberg, H. P. R., 'The open field in Devonshire', *Antiquity*, 23 (1949), pp 180–8

Fogwill, E. G., 'Pastoralism on Dartmoor', *Transactions of the Devon Association*, 86 (1954), pp 89–114

Ford, T. D., and Rieuwerts, J. H. (eds), *Lead Mining in the Peak District* (Peak Park Planning Board, 1970)

Fuller, G. J., 'Early lead smelting in the Peak District', *East Midland Geographer*, 5 (1970), pp 1–8

Gaffney, V., 'Summer shielings', *The Scottish Historical Review*, 38 (1959), pp 20–35

Gant, R. L., 'The townscape and economy of Brecon', *Brycheiniog*, 16 (1972)

Goodridge, J. A., 'Devon Great Consols – a study of Victorian mining enterprise', *Transactions of the Devon Association*, 96 (1964), pp 228–68

Gough, J. W., *The Mines of Mendip* (Oxford University Press, 1931)

Harris, H., *The Industrial Archaeology of the Peak District* (David and Charles, 1971)

Hoskins, W. G., and Finberg, H. P. R., *Devonshire Studies* (Cape, 1952)

Jackson, J. C., 'Open-field cultivation in Derbyshire', *Derbyshire Archaeological Journal*, 83 (1963), pp 66–76

Jenkins, R., 'The Society for the Mines Royal and the German colony in the Lake District', *Transactions of the Newcomen Society*, 14 (1939), pp 225–34

Jones, G. D. B., and Blakey, I. J., 'Dolaucothi – the Roman aqueduct;, *Bulletin of the Board of Celtic Studies*, 19 (1962), pp 71–84

Jones, G. R. J., 'The pattern of settlement on the Welsh Border', *Agricultural History Review*, 8 (1960)

—— 'Post-Roman Wales', in Finberg, H. P. R. (ed), *The Agrarian History of England and Wales, AD 43–1042* (Cambridge University Press, 1972)

—— 'Anglesey protrayed', *Anglesey Antiquarian and Field Club Transactions* (1974), pp 109–17

Kirkham, N., and Ford, T. D., *The Ecton Copper Mines*, Peak District Mines Historical Society Special Publication No 1 (1967)

Manning, W. H., 'The Dolaucothi gold mines', *Antiquity*, 42 (1968), pp 299–302

Miller, R., 'Land use by summer shielings', *Scottish Studies*, 2 (1967), pp 193–221

Monkhouse, F. J., 'Some features of the historical geography of the German mining enterprises in Elizabethan Lakeland', *Geography*, 28 (1943), pp 107–13

Nixon, F., *The Industiral Archaeology of Derbyshire* (David and Charles, 1969)

Pennant, T., *A Tour in Wales, 1770* (1781)

Plint, R. G., 'Stone-axe factory sites in the Cumbrian Fells', *Transactions of the Cumberland and Westmorland Antiquarian and Archaeological Society*, 62(NS) (1962), pp 2–26

Raistrick, A., and Jennings, B., *A History of Lead-Mining in the Pennines* (Longman, 1965)

Raleigh Radford, C. A., 'Tretower: the castle and the court', *Brycheiniog*, 6 (1960)

Rees, D. M., *The Industrial Archaeology of Wales* (David and Charles, 1975)

Rollinson, W., *A History of Man in the Lake District* (Dent, 1968)

Rowlands, J., 'Copper Mountain', in *Studies in Anglesey History*, Vol 1 (Anglesey Antiquarian Society, 1966)

Rowley, R. T., 'The Clee Forest – a study in common rights', *Transactions of the Shropshire Archaeological Society*, 58 (1965–8)

Sayce, R. U., 'The old summer pastures', *Montgomeryshire Collections*, 54 (1955–6)

Tate, W. E., 'Field systems and enclosure movements in Cumberland', *Transactions of the Cumberland and Westmorland Antiquarian and Archaeological Society*, 43(NS) (1943), pp 175–85

Wood, P. D., 'Open field strips: Forrabury Common near Boscastle', *Cornish Archaeology*, 2 (1963), pp 29–33

## 6   The Taming of the Uplands

Dodd, A. H., *The Industrial Revolution in North Wales* (University of Wales, 1951)

Gaffrey, V., 'The Lordship of Strathavon', *Third Spalding Club, Aberdeen* (1960), pp 34–61

Gaskell, P., *Morven Transformed* (Cambridge University Press, 1968)

Hyde-Hall, E., *Description of Caernarvonshire ( 1809–1811)*, Caernarvonshire Historical Society Records Series, 2 (1952)

Inglis-Jones, E., *Peacocks in Paradise – the story of Hafod in Cardiganshire* (Faber and Faber, 1953)

Kay, G., 'The landscape of improvement', *Scottish Geographical Magazine*, 78 (1962), pp 100–8

Linnard, W., 'Thomas Johnes of Hafod – pioneer of upland afforestation in Wales', *Ceredigion*, 6 (1968–71), pp 309–18

Messman, F. J., *Richard Payne Knight – the twilight of virtuosity* (Mouton, 1974)

Millman, R., *The Making of the Scottish Landscape* (Batsford, 1975)

Mitchison, R., *Agricultural Sir John – the life of Sir John Sinclair of Ulbster* (Bles, 1962)

Omand, D., *The Caithness Book* (Highland Printers, 1973)

Orwin, C. S., and Sellick, R. J., *The Reclamation of Exmoor Forest* (David and Charles, 1970)

Phillipson, J., and Mitchison, R. (eds), *Scotland in the Age of Improvement* (Edinburgh University Press, 1970)

Symons, J. A., *Scottish Farming* (Oliver and Boyd, 1959)

Turnock, D., 'The improving movement on a West Highland estate', *Scottish Geographical Magazine*, 85 (1969), pp 17–30

——   *Patterns of Highland Development* (Macmillan, 1970)

## 7   The High Ways

Bowen, R., and Gresham, C., *History of Merioneth*, Vol 1 (Merioneth Historical and Record Society, 1967)

Chitty, L. F., 'The Clun–Clee ridgeway', in *Culture and Environment: essays in honour of Sir*

*Cyril Fox* (Cambridge University Press, 1963)

Colyer, R. J., *Welsh Cattle Drovers* (University of Wales Press, 1976)

Godwin, F., and Toulson, S., *The Drover's Roads of Wales* (Wildwood House, 1977)

Grinsell, L. V., *The Archaeology of Exmoor* (David and Charles, 1970)

Grundy, G. B., 'Ancient highways in Devon', *Archaeological Journal*, 98 (1941), pp 131–64

Haldane, A. R. B., *The Drove Roads of Scotland* (Nelson, 1952)

—— *New Ways through the Glens* (Nelson, 1962)

Hughes, P. G., *Wales and the Drovers* (Foyles Welsh Co, 1943)

Jerman, H. N., 'From moss to macadam', *Montgomeryshire Collections*, 43 (1934), pp 11–32

Marshall, J. D., *Old Lakeland* (David and Charles, 1971)

Peel, J. H. B., *Along Roman Roads* (Pan, 1976)

Phillips, R., 'The last of the drovers', *Transactions Honourable Society of Cymmrodorion* (1968), pp 110–21

Raistrick, A., *Old Yorkshire Dales* (Pan, 1967), Ch 8, pp 121–36

—— *Malham and Malham Moor* (Dalesman Publishing Co, 1976)

—— *Green Roads of the Mid-Pennines* (Moorland, 1978)

Sedgley, R., 'The Roman milestones of Britain', *British Archaeological Reports*, 18 (1975)

Sellick, R. J., *The West Somerset Mineral Line* (Phoenix, 1962)

Turner, K., *Snowdon Mountain Railway* (David and Charles, 1973)

Vallance, H. A., *The Highland Railway* (David and Charles, 1963)

Wright, G., *The Yorkshire Dales* (David and Charles, 1977)

# Appendix: Time Scales

**Geological column and time scale**

| Era | System | Approximate age (millions of years before present) | Main upland areas where formations occur |
|---|---|---|---|
| Cainozoic (Tertiary) | Holocene | | |
| | Pleistocene (Ice Age) | | Veneer of glacial beds in Scotland, Pennines, N Wales. Deposits of head on Exmoor |
| | | 1 | |
| | Pliocene | | |
| | | 11 | |
| | Miocene | | |
| | | 25 | |
| | Oligocene | | |
| | | 40 | |
| | Eocene | | Volcanic beds of the Inner Hebrides, including |
| | | 60 | |
| | Palaeocene | | Skye |
| | | 70 | |
| Mesozoic | Cretaceous | | |
| | | 135 | |
| | Jurassic | | Scattered deposits in Inner Hebrides |
| | | 180 | |
| | Triassic | | |
| | | 225 | |
| | Permian | | |
| | | 270 | |
| | Carboniferous | | Pennines (Mountain Limestone) |
| | | 335 | |

| Era | System | Approximate age (millions of years before present) | Main upland areas where formations occur |
|-----|--------|------|------|
| Palaeozoic | Devonian (Old Red Sandstone) | | Quantocks, Exmoor, Caithness |
| | | 400 | |
| | Silurian | | N Wales and Southern Uplands of Scotland |
| | | 440 | |
| | Ordovician | | N Wales and Lake District |
| | | 500 | |
| | Cambrian | | Quartzite of N W Highlands, Lake District |
| | | 600 | |
| Pre-Cambrian | Torridonian | | N W Highlands of Scotland |
| | Lewisian | 2600 | Outer Hebrides |

## The chief stages of prehistory in Britain

| | |
|---|---|
| The Romans occupy Britain<br><br>43 AD | First towns and planned systems of made roads. Forts and signal stations, Hadrian's and Antonine walls mark occupation of north and west |
| Iron Age<br><br>500 BC | Climatic deterioration and great increase in area of blanket bog in uplands. Evidence for abandonment of settlements above 1,000ft contour. Hill-forts, *duns* and *brochs* |
| Bronze Age<br><br>2000 BC | First metal-working – exploitation of gold, copper, tin resources of upland Britain. Clustered hut settlements and associated field systems. Extensive forest clearance in highland Britain after 1200 BC – moorland appears – degradation of upland soils |
| Neolithic<br><br>3300 BC | First immigrant farmers – forest clearance, from evidence of the elm decline. Chambered tombs, passage graves and, towards end of period, 'henge' monuments and stone circles. First fields |
| Mesolithic<br><br>8000 BC | General amelioration of climate. Spread of birch, pine, hazel and later mixed oak forest. Rising sea levels and great loss of land around Britain. Hunting and food-gathering peoples – some evidence for beginnings of forest clearance towards end of period |
| Upper Palaeolithic<br><br>35000 BC | Tundra. Hunting and food-gathering peoples. Horses and reindeer appear |
| Lower Palaeolithic | Hunting, food-gathering communities of the Ice Age |

# Index

237

239